Employment Regimes and the Quality of Work

Edited by

Duncan Gallie

OXFORD

UNIVERSITY PRESS

OXFORD
UNIVERSITY PRESS

Great Clarendon Street, Oxford OX2 6DP

Oxford University Press is a department of the University of Oxford.
It furthers the University's objective of excellence in research, scholarship,
and education by publishing worldwide in

Oxford New York

Auckland Cape Town Dar es Salaam Hong Kong Karachi
Kuala Lumpur Madrid Melbourne Mexico City Nairobi
New Delhi Shanghai Taipei Toronto

With offices in

Argentina Austria Brazil Chile Czech Republic France Greece
Guatemala Hungary Italy Japan Poland Portugal Singapore
South Korea Switzerland Thailand Turkey Ukraine Vietnam

Oxford is a registered trademark of Oxford University Press
in the UK and in certain other countries

Published in the United States
by Oxford University Press Inc., New York

First published 2007
First Published in Paperback 2009

British Library Cataloguing in Publication Data
Data available

Library of Congress Cataloging in Publication Data
Data available

Typeset by SPI Publisher Services, Pondicherry, India
Printed in Great Britain
on acid-free paper by the
MPG Books Group, Bodmin and King's Lynn

ISBN 978–0–19–923010–5
      978–0–19–956603–7 (Pbk.)

1 3 5 7 9 10 8 6 4 2

Employment Regimes and the Quality of Work

Contents

Contents

List of Figures

List of Tables

List of Contributors

Martina Dieckhoff is postdoctoral research fellow at the Danish National Institute of Social Research in Copenhagen.

Duncan Gallie is an official fellow of Nuffield College, Oxford, and professor of sociology of the University of Oxford.

Jean-Marie Jungblut is a researcher and project leader at the Centre of European Social Research (MZES) in Mannheim.

Philip J. O'Connell is research professor and head of the Education and Labour Market Research Division at the Economic and Social Research Institute in Dublin.

Stefani Scherer is a research fellow at Milano-Bicocca University, Department of Sociology and Social Research.

Nadia Steiber is a research associate at the Institute of Sociology and Social Research at the Vienna University of Economics and Business Administration.

Michael Tåhlin is professor of sociology at the Swedish Institute for Social Research (SOFI), Stockholm University.

Serge Paugam is professor of sociology and director of the department of doctoral studies in sociology at the EHESS (Paris). He is also director of a research team on social inequalities in the Centre Maurice Halbwachs (CNRS/EHESS/ENS).

Ying Zhou is research officer at Nuffield College, Oxford.

Acknowledgements

This book is the result of a collaborative research project among members of the Economic Change, Quality of Life and Social Cohesion (EQUAL-SOC) Network of Excellence, funded by the European Commission (DG Research) as part of the Sixth Framework Programme. The network (coordinated by Robert Erikson of the Swedish Institute of Social Research) has provided the opportunity and resources for the authors to meet on a regular basis to discuss underlying issues, comment upon each others' chapters, and think through their theoretical implications.

We are very grateful to the various bodies that have provided the data used in our analyses. Chapter 2 draws on the second wave of the European Social Survey (ESS); Chapter 3 on the European Community Household Panel (ECHP); Chapter 4 on the second and third European Working Conditions Survey (EWCS); Chapter 5 on the International Social Survey Programme's Gender Role module of 2002; and Chapters 5 and 6 on the Eurobarometer surveys 44.3 and 56.1. We are grateful to Eurostat for making available the ECHP. Roger Jowell and his colleagues deserve thanks for their vision in developing and implementing the European Social Survey series (for which they have received the Descartes Prize from the European Union). The Eurobarometer surveys 44.3 and 56.1 were specially commissioned by DG Employment (formerly DG V) and the versions used here were made available by INRA, which conducted the fieldwork. The EWCS was provided by European Foundation for the Improvement of Living and Working Conditions (http://www.eurofound.europa.eu/ewco/surveys). The ISSP was kindly provided by the Central Archive for Empirical Social Research (ZA), University of Cologne, Germany. We have also made use of a number of national surveys. The versions of the British Skills Survey series were those held by Nuffield College, Oxford. The German BIBB/IAB surveys were provided by the Central Archive (ZA), Cologne. The French surveys 'Conditions de travail' were provided by the Institut du Longitudinal

(LASMAS), with the help of Alexandre Kych. The Swedish Living Standards Survey was made available by Statistics Sweden (SCB). We would like particularly to thank Martin Hällsten of the Swedish Institute of Social Research (SOFI) for the data runs on which our tables draw in Chapter 4 and Nadia Steiber for her help in the analysis of the BIBB/IAB surveys. Jane Roberts of Nuffield College, Oxford, also has been a very valuable source of help in acquiring access to data and relevant technical information.

Neither the funders of the programmes nor the data providers mentioned above bear any responsibility for the interpretations presented here. The views expressed in the book, as well as any errors, are the authors' responsibility.

We owe special thanks to Min Zou, Nuffield College, for his work in preparing the manuscript and constructing the index.

List of Abbreviations

AFL:	Working Life Fund
BAuA:	Federal Institute for Occupational Safety and Health
BHPS:	British Household Panel
BIBB:	Federal Institute for Vocational Education and Training
BNSG:	British National Survey of Graduates and Diplomats
CATEWE:	Comparative Analysis of Transitions from Education to Work in Europe
CME:	coordinated market economies
CVTS:	Continuing Vocational Training Survey
EB:	Eurobarometer surveys
ECHP:	European Community Household Panel
EGP:	Erikson-Goldthorpe Portocarero class model
EIB:	Employment in Britain Survey
EQUALSOC:	Economic Change, Quality of Life and Social Cohesion Network of Excellence
ESEC:	European Socio-Economic Classification
ESF:	European Science Foundation
ESRC:	Economic and Social Research Council
ESS:	European Social Survey
ESWC:	European Survey on Working Conditions
EU:	European Union
EWCS:	European Working Conditions Survey
FWC:	family–work conflict
GSOEP:	German Socio-Economic Panel
HI:	high quality insecure integration
HS:	high quality secure integration
IAB:	Institute for Employment Research
INSEE:	National Institute of Statistics
ISCO:	International Standard Classification of Occupations
ISSP:	International Social Survey Programme

LASMAS:	Institut du Longitudinal
LFS:	Labour Force Survey
LI:	low quality insecure integration
LME:	liberal market economies
LNU:	Level of Living Surveys
LO:	Landsorganisationen (The Swedish Trade Union Confederation)
LS:	low quality secure integration
MZES:	Centre of European Social Research
NDUs:	National Data Collection Units
NSD:	Norwegian Social Science Data Services
OECD:	Organisation for Economic Co-operation and Development
OMC:	Open Method of Coordination
OSR:	occupational skill requirements
PPS:	purchasing power standards
SCB:	Statistics Sweden
SEP:	Socio-Economic Panel Survey
SKOPE:	Centre for Skills Knowledge and Organizational Performance
SOFI:	Swedish Institute of Social Research
ULF:	Swedish Surveys on Living Conditions
WFC:	work–family conflict
WSII:	Welfare State Intervention Index
ZA:	Central Archive for Empirical Social Research, Cologne

1

Production Regimes, Employment Regimes, and the Quality of Work

Duncan Gallie

The Place of Quality of Work in the Social Agenda

After a marked, but transitory, flourishing in the 1960s and 1970s, quality of work issues returned to an increasingly central place in the social agenda of many European societies in the last decade of the twentieth Century. The first period of serious policy concern had been triggered by the strike waves of the late 1960s, which many interpreted as a reaction to the inhumane working conditions of Fordism, symbolized by the assembly lines of the giant car factories. There were significant policy initiatives to encourage the enrichment of jobs in countries as diverse as France, Germany, and Sweden. In the United States a major series of quality of work surveys were commissioned (Quinn and Staines 1979). In Britain a Royal Commission was established to examine the feasibility of extending 'industrial democracy' in private companies (Bullock 1977), while in Sweden a new Co-Determination law was introduced despite strong employer resistance (Kjellberg 1998).

But the political success of neoliberalism in both the United States and the UK brought an abrupt end to such initiatives in the Anglo-Saxon countries in the 1980s, and, after a brief radical phase of French Socialist government, they became increasingly marginal in the Continental European countries by the late 1980s (Piotet 1998; Van de Velde 2005). It was only in the Nordic countries that active programmes of work improvement continued to be a central preoccupation of both the social partners and government, with the introduction of increasingly large-scale programmes to diffuse the growing body of systematic research evidence on the social consequences of job design and to provide incentives for companies to reorganize work in consultation with their employees (Gustavsen et al. 1996). Even in Sweden, the country that had gone furthest in raising the policy profile of work quality, the closure in 1993 of Volvo's exemplar Uddevala plant after only four years raised the issue of the viability of such programmes, faced by growing international competitiveness and the spread of new 'lean' forms of production more strongly influenced by the Japanese production model.

The new impetus behind work quality issues in Europe that developed in the 1990s was partly propelled by the elaboration of an increasingly ambitious social and employment agenda by the European Union (EU) (now reinforced by the membership of the Nordic countries). The early 1990s saw the introduction of the new Health and Safety Directive, which although implemented in very varied ways in different countries gave a new salience to issues of job design (Frick et al. 2000). Other directives obliged member states to think seriously about the treatment of 'marginal' categories of employee—such as part-timers and temporary workers—and about working hour times (Quintin and Faverel-Dapas 1999). The prolonged discussion about employee consultation rights at least raised the public profile of such issues. The Employment Policy initiatives that followed the Luxembourg summit of 1997 not only gave a central place to continuing training as a way of reducing risks of social exclusion but introduced a new system of collaboration between national governments on policy development—the Open Method of Coordination (Rodrigues 2003; Begg 2004). A notable feature of this was the move to develop broadly comparable indicators of progress, a development that reached an important turning point with the Lisbon Summit's addition of better quality jobs to the central mission objectives of the EU and the subsequent adoption under the Belgium Presidency in December 2001 of agreed indicators to monitor the effectiveness of national policies both with respect to social inclusion and the quality of work (European Commission 2001*a*, 2002, 2003).

Such higher-level policy initiatives, however, chimed with new developments in management thinking that affected at least a sector of influential larger companies. While in the 1980s the discourse of 'flexibility' had been heavily dominated by an Anglo-Saxon emphasis on deregulation, in the 1990s there a growing interest in the notion of 'high-performance' management, with a focus on skill development, teamwork and motivation (Frohlich and Pekruhl 1996; Murray et al. 2002). At the same time research was underlining in an ever more persuasive way the deleterious implications not only for employee motivation, but for employee health, of the way in which jobs were designed (Johnson and Johansson 1991). As the conviction grew that the economic sustainability of European economies depended on high skills, creativity, production quality, and customized output, the need to rethink the principles underlying work organization to ensure that employees were encouraged to make best use of their discretionary abilities and to enhance work skills could only appear more pressing.

Despite the broad trend for a growing salience of work quality issues in terms of policy, not only did policy formulation differ between countries, but policies were refracted through the (very different) social structural contexts in specific countries. A range of arguments in the literature point to the central importance for the nature of jobs of changes in competitive pressure, in the technological infrastructure of work, and in the sectoral composition of the economy (Gallie et al. 1998). It is possible such factors are even more powerful determinants of job quality than either government policy or employer philosophies of management. The predictions made are very diverse, but some point to a very bleak view of likely trends. The conviction that work quality was of importance may have grown stronger, but changes in economic structure may have led to deterioration rather than improvement in the quality of work.

In practice, we still know very little empirically about how key aspects of the quality of work actually changed in different countries over the last decade. What were the general trends in work quality in terms of employees' everyday experiences of their jobs? Did some countries prove more successful than others in enriching jobs? If there were differences, how far are these explicable in terms of the policy orientation of particular governments or of other social structural factors? Were trends quite general across the workforce or were improvements to the benefit only of specific groups, thereby potentially leading to greater polarization within the workforce? The objective of this book is to examine how far the available national and cross-national evidence for some of the major European societies enables us to address these questions and to begin to explore a range of arguments about the major determinants of work quality and their relative importance.

Dimensions of the Quality of Work

Discussion and research on the quality of work have primarily focused on the nature of the work task and the organizational environment in which work is carried out. The emphasis has been on the factors that contribute to the capacity for self-realization and development of employees at work rather than on the material rewards of work. Over time, however, there has been a marked extension of the range of work dimensions that have been regarded as important, in part reflecting changes in economic experiences in Western societies and in part broad changes in cultural values.

The initial focus of discussion and research on the quality of working life was on the characteristics of the job task itself. This derived from two rather different perspectives on the organization of work. The first was rooted in a Marxian tradition that pointed to tendencies to deskilling, and to a growing separation of conception and execution in work, as the prime source of alienation. In this view, it is through their capacities to both design and produce that employees have the necessary conditions for self-realization and self-development. But changes in the organization of work had increasingly undercut such opportunities as a result of the growing dominance of Taylorist principles of management. This was reinforced by technological change, in particular the spread of Fordist production techniques involving machine-paced work controlled by assembly lines, and the consequent isolation of individual work posts. The second perspective was more managerialist in approach and was concerned with the factors that affected job satisfaction and employee motivation. An impressive array of studies was carried out demonstrating the critical importance of a range of job characteristics for employee satisfaction (Blauner 1967; Caplan et al. 1980; French, Caplan, and Harrison 1982). Indeed a consistent finding of job satisfaction research has been that intrinsic job characteristics are the strongest predictors of job satisfaction.

The broad conclusions of the two approaches were very similar. Both placed a central emphasis on skill utilization, the variety of work, and opportunities for learning—all of which were intimately linked to the skill level or task complexity of the job. Second, they both underlined the importance of the scope the job provided for the use of initiative (or autonomy) in carrying out the immediate job task.

From the 1980s, with the greater turbulence of labour markets and the return of large-scale unemployment, discussions of the quality of work began to become more comprehensive. In particular, the literature on labour market segmentation highlighted two further aspects of jobs as central to the notion of job quality: the availability of opportunities for skill development and hence career progression on the one hand and the stability of employment on the other (Doeringer and Piore 1971; Berger and Piore 1980; Rubery 1988: 251–80). These theorists depicted a divide between a 'primary' sector of the workforce that had high levels of job security and where employment involved a career within an internal labour market and a 'secondary' sector of poor jobs where employees were involved in dead-end jobs and were subject to chronic job insecurity.

By the early 1990s, 'flexibility' theories had built on and extended these arguments, placing a particular emphasis on the significance of contractual status for job quality (Rosenberg 1989; Mangan 2000; Felstead and Jewson 1999; Barker and Christensen 1998). Employers, it was argued, were seeking to gain flexibility in adjusting to an increasingly competitive and volatile world market by making greater use of employees on a variety of non-standard contracts (temporary, part-time, and self-employed). Such workers were less well protected by existing forms of employment protection and therefore could be disposed of more rapidly in periods of economic downturn. As a result the workforce, it was suggested, was becoming increasingly fragmented between a 'core' of relatively secure and privileged employees and an insecure 'periphery'. Certainly, a wide array of research has shown that job security is of major importance for employees' experience of their working lives (Sverke, Hellgren, and Naswall 2006). The results are parallel to those of research into unemployment, consistently showing that low job security leads to significant psychological distress (Warr 1991).

In the course of 1990s, reflecting the growth of female labour market participation, a fifth major dimension was introduced into the discussion of job quality, namely the extent to which work was organized in ways that enabled people to reconcile work careers with their family lives, thereby preventing high levels of work–family stress (see Scherer and Steiber, Chapter 5, this volume). This placed on the agenda issues such as the length of work hours, the extent to which work hours were 'unsocial' in terms of their scheduling, and the ability to vary work hours or take time off to meet family obligations.

There are other dimensions of jobs that have entered into discussions of job quality, but there has been less consensus about their status. Work pressure is a case in point. Some writers have argued that there has been an intensification of work and that work pressure should be an important dimension of job quality. But counter to this it can be argued that some element of job pressure is inherent in skilled and responsible work and indeed may be a source of challenge and creativity. It is notable that job pressure measures tend to correlate very highly with skill, with those in more skilled jobs reporting higher levels of pressure. Further, there is an issue of whether work pressure is an inherent characteristic of the job or results from decisions by employees themselves. Significant sources of pressure—such as long hours of work—may reflect organizational con- straint or employee choice. Defining the difference between creative and negative job pressure may be empirically tricky. There is also a substantial literature that suggests that job pressure per se does not undermine the psychological well-being of employees, but rather that its implications depend on the degree of control that employees have at work. It is where high job pressure is associated with low discretion on the part of employees with respect to how they carry out their work that its effects are held to be negative. Finally, it could be argued that it is only where job pressures are such that they place major strain on other aspects of people's lives that they become an important matter of concern. Given this, the degree of work–family conflict may be one of the most pertinent measures of negative work pressure.

Finally, it is notable that discussions of job quality rarely dwell on pay. This is partly a definitional issue, with the notion of 'job' focusing primarily on the intrinsic characteristics of work experience in contrast to 'conditions of employment' which are concerned with the extrinsic features of work. But it may also reflect the fact that, to a greater extent than for many other characteristics of work, the implications of any given level of pay may vary substantially between individuals depending on their household situation. The most obvious issue of concern with respect to job quality would be low pay. But research has shown that the association between low pay and poverty is relatively weak because such employees are usually in households where the income of partners provides protection against financial deprivation. However, it is clear that where individuals do not have the support of other household members, the level of pay of their job is likely to have direct and severe consequences for their well-being.

For the analyses of the book, we have taken the core dimensions of job quality to be skill level, the degree of task discretion or autonomy, the opportunities for skill development, job security, and the extent to which jobs are compatible with work–family balance. However, the issue of work pressure is also addressed in the context of work–family conflict and that of pay in the context of changing skill profiles.

Job Characteristics or Job Satisfaction? Approaches to Work Quality

There have been two rather distinct approaches to the measurement of job quality. The first has focused on the way in which the 'objective' nature of working conditions affects the competencies and opportunities of employees. Initially deriving from the neo-Marxist tradition, this primarily sought to assess the implications of the changing nature of work for people's skills conceived in a broad way to include both the 'complexity' of the work task and the degree of 'autonomy' or 'discretion' that they can exercise over it. A central concern of this approach has been with how far jobs provide contexts for self-development, so that people can enhance their skills over time. This has tended to be associated with a case study methodology in which researchers provide detailed descriptions of specific types of work context and their associated work roles, although there is also a substantial body of work that characterizes the features of the work situation on the basis of employees' own accounts of them. This was very much the approach of the French tradition of 'sociologie du travail' (Rose 1987; Gremion and Piotet 2004), but it was also influential in the Anglo-Saxon countries among researchers building on the ideas of Braverman (Nichols and Beynon 1977; Crompton and Jones 1984).

The second approach has taken as its point of departure the factors that affect the degree of satisfaction or dissatisfaction that people feel in their jobs (Blauner 1967; Clark 2005). Good jobs are those that people are happy with. In principle this is an important distinction. Whereas the first approach relies upon the analyst's stipulation of what is important for people, whether on the basis of theoretical assumptions about human nature or research evidence on the consequences of different job structures, the second allows people to judge for themselves what is important about a job. Most typically this approach has relied upon survey research evidence in which respondents evaluate different aspects of their work situation.

Both approaches are open to criticism. It can be argued that the 'objective' approach fails to allow for significant differences between individuals in their values and simply assumes that employment is a centrally important experience for people's lives. It is arguable that there are profound differences between people in the relative importance they attach to paid work relative to other significant life spheres such as the family. If people give priority to their family lives, jobs that offer responsibility and skill development may be an undesirable source of strain. They may prefer undemanding jobs, while their self-development may be better served through their non-work lives. Alternatively people may prefer work that provides relatively high income even though it does little for their skill development, since it provides them with the resources to make better use of their leisure.

Critics of a 'job satisfaction' approach argue that people may be blinded to their true interests by the pressures of consumerism, they may myopically focus on short term benefits rather than their longer-term interests or that there may be powerful processes of psychological adaptation whereby they resign themselves to what they have or to what they feel to be realistically within their reach. Measures of job satisfaction are also open to criticism that they are relatively weak indicators of positive attachment to work. A person can be 'satisfied' without having any strong sense of emotional involvement.

In practice the implications of these differing perspectives for the choice of indicators of the quality of work are less drastic than might anticipated. While those working from the 'objective' and 'job satisfaction' perspectives differed substantially in their methodological starting points, they showed a remarkable convergence in terms of the aspects of work that they concluded were crucial for well-being. This reflects the fact that people do in general attach importance to those aspects of their jobs that analysts have pointed to as major determinants of their well-being (see Table 1.1). While there is clearly variation in the relative importance attached to different job characteristics, the broad patterns are very similar across different European societies and for both men and women. Where employees are in jobs with lower skill levels, with less discretion over how they do the work, where there are fewer training opportunities, less security and greater difficulties in reconciling work and family life, they are also significantly less satisfied with their work.

Table 1.1. Correlations of job characteristics and overall job satisfaction (employees in the EU-15)

	All employees	Male employees	Female employees
Skill (ISCO class)	0.12	0.12	0.14
Task discretion	0.28	0.30	0.26
Employer training	0.12	0.14	0.11
Job security	0.32	0.33	0.30
Work–family balance	0.23	0.20	0.25

Source: Pooled data from Eurobarometers 44.3 (1996) and 56.1 (2001).

It is notable, however, that among these different factors it is discretion at work, job security, and work–family balance that have the most marked impact on job satisfaction. There are some variations between men and women. Task discretion appears to matter more strongly for men than for women, while work–family balance has greater importance for women's satisfaction. But these differences are relatively minor and the more striking point is the high level of similarity in pattern for the two sexes.

The approach adopted in this book is rooted in the job characteristics tradition rather than that of job satisfaction. It is concerned with the extent to which jobs provide for the development of capabilities and offer protection against conditions that have been shown to be damaging for employee psychological health. But the factors that it is focusing upon are also subjectively important for employees and they powerfully affect their satisfaction with their jobs.

Perspectives on Changing Job Quality

There exist very diverse scenarios in the literature about the broad trends in the quality of work, underpinned by rather different assumptions about the key causal determinants of work patterns. Drawing selectively from a rather large and diverse literature, we would highlight three particularly interesting approaches: universalistic theories (which subdivide into optimistic and pessimistic versions), production regime theory (which emphasizes the importance of employer choices and skill formation systems), and finally an employment regimes approach which underlines the importance of employment policies and of the power of organized labour within particular countries.

Universalistic Theories

The common feature of the various universalistic approaches is the view that the broad trends in the nature of work will be very similar across at least the more advanced economies. The optimistic versions pointed to the determining power of technology in the broad sense of the term. In the 1960s, this perspective was primarily associated with the theory of industrialism. It received its most powerful formulation in Kerr et al.'s *Industrialism and Industrial Man* (Kerr et al. 1960), which argued that advanced industrial technology led to higher levels of skill, increased skill specialization, and more consensual patterns of work relations that reflected recognition of the enhanced role of employees in the production process. A particularly influential study that appeared to offer empirical support for this perspective was Robert Blauner's *Alienation and Freedom* (Blauner 1964). This linked trends in work quality to the growing interest in the implications of automation. While accepting that earlier periods of technological development, in particular that of assembly line production, may have had very negative effects for work quality, Blauner argued that the arrival of automation reversed earlier trends to an ever greater division of labour and fragmentation of work tasks. Instead, it brought higher levels of skill involving a reunification of the conception and execution of work, led to greater discretion for employees both individually and as members of teams and was conducive to a stronger sense of social integration in the workplace. While the type of automation that Blauner focused upon—large-scale capital intensive plant—proved suitable only for special sectors of production, many of his arguments were redeployed by Piore and Sabel (Piore and Sabel 1984) in the 1980s in the context of the new more flexible forms of automation made possible by microprocessor technology.

From the 1970s, the 'industrialism' perspective was increasingly replaced by the theory of post-industrialism. This gave less emphasis to technology in the sense of production equipment and shifted the focus to the growing importance of 'knowledge' as the key driver of economic growth (Bell 1974). It retained however the broadly optimistic view of developments in skill structure, predicting a steady growth in the proportion of the workforce in higher-level professional, technical, and managerial occupations. Whereas the theory of industrialism was mainly premised on the view that manufacturing was the core industrial sector, the theory of post-industrialism was able to generalize many of its tenets to the rapidly expanding service sector. The emphasis on knowledge as the key to economic progress in the advanced economies also echoed with the growing concern with international competition in the 1990s. While the developing economies had the advantage of low labour costs, the advanced economies it was argued could retain their competitive position through an increasing shift towards high value products requiring large-scale research investment and a highly skilled workforce. In the 1990s variant versions of the same underlying thesis emerged, emphasizing the centrality of information technologies rather than knowledge per se (Castells and Aoyama 1994; Aoyama and Castells 2002). Many of the ideas underlying this schema appear to have fed into the EU's commitment in 2000 to develop the most competitive and dynamic knowledge-based economy, with more and better jobs and greater social cohesion (Rodrigues 2002).

The pessimistic version of universalistic theory had its roots in the long tradition of Marxian theory of capitalist development. This predicted a general tendency for an increasing division and intensification of labour, with work tasks becoming highly fragmented, deskilled, and closely supervised. An influential development of this view, inspiring a large body of case study research in the 1950s, was by the French industrial sociologist Georges Friedmann (Friedmann 1964). However, the sharp rise of interest in this perspective in Anglo-Saxon sociology in the 1970s was largely associated with the publication of Braverman's Labor and Monopoly Capital (Braverman 1974). While redeploying many of Friedmann's themes, Braverman gave the argument a new lease of life by extending it to embrace the service sector and white-collar work. As in earlier analyses, he was sharply critical of the view that advanced automation in manufacturing was leading to an improvement in the conditions of manual work. Rather, it merely accentuated the long-term trend towards the degradation of labour. But most crucially, in sharp contrast to Bell's vision of the growth of non-manual work, involving a general tendency to rising skill levels, Braverman argued that non-manual work was subject to the same general law of the capitalist division of labour as manual. After an initial period of expansion it became the object of the same strategies for enhancing employer control: with the increasing subdivision of work and mechanization of the office, the skills and autonomy of clerical and service sector workers were being progressively eroded until they would become indistinguishable from those of manual workers.

In the 1980s, the pessimistic view of developments in the quality of work re-emerged in a rather different form. The argument was no longer that there was a general process undermining the quality of jobs, but rather that the labour market was segmented into quite distinct sectors of 'good' and 'bad' jobs. The major early influences were the work of the American economists Michael Piore and Richard Edwards (Doeringer and Piore 1971; Edwards 1979; Berger and Piore 1980). They pointed to a critical distinction between a 'primary' sector of relatively skilled, highly paid and secure jobs, which at least in its upper tier offered significant promotion opportunities, and a secondary sector of low-skill, poorly paid, insecure and dead-end jobs. Despite the similarity in the description of the labour market, the arguments differed in the explanatory factors thought to be at work, with Piore giving a more central role to technological change (with its implications for skill and internal labour markets) and

Edwards renewing in more sophisticated form the argument about capitalist control strategies. While segmentation theory provided a relatively static vision of labour market divisions, its successor 'flexibility theory'—drawing on the same underlying schema of core and periphery—offered a even darker image of labour market development. Driven by ever greater international competition and more volatile product markets, employers, it was argued, would seek to maximize their flexibility to restructure their workforces by placing an increasing proportion of their employees on non-standard contracts (whether temporary, part-time, or pseudo-self-employed). Since this peripheral workforce was designed to bear the brunt of adjustment costs, this perspective offered a polarization scenario in which a protected 'core' of skilled workers was complemented by an increasingly vulnerable periphery of the lower skilled.

Finally, a new version of the polarization argument emerged from economists in the 1990s, re-engaging with some of the earlier debates about the implications of automation. The early automation studies had predicted a positive effect on skill arising from the elimination of the least skilled jobs, which were also the jobs with the poorest job quality. The new twist to the argument involved a re-specification of the types of jobs that were most likely to automated (Autor, Levy, and Murnane 2003). These, it was suggested, were jobs with clearly defined rule structures that could be converted into programmed instructions. Such jobs were not primarily those of the least skilled, where work routines were likely to be relatively haphazard, but those of skilled manual and lower clerical work. The progress of automation then would lead not to overall upgrading of the occupational structure, but rather to the hollowing out of the middle and increased polarization of work between the highly skilled and the low skilled (Goos and Manning 2007; Manning 2004).

The different scenarios discussed above point to deep trends in the underlying infrastructure of advanced societies that are likely to lead to broadly similar pattern of development in work tasks and work organization. More recently, however, there has been a growing interest in how patterns of work are affected by institutional patterns and cultural norms. Common economic pressures are held to be mediated by the nature of the historically developed institutional frameworks of particular countries or groups of countries. There are two versions of the 'institutionalist' argument that are of particular interest to us here. The first distinguishes countries in terms of their production regimes, the second in terms of their employment regimes.

Production Regimes, Skill Formation Systems, and the Quality of Work

Theories of production regimes are perhaps most naturally seen as heirs of the corporatism tradition, but shifting the focus from national to meso and company level (Soskice 1999; Estevez-Abe, Iversen, and Soskice 2001; Hall and Soskice 2001a, 2001b; Soskice 2005). The central argument is that quite different employment dynamics can be found between capitalist societies depending on the way that firms try to solve their coordination problems with respect to industrial relations, vocational training, corporate governance, inter-firm relations, and the cooperation of their employees. Very broadly it is suggested that there is a critical difference between liberal market economies (LMEs), which coordinate their activities primarily in terms of hierarchies and competitive market arrangements, and coordinated market economies (CMEs) which depend more heavily on non-market arrangements.

Although there are variants of CMEs, it is those in which coordination takes place through the industrial sector (industry-coordinated economies) that are characteristic of certain European societies. Within Europe, the closest examples to the ideal-typical coordinated model are Germany and the Scandinavian countries. While initially a distinction could be drawn between a 'centralized egalitarian model' of coordination more characteristic of the Scandinavian societies and a 'flexibly coordinated' model more characteristic of the Germanic countries, there has been subsequent convergence on a single 'flexibly coordinated' model. The countries closest to the ideal-typical LME are Britain and Ireland.

A potentially attractive feature of the theory is that it provides an account of the inter-linkages of many different institutional characteristics, affecting diverse spheres of social interaction. For our purposes, however, the point of central interest is that the nature of the production regime is held to affect a number of aspects of work experience that have been shown to be critical for the quality of employment and that have important consequences both for worker's job satisfaction and psychological health. This is particularly the case with respect to skill level, the degree of job control, participation at work and job security. The argument is most systematically presented by David Soskice (Soskice 1999).

Many of the factors crucial for employee well-being are held to be substantially better in CMEs. To begin with these production regimes emphasize product market strategies based on complex 'diversified quality products' (Streeck 1992) that 'depend on skilled and experienced employees'. There will be a need to foster, through strong initial vocational training systems, specialized skills across the broad spectrum of the workforce (skilled manual workers, technicians, and engineers). Such skills will combine both industry-specific technological knowledge with company-specific knowledge of organization, processes, and products.

Higher skill levels in turn reinforce other institutional characteristics that are usually associated with a higher quality of employment. Complex products favour the devolution of decision-making responsibilities to employees. Devolved responsibility will be reinforced by new forms of work organization. This type of production requires its skilled employees 'to work in ways (especially autonomous group environments) that are costly for management to monitor and impossible to explicate contractually'.

The fact that, with high skill levels and new forms of work organization, employees themselves possess key problem-solving knowledge has major implications for industrial relations. Unilateral control over decisions is less efficient than consensus-based approaches to decision-making. It is a process of production that leads to more cooperative industrial relations at company level 'to ensure cooperation from highly skilled and hence powerful employees', with employee elected bodies playing a significant role in company decision-making. There will be effective works councils (or other employee representational bodies) within the company linked to industry unions outside it that themselves play an important part in the industrial relations system.

Finally, skill specificity will make employers reluctant to casually hire and fire employees, because of the training costs to develop company-specific skills and the market power of those with industry-specific skills. Cooperative industrial relations also require the ability of companies to commit to long-term relations with employees, and hence are conducive to greater job security. This is reinforced by the fact that higher specialized skills are thought to have implications for welfare systems: the need to encourage investment in industry-specific skills is conducive to the creation of strong welfare safety nets that protect income in the event of unemployment (Estevez-Abe, Iversen, and Soskice 2001; Iversen and Soskice 2001; Mares 2003).

In most respects LMEs are held to provide a mirror image of the employment conditions of the coordinated economies. Although in early formulations of the theory, these were described as societies based on a low-skill equilibrium, more recent discussions characterize them in terms of a highly polarized skill structure. The lack of a strong vocational training system at post-compulsory secondary education level means that lower-level workers have especially weakly developed skills. But, given that it is a production system more orientated to internationally competitive service provision and innovative development of complex systems (such as telecoms and defence), it also requires significant numbers of 'highly trained and mobile' professionals. The emphasis on rapid technological innovation encourages organizational structures that allow high levels of unilateral managerial control, and the consequent marginalization of unions, while the need to take advantage at short notice of new skills on the labour market requires a regulative system that allows employers to hire and fire employees at low cost.

A particularly interesting feature of production regime theory for analyses of the quality of work is the central role it attributes to systems of skill formation. A somewhat later development in production regime theory was recognition that the structuring quality of skill regimes could have rather different consequences for men and women (Estevez-Abe 2005; Soskice 2005). As Estevez-Abe (2005: 180–215) has argued, the emphasis on specific skills in the CMEs may be primarily beneficial for men, while making women's entry into private sector jobs, particularly higher-level jobs, considerably more difficult than in liberal market regimes. This reflects the greater difficulty and lower incentives for women to acquire specific skills compared to general skills, given the likelihood of career interruptions and a higher risk of statistical discrimination by employers reluctant to train employees who they think may have extended periods away from work. The implications of this for women's labour market participation differ however fundamentally between the Scandinavian countries and other coordinated market regimes. In the former, the state has taken an active role in expanding public sector employment, which provides good employment opportunities for women (albeit at the cost of very marked sex segregation in employment) and a level of childcare provision that makes it possible for women to take up such jobs. In contrast, in a country such as Germany, the lack of private sector opportunities is reflected in relatively low levels of female participation in the labour market.

Following the same logic about the disadvantages in coordinated regimes of those who have difficulties acquiring specific skills, the argument could be extended to expect relatively strong labour market stratification by contract type, since those on non-standard contracts will have little chance to receive specialized training. In short, it is a scenario that implies significant dualism with respect to the quality of work whether in terms of sex or contract. In contrast liberal market regimes are likely

Table 1.2. Production regimes and polarization risks (+ high polarization risk; = low polarization risk)

	Class	Industry	Temporary	Part-time	Gender
Liberal					
Skill	+	+	=	+	=
Training	+	+	=	+	=
Task discretion	+	+	=	+	=
Job security	+	+	=	+	=
Coordinated					
Skill	=	=	+	+	+
Training	=	=	+	+	+
Task discretion	=	=	+	+	+
Job security	=	=	+	+	+

to lead to polarization primarily along skill (or class) lines, although this in turn may produce skill-related differences between workers in different industries and between full-time and part-time employees (Table 1.2).

Employment Regimes and the Quality of Work

In developing their argument, theorists of production regimes, with their strong emphasis upon the centrality of the role of employers, placed themselves in conscious opposition to a rival approach that had held the field in comparative analyses of European social structure. This sought to account for variations in institutional structures in terms of a 'power resources' perspective, which emphasized the relative organizational capacity of employers and labour and the way this was mediated through the state. This was closely related to earlier Marxian theories of class formation and class conflict, but it gave the tradition a distinctive twist through its emphasis on the way in which democratic institutions could provide a non-violent channel for class forces to modify capitalist social structure. Perhaps the most systematic development of this approach was by Walter Korpi (Korpi 1978, 1983), although it informed a good deal of analysis of welfare state development, in part from other Nordic researchers (Palme 1990; Kangas 1991), but also from wider afield (see in particular, Stephens 1979; Esping-Andersen 1990; Fligstein and Byrkjeflot 1996).

Much of the theorization and empirical work linked to this approach has focused on welfare regimes. However Esping-Andersen's work brings out strongly the mutual implications of welfare regimes and employment policies. Fligstein and Byrkejeflot explicitly linked the power resources approach to a notion of 'employment systems', which reflect a political compromise by the major social actors, that at least for a period informs a set of cultural practices and understandings framing patterns of social interaction. In a rather similar way to production regime theorists they give a central position to systems of skills formation in developing their contrast between systems based on vocationalism, professionalism, and managerialism. In sharp contrast, however, to the production regime perspective, they depict the strong German vocational system as the reflection of powerful labour organizations at an earlier historical period, whereas a reliance on general education and firm-specific job training is a product of managerialist systems where labour has been historically weak. A central structuring feature of the institutional compromise was the level of state intervention, which in turn was seen as reflecting the labour market power of workers, rooted partly in skill and partly in the ability to control labour and skills supply.

Given the central emphasis in this approach on the power resources of labour, it would seem more relevant to distinguish institutional structures in terms of the employment and industrial relations policies that underlie them. In this light, one could distinguish between three principal models of employment regime: inclusive, dualist, and market regimes. Inclusive employment regimes are those where policies are designed to extend both employment and common employment rights as widely as possible through the population of working age. Dualist regimes are less concerned about overall employment levels but guarantee strong rights to a core workforce of skilled long-term employees, at the expense of poor conditions and low security of the periphery. Finally, market employment regimes emphasize minimal employment regulation and assume that market adjustments will naturally lead in the longer term to relatively high employment levels, while employees' benefits will be strictly related to their marginal productivity. The three employment systems differ in a relatively systematic way in terms of the extent of involvement of organized labour in decision-making, the principles underlying employment policy, the role attributed to the public sector, the salience of quality of working life programmes, the institutional provision to support the combination of paid work and family and the level of welfare protection offered to the unemployed.

The starting point of such a perspective, which provides the central dynamic for the other features of employment relations, is the role attributed to organized labour in employment policy and employment regulation. In inclusive employment systems, organized labour has a strongly institutionalized participation in decision-making, both in its own right and through its influence over the party in government. It will tend to use those resources to develop policies that will both benefit its membership and reinforce its own power resources. A central issue is the level of employment: organized labour will push for employment generation since high employment levels not only protect its members from unemployment and poverty, but increase the relative power of labour by creating greater skill scarcity. A policy geared to high employment is in turn likely to see stronger state intervention to create jobs in the public sector. A relatively tight labour market will strengthen employees' power at workplace level, will be conducive to greater participation at work, and will broaden concern about the quality of work. High employment policies will also encourage the development of work–family policies that make it easier for women to enter and remain in the labour market. Finally, a concern to provide security and welfare to employees will lead to policies that provide higher levels of support to the unemployed—both in terms of financial assistance and in terms of active labour market policy to help re-entry to work. This type of employment regime then minimizes differentials between different types of employee and provides a strong safety net for weaker categories of employee (Table 1.3). Polarization tendencies therefore should be strongly contained.

Dualist employment regimes will be characterized by a consultative involvement of labour in the decision-making system, reflecting its

Table 1.3. Employment regimes and polarization risks (+ high polarization risk; = low polarization risk)

	Class	Industry	Temporary	Part-time	Gender
Market					
Skill	+	+	=	+	=
Training	+	+	=	+	=
Task discretion	+	+	=	+	=
Job security	+	+	=	+	=
Dualist					
Skill	=	=	+	+	+
Training	=	=	+	+	+
Task discretion	=	=	+	+	+
Job security	=	=	+	+	+
Inclusive					
Skill	=	=	=	=	=
Training	=	=	=	=	=
Task discretion	=	=	=	=	=
Job security	=	=	=	=	=

weaker organizational strength. Its influence then will be contingent on the political orientation of the government. In Dualist systems organized labour tends to draw its strength primarily from a more easily mobilizable core workforce of employees in larger firms. The nature of employment regulation will tend to reflect this providing strong employment protection, good employment conditions, and generous welfare support for the core workforce, but much poorer conditions for those on non-standard contracts. Given a less strong commitment to high employment levels, provision to assist women to combine paid work and the family will be rudimentary. Unemployment protection will distinguish sharply between employees in the core and the periphery. In short, one would expect sharp contrasts between the conditions of employees on standard and non-standard contracts and significant vulnerability of those in more vulnerable labour market positions (Table 1.3).

Finally, in market employment regimes, the assumption is that employment levels and job rewards are self-regulated by a well-functioning market and that institutional controls by organized labour are negative rigidities. Labour is then excluded from a significant role in decision-making, the level of employment is not regarded as an appropriate political objective—with the exception of policies to remove market rigidities, the public sector is kept to a minimum, employment conditions are regarded as the concern of individual employers, and provision of welfare, whether in terms of work–family support or unemployment benefit, is highly restricted. As a market regime, differentials should primarily reflect skill differences (Table 1.3). Stratification will be particularly strong by class. There are also likely to be high differentials between routine services and manufacturing, and between full-time workers and part-time workers, but this should primarily result from underlying skill differences. Since there is a very weak safety net for more vulnerable groups, there should be relatively high risk of polarization. In contrast sex differences should be relatively small reflecting the convergence of men and women's qualification levels. Similarly, since there are only weak restrictions on employers' rights to hire and fire even permanent workers, differentials between permanent and short-term contract workers should be relatively small.

The Country Comparisons

Our aim has been to focus on country contrasts that will provide relatively strong tests of the expectations of these different perspectives. The models are of ideal-type nature and countries can only regarded as more or less proximate to any specific type. Yet those who have developed production regime and power resource theory have been relatively explicit about the countries that they regard as reasonably close exemplars of particular types of regime. We focus particularly upon Britain, France, Germany, Spain, and Sweden as core examples of different regime types.

The Scandinavian countries (with the honorary inclusion of Finland) are held to be particularly good examples of the CMEs. They also have been usually taken as the models of countries where organized labour has a strongly institutionalized position and protection is relatively universalized. We have taken Sweden as in many respects the paradigm country with respect to the development of active labour market policies and quality of work programmes. However, the analysis of training focuses on Denmark and Finland for which the data is more comparable with other European societies.

Britain is usually presented as the polar opposite to the Scandinavian countries, as the European exemplar of liberal or market-orientated policies. It has to be said that this was clearest in the period of the Thatcher and Major governments (although these were in power for much of the period for which we have good comparative data). While Ireland is also sometimes cited as 'liberal', it is recognized that its industrial relations system poses significant problems with respect to that classification.

Germany has a very different theoretical position in the two schemas. It is placed together with the Scandinavian societies as a coordinated regime in production theory, and indeed, given the thesis of convergence between types of coordinated economies, it is very much taken as the prime example of such societies. But, within an employment regime perspective, it is viewed as a dualist regime that is quite distinct from the Scandinavian inclusive model.

Spain and France are recognized to be tricky to fit into the typology of production regimes, although there is a tentative suggestion that they may belong to a third, theoretically unelaborated, regime type— the 'Mediterranean', where the state has played a significant coordinating role, while retaining relatively liberal arrangements in the sphere of labour relations. They are taken here primarily as examples of dualist regimes with strong insider protection, reflected particularly in Spain by very high levels of temporary employment.

A first step is to consider more closely how these countries differ in terms of the key institutional factors that are thought to lead to variations in the quality of working life between countries—the skills formation system on the one hand and the coordinating power of labour and the strength of integrative policies—on the other.

Skill Formation Systems

Although production regimes are viewed as highly integrated complexes of mutually reinforcing institutions, the emphasis in much of the detailed causal discussion—particularly with respect to the quality of work, but also in the analyses of welfare systems and sex differences in employment opportunities—is placed on their distinctive systems of initial skill formation.

INITIAL SKILL FORMATION SYSTEMS

There is a reasonable consensus that Britain and Spain represent systems with low levels of pre-entry vocational training (Cruz-Castro and Conlon 2001), while France and Sweden have schools-based industry-specific training and Germany and Denmark dual system industry-specific training.

The strength of a pre-vocational training system depends partly upon the proportion of the age group that enters upper secondary education and partly on the relative size of the vocational and general streams within secondary education. Estimates for France and Britain vary substantially upon whether one takes all upper secondary or excludes short-term upper secondary. The latter is probably more relevant since short-term pupils may be primarily retaking earlier exams. We take then as the effective participation rate in full upper secondary education, the participation rate at age 17. Programmes in upper secondary education can be divided into those that are general and those that are vocational in terms of 'orientation'.

On the basis of these estimates (Table 1.4, column 3), Germany emerges as having the strongest pre-entry vocational training system and Spain the weakest. Taking those countries with more than a third of the age cohort in vocational training as 'strong vocational systems', Germany, France, Finland, Denmark, and Sweden have strong vocational systems and the UK and Spain can be classified as 'general' systems. Among the strong vocational, we can distinguish two countries that rely heavily on the dual system (Denmark and Germany), whereas Finland, France, and Sweden are schools-based.

The evidence broadly supports then the distinctions between initial skill formation regimes in the production regime literature, with the addition

Table 1.4. Initial vocational training

	Participation in education at age 17 1998	Proportion of upper secondary vocational	Proportion of cohort with pre-entry vocational training	Proportion of upper secondary enrolments 'dual'
Denmark	82	51.8	42.5	51.3
Finland	93	52.0	48.4	10.5
France	90	56.4	50.8	11.2
Germany	92	64.6	59.4	49.1
Spain	79	21.5	16.9	2.7
Sweden	97	40.6	39.3	ND
UK	68	47.1	32.0	NA

Sources: OECD *Education at a Glance* (2000) and ONS *Social Trends* (2001).

that France would appear to be closer to the model characteristic of the coordinated regimes.

CONTINUING VOCATIONAL TRAINING

A more recent turn to the debate, however, has been to question whether such initial vocational training is as important as it once was for the skill needs of the modern workplace. By emphasizing one particular source of skill development, it could give a misleading picture of the overall distribution of relevant training. Taking account of in-career training may provide a much higher skill profile than would be indicated by measures based on initial training alone (Finegold and Wagner 1999).

These arguments have been developed forcibly by Herrigel and Sabel (Herrigel and Sabel 1999). While the German craft-type skill formation system certainly provided more flexibility than Taylorism, it also contained important forms of rigidity which, it is suggested, made transition difficult to the most effective types of production organization that were developing in the 1990s. This in turn might help to explain the decline in the 1990s in the proportion of German firms that provided apprenticeship training and in the number of apprentices within those firms that did train.

The view that the pace of technical and organizational change is accelerating in an increasingly competitive international economy also underlies the increased attention given to the provision by firms of continuing training. Arguably this is likely to be particularly important for the quality of work life of employees, since it provides the opportunities for skill renewal that safeguard against the risk of labour market marginalization in the later career phase when the skills acquired in initial training have become outdated.

Table 1.5. Participation rates of employees in vocational training over one year

	ECHP 1994	ESWC 2000	CVTS 1999	Average hours per trainee per year	Training as % total labour costs
Denmark	44.0	48.3	53.0	41	3.0
Finland	57.5	53.7	50.0	36	2.4
France	14.9	23.3	46.0	36	2.4
Germany	24.6	30.1	32.0	27	1.5
Spain	11.2	17.8	25.0	42	1.5
Sweden	n.d.	46.0	61.0	31	2.8
UK	22.4	47.6	49.0	26	3.6

Notes: The CVTS is an enterprise survey covering establishments with at least ten employees and therefore excludes a significant group of employees.

Sources: Figures from Ok and Tergeist (2003: 10), apart from ECHP which are from Martina Dieckhoff (see Chapter 3, this volume). ECHP figures for France are for 1995 and for Finland 1996, as joined the survey in the third wave. Third European Survey on Working Conditions 2000; Continuing Vocational Training Survey 1999.

The relative position of countries in terms of initial and continuing training may be very different. While estimates of continuing training from different sources have to be handled with considerable care (Ok and Tergeist 2003; Bainbridge et al. 2004), there are three main comparative sources for the 1990s—the European Community Household Panel (ECHP), the Third European Survey on Working Conditions, and the Continuing Vocational Training Survey (a survey conducted in 1999 of establishments with at least ten employees).

Looking at the broad pattern that emerges from these (Table 1.5), Denmark, Finland, and Sweden have relatively high levels of participation (with a participation rate of over 40 per cent in all surveys); together with Britain (two surveys give figures higher than 40 per cent, although the ECHP data from earlier in the decade are rather lower). The three countries with low levels of continuing training are Germany, Spain, and France. All the estimates indicate that less than a third of German employees participate and a quarter or less of Spanish employees. The figures are most volatile for France where estimates are 15 per cent from the ECHP, 23.3 per cent from ESWC, and 46.0 per cent from CVTS. The higher figure for France comes from the establishment survey, which excludes small establishments, perhaps indicating a higher degree of segmentation in French training provision than in other countries. Taking the majority verdict, however, France too falls into the low continuous training category.

The picture could be developed by taking into account, together with the participation rate, potential quality indicators. One might be the average number of hours spent in training by each trainee. This is only possible with the CVTS data. Participation rates and hours per trainee are

Table 1.6. A classification of skills formation systems

Pre-entry	Continuing VT	
	High	Low
Strong vocational		
Dual	Denmark,	Germany,
schools-based	Sweden, Finland	France
General	UK	Spain

not in general very highly correlated. Germany remains a low-level provider, but France and Spain, despite their low levels of participation, have course durations comparable to those of the Nordic countries. The UK comes out as relatively weak in terms of course duration. Alternatively one could take the costs of training to companies as a percentage of total labour costs. This confirms the picture of Germany and Spain as poor providers, but France again is comparable to the Nordic countries. The UK comes out as particularly strong on this indicator.

Taking together initial and continuing training provision gives the overall typology of skill formation systems shown in Table 1.6. Ideally it would be helpful to be able to distinguish degrees of specificity of continuing vocational training, but this is a controversial area where there is little consensus about the nature of the skills acquired under the different systems. With respect to the Scandinavian countries, taking account of continuing training reinforces their already strong position with respect to vocational training. Germany on the other hand has a strong initial training system but weak continuing training provision. This would suggest that the types of effects claimed for specific skills systems may be even clearer in the Scandinavian countries than in Germany. In terms of the assumptions of production regime theory the most problematic country is the UK, which combines a very low level of initial training with a high level of continuing training. Clearly an important empirical issue is whether the nature of this continuing training is such that it provides significant compensation for weak initial training, thereby counteracting the effects attributed to its 'general' pre-entry system.

Employment Policies

The distinctions emphasized by the employment regime perspective draw attention to the strength of organized labour and to policies that facilitate the labour market integration of potentially marginal groups. Inclusive regimes are those that have high levels of union coordinating capacity, and strong policies for the integration of more vulnerable categories of labour both within the workplace and within the labour market. Dualistic regimes will have labour movements with moderate or weak coordinating power, strong protection at work of well-established employees, and weak policies to facilitate labour market integration. Market regimes will have weak labour movements, and little in the way of either workplace or labour market integrative policies.

THE POSITION OF ORGANIZED LABOUR

The coordinating strength of organized labour depends upon the capacity to exercise influence at both central and local level. Influencing decision-making at national level is important for the degree of uniformity of norms, while influence at local level is likely to be a condition of effective implementation. The European Commission has constructed an index of the centralization of wage bargaining over the period 1990 to 2003 (European Commission 2004: 43). This takes account both of the relative importance of higher-level national and sectoral-level bargaining and of the degree of union fragmentation. Sweden, Finland, and Denmark stand out very clearly as having highly centralized systems, Germany and Spain are at an intermediate level, while France and the UK have very low levels of centralization (Table 1.7).

In general it can be assumed that the influence of the unions at work-place level will be closely related to the strength of union membership. It is notable that union density varies sharply between the Scandinavian countries and the other countries. A recent comparative assessment of union membership (Visser 2006) that adjusts for variations in

Table 1.7. The coordinating strength of labour organizations

	Bargaining centralization 1990–2003 (1)	Union density 2003 (2)
Denmark	0.53	70.4
Finland	0.57	74.1
France	0.17	8.3
Germany	0.47	22.6
Spain	0.30	16.3
Sweden	0.61	78.0
UK	0.13	29.3

Source: (1) European Commission (2004: 43) and (2) Visser (2006: 38–49).

Note: Bargaining centralization indices have been averaged over the three time points given in the source.

membership criteria (by taking out of the count those who have not paid, the retired, the unemployed, and the self-employed) shows that membership was exceptionally high in the Scandinavian countries. Taking the figures for 2003, given in the second column of Table 1.7, more than 70 per cent of employees were union members in the Scandinavian countries. In contrast, density levels were even lower in Germany (22.6%) than in the UK (29.3%) and exceptionally low in Spain (16%) and France (8%).

Despite the suggestion of a convergence within the group of coordinated economies, this difference between the Scandinavian countries and Germany has been growing greater over time. As Visser (2006) has shown, between 1970 and 2003, union density increased by 22.8 percentage points in Finland, 10.3 in Sweden, and 10.1 in Denmark. Spain also experienced a small increase in union density (3.4 percentage points). In contrast in Germany, France, and the United Kingdom the period saw a marked decline in union strength (−9.5%, −13.4, and −15.5 percentage points respectively).

A final point to note is that sex differences in membership are rather different in the Scandinavian countries compared to Germany. Women were more likely to be unionized than men in Denmark (78% vs. 73%), Finland (75% vs. 69%), and Sweden (90% vs. 83%). In contrast, British, French, and German men were more likely to be union members than women, with the gap particularly marked in Germany (30% of men, but only 17% of women) (Visser 2003). Not only then is the strength of unions at workplace level much weaker in the non-Scandinavian countries, but it appears to be more strongly orientated to the defence of the interests of male employees.

In the case of Germany, it might be argued that the relative weakness of the unions at workplace level is compensated by the existence of the works council system. German works councils certainly have significant co-determination rights—for instance with respect to working hours, principles of pay, overtime, holidays, and health and safety. In principle, this should provide rather comprehensive representation for employees since works councils can be established in any establishment with five or more permanent employees. Moreover, procedures for implementing the legislation are relatively straightforward (Addison et al. 2002). Over time the powers of works councils have been extended to enhance their control over changes in work organization. Significant legislation was passed in 2001 to facilitate the coverage of works council representation.

There is a notable absence of official statistics on works councils and the best estimates have to be drawn from establishment surveys. These suggest that the number and coverage of works councils declined in the 1980s and again after 2000 (Addison, Schnabel, and Wagner 2006).

Using the IAB panel data, Addison et al. found that the prevalence of works councils had become highly restricted by the end of the 1990s. Only 16 per cent of eligible establishments had a works council (and in the private sector only 12.3%). Whether establishments had works councils was strongly related to organizational size (the conventional picture of representation for Germany is predominantly a picture for larger establishments). This implies that coverage rates for employees are higher than might be suggested by figures on prevalence in establishments. Nonetheless, taking the workforce as a whole, only just over half of all-German workers (53%) have access to works council representation (and only 46% of those in the private sector).

Overall, the German works council system is unlikely to provide anything like the level of workplace representation for employees available through the high prevalence of union influence in the Scandinavian countries. The picture that emerges for Germany is rather one of a segmented workforce, in which employees in medium or smaller firms have relatively weak representation in the workplace through either unions or works councils.

WORK INTEGRATION POLICIES

Inclusive regimes will tend to have policies that will reduce differences in the work and employment conditions of different categories of the workforce, whereas dualist regimes will tend to enhance differentiation through policies designed to favour 'core' employees. This should be reflected in differences in approaches to wage bargaining, the salience of work reform programmes, and the strength of insider protection from job loss.

The unions in the Scandinavian countries were distinctive in placing a stronger emphasis on 'solidaristic' wage bargaining, which was designed to curb pay differentials (Gourevitch et al. 1984) and give higher pay rises to the lower paid. Sweden was the exemplar case of this. Although, from the 1980s in Denmark and Sweden and from the early 1990s in Finland, employers sought to reduce the effectiveness of this policy by increasing the decentralization of pay bargaining (Kjellberg 1998; Lilja 1998; Scheuer 1998), in practice change was gradual, informal comparison processes remained strong and the effects of the policy are still reflected in the level of earnings dispersion. The first column of Table 1.8 takes the ratio of the 90th to the 10th earnings percentile as a measure. It shows wage

Table 1.8. Work integration policies

	Earnings dispersion P90/P10 1995–9 (1)	National work reform programmes	Employment protection index 2003 (2)
Denmark	2.16	High	1.8
Finland	2.36	High	2.1
France	3.07	Medium high	2.9
Germany	2.87	Medium	2.5
Spain	n.d.	Low	3.1
Sweden	2.23	High	2.6
UK	3.45	Low	1.1

Source: (1), (2) OECD 2004.
Note: Data for earning dispersion for Denmark are for 90–4.

compression to be substantially greater in Denmark, Finland, and Sweden than in other countries. Wage dispersion was highest in the UK, followed by France and Germany. No data is available for Spain, but given its overall degree of income dispersion, it is probable that it is high there too.

The Scandinavian countries also took the lead in developing policies for the reform of work organization, particularly with a view to increasing the variety of work tasks and the initiative that employees could exercise in work through more autonomous team working practices. These were primarily aimed at improving the work situation of less skilled workers. While Norway pioneered these developments, Sweden began larger-scale and better resourced reform initiatives from the 1980s (Gustavsen 1983; Thorsrud 1984; Gustavsen et al. 1996; Huzzard 2003). An important stimulus came from the Work Environment Act 1978, which broadened the definition of health to include both psychological and physical health. It established the concept that worker control was an integral feature of a healthy working environment (Gunningham and Johnstone 2000). In 1990, the Swedish manual worker union (LO) made the extension of 'developmental work' a central strategic objective, while Sweden launched a vast programme of working life reform—the Working Life Fund (AFL)—which in a four-year period stimulated 25,000 projects, estimated to have affected approximately half of all employees across a wide range of industrial sectors. Similar developments began to take place in Denmark from the 1980s, though primarily driven by a major extension of the occupational health and safety agenda. As in Sweden, the concept of 'unsafe' work was extended to include factors leading to psychological stress (Karageorgiou et al. 2000) and the unions gave a prominent place to the demand for 'developmental work'(Hvid 1999). From the early 1990s, Denmark introduced a far reaching reform to introduce procedures of internal control for health and safety, in which concepts of risk reflected shop floor concerns and involved employee representatives in the risk assessment process (Frick et al. 2000; Nielson 2000). While there were similar developments in Finland, there has been more questioning of their efficacy in the light of the high unemployment rates in the early 1990s (Lehto and Sutela 1999; Frick and Wren 2000). The high level of in-career training in the Scandinavian countries, noted in the previous section, is consistent with the strong policy emphasis in these societies on providing employees with better opportunities for use of their skills and initiative.

However, in other countries, work life reform policies were much more modest. France perhaps came closest with its introduction of a legislative reform (the Lois Auroux) to oblige employers to give employees a 'right of expression in the workplace' (Martin 1994; Goetschy 1998; Jefferys 2003), but its ongoing programme to improve the quality of work tasks was poorly resourced and lost momentum from the 1980s (Piotet 1988; Van de Velde 2005). The German 'humanization of work' programme also lacked the scale and resources to bring about widespread changes in work organization (Fricke 2003; Steiber 2005). In Britain and Spain the issue of work life reform made little impact at all.

A third aspect of work integration policy is that of employment protection. However, this type of integration, especially when related to length of service, can be expected to encourage dualism rather than inclusiveness. Where a high level of protection gives existing employees the leverage to obtain relatively good conditions and high financial rewards, employers may be likely to look to workers on non-standard contracts as a way of enhancing flexibility and reducing costs (Berger and Piore 1980). The most commonly used indicator of the strictness of employment protection regulation is the OECD's EPL measure (OECD 2004). The initial version of this, constructed in 1999 and drawing on the earlier work of Grubb and Wells (Grubb and Wells 1993), was superseded by a considerably modified version in 2004. Rather than just taking severance pay, it assesses the strength of employment protection across a number of different dimensions of employment regulation including rules about notification procedures, grounds for individual dismissal, conditions for the use of temporary workers, and constraints on collective dismissals. While the summary indicator necessarily involves judgements about the scoring and weighting of different items, and is based on formal procedures rather than the way these are implemented, the rankings it produces are held to be consistent with measures from employers' surveys of flexibility with respect to job security. The index shows relatively high levels of employment protection in France, Germany, and Spain as would be expected from 'dualist systems'. The Scandinavian countries diverge with Denmark and Finland having a relatively low, but Sweden a considerably higher rank. Finally, Britain is confirmed as the country where employers have the greatest freedom to hire and fire.

Taking the three aspects of work integration, the Scandinavian countries generally stand out as having stronger policies to benefit the less advantaged sectors of the workforce. This was particularly the case for Denmark and Finland. It was also true for Sweden with respect to wage compression and work reform, although the level of employment closure in Sweden was closer to that of the 'dualist' countries.

EMPLOYMENT INTEGRATION POLICIES

An inclusive employment strategy is one that combines high employment levels with the provision of support for those in more vulnerable labour market positions to enable them to have access to jobs with good employment conditions.

The overall employment rate was certainly high in the Scandinavian societies—particularly in Denmark and Sweden where it was 76 per cent and 72 per cent respectively. But Britain had a very similar employment rate (76%) to Sweden and a rate that was substantially higher than that of Finland. A similar pattern emerges taking women's employment rates with two-thirds or more of women of working age in employment in the Scandinavian countries (and Britain in this case very close to Finland). In contrast, France, Germany, and Spain had lower employment rates overall and this was particularly reflected in their much lower female employment rates. In Spain less than half of women of working age were in jobs.

But if Britain and the Scandinavian countries were similar with respect to the level of employment, they were very different in terms of the support given to potentially vulnerable labour market groups. The Scandinavian countries had stronger policies for facilitating women's access to stable employment, through the provision of parental leave and support for childcare, as well as developing job opportunities through an extensive public sector. Mandel and Semyonov (2006) have developed a 'Welfare State Intervention Index' to capture state interventions (both family policies and state employment) that facilitate women's employment. It includes three indicators: the number of fully paid weeks of maternity leave, the percentage of preschool children in publicly funded day-care facilities, and the percentage of the workforce employed in the public welfare sector. As can be seen from Table 1.9, Denmark and Sweden come out

Table 1.9. Employment integration policies

	Employment rate overall 2004 (1)	Employment women 2004 (2)	WSI index (3)	At-risk-of-poverty rate unemployed 2003 (4)	LPM expenditure per LFS unemployed 2004 (PPS) (5)
Denmark	75.7	71.6	93	33	39.1
Finland	67.6	65.6	57	33	16.0
France	63.1	57.4	50	34	15.6
Germany	65.0	59.2	20	46	18.3
Spain	61.1	48.3	43	40	9.1
Sweden	72.1	70.5	100	26	19.8
UK	71.6	65.6	27	54	9.5

Sources: (1), (2), (4) European Commission (2006: 152, 157); (3) Mandel and Semyonov (2006: 1910–49); and (5) Eurostat (2006: 1–7).

as providing by far the strongest support for women's access to employment, followed at some distance by Finland. Spain, the UK, and particularly Germany have relatively low provision. In contrast, France has a relatively high position on the index, coming next in rank to Finland.

Finally, there are wide country variations in the level of state support for the integration of the unemployed (Gallie and Paugam 2000). In particular countries differ in the extent to which they provide benefits that maintain the living standards of the unemployed and in the expenditure on training provision and assistance in finding new work. One measure of the success of support is the proportion of the unemployed at risk of poverty. The Scandinavian countries have relatively low poverty risks. It should be remembered that poverty risks are not purely a result of the level of benefits, they can also be affected by household structure. But Nolan and his colleagues (Nolan, Hauser, and Zoyem 2000) have shown that the transfer system does play a major role in determining poverty risks. Moreover, given their relatively high proportion of people in single person households, the low poverty level of the unemployed in the Scandinavian countries is unlikely to reflect greater income from other partners. France also has low poverty risks but other household income may play a more important role in accounting for that, since the French unemployed are more than twice as likely as the Danish to be living in a household with other people (Paugam and Russell 2000). The unemployed in Spain and Germany are substantially more likely to be at risk of poverty. Britain is the most extreme case of low living standards for the unemployed, with over half the unemployed (54%) at risk of poverty. This is wholly consistent with its very low-level, primarily means-tested, benefits system.

Denmark and Sweden are also countries that stand out in terms of the resources that they allocate to the training and labour market placement of the unemployed. The measure taken is expenditure on labour market policies per unemployed person. This is estimated in purchasing power standards (PPS), which largely eliminates the effect of price differentials. Germany, France, and Finland have very similar intermediate levels of support. In contrast, Britain and Spain are notable for very low levels of expenditure.

The employment regime classification involves the use of ideal types and as such the institutional structures of specific countries are unlikely to fit particular types in any perfect way. But they may be closer to one type rather than another. In general the Scandinavian countries—Denmark, Finland, and Sweden—appear to be closer to the inclusive employment regime type. Organized labour has a relatively high level of coordinating capacity, there are policies to reduce differentials between different employee categories at work through reducing pay dispersion and improving the quality of job tasks for less skilled employees, and there is relatively strong support for both women and the unemployed to gain access to stable employment. Within this pattern, however, there are differences particularly with respect to the relatively high level of employment protection of existing employees in Sweden.

France, Germany, and Spain approximate more to the dualist employment regime category, given their medium or weak unions and strong employment protection for established employees. Germany and Spain also have relatively low levels of support for the employment integration of women and the unemployed, but France gives substantially higher levels of support. Whereas Germany and Spain approximate the dualist model on all three of the main dimensions, France is allocated more tentatively on the basis of two. Finally, Britain is closest to the criterion for a market employment regime with relatively weak unions and policies for the integration of more vulnerable groups (although more recently government policies have been developing with respect specifically to employment integration).

The Chapters

The chapters that follow take up in turn the major dimensions of work quality. They seek to assess how far patterns are common or vary between countries and, in the case of variation, the plausibility of the two main institutional accounts presented in the second part of the introduction. They also examine the differences of experience of different categories of employee and the evidence for whether there has been a process of polarization.

Michael Tåhlin in Chapter 2 compares countries in terms of skill levels and skill trends, as well as considering the implications of skill for pay dispersion. Martina Dieckhoff, Jean-Marie Jungblut, and Philip O'Connell continue the theme of skill development in Chapter 3, turning to the issue of the level and distribution of employer training and its implications for careers as proxied by earnings. In Chapter 4, Duncan Gallie compares the degree of task discretion between countries, the trends over time and whether there has been convergence or divergence between different types of employee. Stefani Scherer and Nadia Steiber take up in Chapter 5 the issue of work–family balance, in particular looking at the implications of different types of welfare support. In Chapter 6, Serge Paugam and Ying Zhou compare levels of job security, the way job security relates to other aspects of job quality and the implications of this for overall levels of work integration. Finally, Chapter 7 draws out some of the major conclusions of the book. Details of the data sources for each of the chapters are presented in the Appendix.

2

Skills and Wages in European Labour Markets: Structure and Change

Michael Tåhlin

Introduction

Skills and economic inequality are commonly supposed to be tightly linked. The increase in wage dispersion over recent decades that has been observed in several (but not all) OECD countries has often been attributed to a supposed excess demand for skills (Acemoglu 2002; cf. Green 2006). Aside from their links to market factors, skills may be assumed to play an important institutional role. In the production regimes perspective, for instance, the structure of skills is a key determinant of labour market institutions that in turn shape or modify the social stratification of economic rewards. Despite extensive theoretical discussion, however, little is actually known about the empirical variation in the structure and change of skills across national labour markets. Nor do we have a firm grasp of how skills and wages are connected in different countries, and how this connection is tied to fundamental dimensions of social inequality such as class, gender, industry, and contract.

This chapter contains an empirical analysis of the structure and change in skills and wages in five European countries: Germany, Spain, France, Great Britain, and Sweden. I concentrate on the job—or demand—side of skills because my main interest is to assess variations in job quality, but individual skills need to be taken into account as well in order to understand the relation between skills and inequality. I start by looking at the structure of skills, including skill formation and the economic returns to skill, by using cross-sectional micro data from the 2004 wave of the European Social Survey (ESS). In a second empirical section, I examine trends in the level and distribution of skills, again focusing on the demand side. For the change analysis—spanning three decades, 1975–2004—I rely on macro (aggregate micro) data on class location among men and women. Throughout, I consider inequality by class and gender, including a long-term change analysis of gender segregation. In addition to these two fundamental dimensions of stratification, and in line with the general outline of the book, differences in skills and wages by industry and contract are examined.

The chapter is organized as follows. I begin with an overview of previous research in three interrelated fields of relevance for the empirical analyses: (*a*) the structure and change of skill demand in Western Europe and the United States; (*b*) the connections between social class and skills; and (*c*) international variations in educational systems and school-to-work linkages. Based on the reviews in these three sections, I formulate a number of outstanding issues, in need of further empirical analysis. The two empirical sections outlined above are intended to provide some answers to important but previously unresolved questions. In the concluding section, I summarize the empirical findings and discuss some implications of them with a focus on theoretically central issues.

Assessing Skill Demand

Measures of Skill

The literature on skills and wages has to a large extent avoided explicit measurement of the demand side. Instead, skill demand is often inferred from data on skill supply (usually education) and wages. This implicit strategy has been especially common in labour economics, although exceptions have recently emerged (Autor, Levy, and Murnane 2003, Goos and Manning 2007). By contrast, in sociology and in the skill matching tradition in economics that studies overeducation, attempts are made to measure the skill requirements of jobs more directly. There are three main approaches: (*a*) job classification based on some kind of external judgement; (*b*) self-reported (by the job holder) requirements; and (*c*) the average or typical education among job incumbents. We focus on (*a*) and (*b*) below, since (*c*) conflates the supply and demand sides of skill (i.e. workers and jobs). Nonetheless, many empirical descriptions in the literature revert to (*c*) for lack of available alternatives.

The most common version of (*a*) is occupational schemas, such as the American DOT or the Swedish SEI which is very close operationally (if not theoretically) to the Erikson-Goldthorpe (or EGP) class model (see further below). Among employees, the most discriminating criterion across classes is the typical educational requirements of the occupation. Large representative data-sets containing occupational information are available for many countries and several time-points.

In contrast, self-reports of skill requirements have rarely been available in nationally representative data-sets, at least not to an extent sufficient to establish trends and/or allow cross-national comparisons. In Sweden, the Level of living surveys (LNU) contain self-reported educational require-ments comparable across four time-points from 1974 to 2000. Similar measures are available for some other countries for some time-points. The Swedish survey question is phrased: 'How many years of education beyond compulsory school are required in your job?' A similar question is used in the second wave of the ESS, carried out in 2004. We make extensive use of these European data later in this chapter. The correlation between this survey item and occupational class (measured by a set of EGP dummies) is high (0.72 in LNU 1991).

Apart from measuring how much (formal) education is required to get a particular job, it is essential to measure how much training (or learning) on the job is required after the point of hiring. In the Swedish LNU, the question on this dimension of skill requirements reads: 'Apart from the competence needed to get a job such as yours, how long does it take to learn to do the job reasonably well?' Again, a similar item is used in ESS 2004. The correlation with class (EGP) is not as high as the educational requirements indicator, but still substantial (0.40 in LNU 1991).

Together, the self-reported measures of educational requirements and on-the-job training (OJT) predict wage rates roughly as well as class does. In a Mincer model (ln hourly wage regressed on education in years plus experience in years and its square) including a sex dummy, R^2 increases from 0.355 to 0.422 when adding educational requirements and to 0.446 when additionally including the OJT requirements measure. By compar-ison, adding class (EGP) to the Mincer model raises R^2 from 0.355 to 0.465, that is, by more but not much more than the skill requirements measures. Predictions of the residual from the Mincer model (i.e. wages net of differentials by human capital and sex) based on skill requirements (the two self-report measures) and on EGP, respectively, correlate 0.67.

Despite these powerful correlations, it should be noted that the mea-sures of skill requirements are of course far from perfect. In particular, self-reported levels of educational requirements are likely to be affected not only by real job demands but also by, *inter alia*, characteristics of the national schooling system and business cycles (general labour demand relative to supply). It is therefore essential that additional indicators of the skill level of the job are used for validation purposes.

Direct measures of skill demand are typically not however available over time. As discussed in more detail in the next section, under the assumption that structural change (shifts in the distribution of occupations or industries) is the dominant component of shifts in skill demand, an assessment of cross-national variations in the evolution of skill requirements is possible to do on the basis of data on trends in the size of occupational and industrial categories. There is evidence from at least two countries, the United States and Sweden, that structural change clearly dominates within-category (occupations or industries) shifts in skill requirements. It would be of great interest to examine whether any change in skill requirements net of structural change has occurred in other countries in recent decades. Additional empirical evidence on the matter has recently emerged. Preliminary British evidence based on, *inter alia*, the Skills Surveys indicates significant within-category upgrading.[1] Similarly, Spitz-Oener (2006) reports within-occupation upgrading in West Germany. Still, less than fully comparable data and methods across countries so far prevent firm conclusions.

Aside from changes in the average demand for skill, it is important to assess trends in the *distribution* of skill demand. Recent studies of the United States and Britain indicate a combination of general growth in skill requirements with tendencies to polarization. Employment growth over recent decades has been strongest in the high-skill section of the skill demand distribution and slowest in the intermediate section, while low-skill jobs have shown an intermediate growth rate. Overall, the skill-growth pattern in both countries has thus been J-shaped. In Sweden, by contrast, the pattern has been more linear during the same period (1970s through 1990s) with negative employment change in the low-skill section. The decline in the number of low-skill jobs shows a markedly decreasing rate over time, however. The shape of the skill-growth pattern is essential to consider for many purposes, for instance when accounting for changes in earnings inequality, as has recently been shown for Britain (Goos and Manning 2007).

---

[1] I am grateful to Ying Zhou of Nuffield College for running these models.

Technological and institutional factors can be expected to underlie these temporal and international variations. As suggested by several studies (Wright and Dwyer 2002; Autor, Lavy and Murnane 2003; Goos and Manning 2007), recent technological change is not simply skill-biased. Many non-routine tasks that are complementary to technology (such as shelf-filling or house-cleaning) require less skill than many of the routine tasks in which technology substitutes for human labour (such as book-keeping). Hence the J-shaped skill-growth pattern, but with institutional variations: the wage structure in countries like Sweden depresses demand for low-skill service jobs, mainly due to relatively high and rigid minimum wages (making low-skill jobs costly to employers) but also due to relatively low high-skill wages (decreasing the high-skill wage earners' demand for personal services). Accordingly, the Swedish pattern of job growth is closer to a straight slash, that is, a more consistently positive association among jobs between skill content and employment growth rate (Åberg 2004).

Social Class and Skill Change

Despite the considerable advantages of direct measures of skill demand, these are—with few exeptions—not currently available over any significant period of time and it is therefore necessary to look for adequate proxies for the analysis of longer-term change in skill patterns. In this section, I argue that class and skill, in the meaning of skill requirements of jobs, are tightly connected, not only empirically (as indicated above) but also theoretically. While there are several more or less distinct variants of class theory (see Wright (2005) for a recent overview), one particular model has achieved dominance in empirical research over the last two or three decades: the EGP schema (Erikson, Goldthorpe, and Portocarero 1979; Erikson and Goldthorpe 1992: ch. 2; Goldthorpe 2000), also called the Goldthorpe class model. The most recent development in the field is the construction of a new European socio-economic classification— ESeC—which is based rather firmly on the EGP conception of class (see http://www.iser.essex.ac.uk/esec/ and Rose and Harrison 2007).

In current theoretical accounts, social class in its EGP version is based on the notion of employment relations—specifically, among employees, on the distinction between the service relationship and the labour contract (Goldthorpe 2000). However, this theoretical rationale for the class schema has not been empirically validated. While many indirect attempts at validation have been published (see the ESeC website referred to above), only one explicit test has so far been carried out (Tåhlin 2007), with decisively negative results for the theory. By contrast, an important original base of the schema, developed by Robert Erikson in the 1970s—class as occupational skill requirements (OSR)—works very well. The grounds for this claim are the following: (a) OSR—in contrast to employment relations—are highly correlated with class as conventionally operationalized; (b) OSR is strictly a demand-side dimension of stratification, that is, it is a characteristic of the position held by an individual rather than a trait of the individual her/himself, which is crucial since class is supposedly a positional concept; (c) OSR is—in contrast to status or prestige—not tied by construction to any of the determinants or outcomes of stratification that class is supposedly connected to in the empirical world, such as schooling or income; (d) OSR can be expected, however, to be empirically tied to these determinants and outcomes through theoretically sound mechanisms.

These mechanisms revolve around a theoretically central notion that is conspicuously absent from close to all sociological writings on stratification and inequality: productivity. Indeed, 'productivity' (at the individual or firm level) is not even listed in the index of the main current reader on stratification (Grusky 2008). Service class employees would appear to reap benefits from productivity in two ways. First, the productive value of the job is high (at least in the eyes of the employer), who is therefore prepared to pay relatively well for its execution. This mechanism is directly equivalent to 'marginal productivity' in neoclassical economics and related to the more elusive and contested notion of 'functional importance' in the stratification theory of Davis and Moore (1945). It is also supported empirically by many studies (see, e.g., overviews in Gottfredson 1985; Hunter 1986; Farkas et al. 1997; Kerckhoff, Raudenbush, and Glennie 2001). But it is no less compatible with a Marxist perspective on inequality in job rewards among employees (see, e.g. the discussion in Sørensen 1991, 2000). Second, by carrying out complex tasks the employee may become more productive, and can to a large extent take the increased capacity with her/him to make use of in subsequent jobs (with the same or a different employer). From the employer's viewpoint, the provision of general (transferable) training to employees pays off as long as: (a) the output value of the employee is sufficiently large (i.e. exceeding the salary) even during (informal) training; and/or (b) sufficiently many of the employees receiving training (formal and/or informal) stay with the firm long enough for their cumulative output value to exceed the total training costs (including salaries). This mechanism is related to the notion of 'jobs as training slots' (Thurow 1975) and to the impressive array of findings on the mental impact of job complexity by Kohn and Schooler (1983) and their colleagues (see Schooler, Mulatu, and Oates 2004 for a recent overview). The provision by employers of general training, out of line with standard human capital theory, is now widely recognized by labour economists as an empirically pervasive phenomenon and the subject of very active theoretical efforts to account for (see the creative discussion in Acemoglu and Pischke 1999a and the review in Leuven 2005).

It is important to point out that the concept of productivity, even if neglected in most stratification research, is clearly connected to the more standard sociological concept of 'life chances', meaning resources that individuals can use to achieve well-being or other desired life-goals. Economists often refer to these resources as 'human capital'. Regardless of terminology, the thought that inequality in rewards is tied to inequality in resources is highly straightforward and hardly disputed by anyone. While the overlap between the distributions of resources and rewards is obviously not complete, it is no doubt considerable, albeit with significant variations across time and social space. From this point of view, research on class inequality should address three distinct distributional issues: (a) how differences in productivity (or resources) emerge (i.e. inequality of opportunity); (b) how productivity in turn affects rewards; and (c) how differences in rewards, given differences in productivity, emerge. All three issues are central to stratification, and all require taking productivity into account. Without explicit consideration of the productivity–skills dimension, theoretical and empirical analyses of inequality will remain unclear.

A conclusion of the discussion above is that data on changes in the class structure are well suited as a basis for assessing the evolution of skill demand. In the second part of the empirical results below, we make use of this conclusion in a comparative analysis of skill demand shifts over three decades among women and men in Germany, France, Britain, and Sweden.

Educational Systems and School-to-Work Linkages

As outlined in the introductory chapter, there has been a growing interest in the implications of differences between educational systems for skill patterns—a development that has found influential expression in the production regimes literature. But this is not the only body of theory and research on these issues. An equally rich research literature has derived from work on the consequences of educational systems for the transition from school to work, which is a crucial phase for young people's entry into adulthood.

In recent decades, the period between school and work has tended to become longer and more problematic in many countries (OECD 1999*a*; Blanchflower and Freeman 2000; Müller and Gangl 2003). Finding a good job has become more difficult, and spells of unemployment have increased in frequency (see, e.g. Blossfeld et al. 2005). Relative youth wages have also tended to decline, at least in the US and the UK (see, e.g. Ryan 2001).

There is a substantial variation across nations, however, in how young individuals fare as they switch from full-time education to the search for stable employment (OECD 1999*a*; Schröder 2000; Ryan 2001). One important source of this variation is international differences in educational institutions (Shavit and Müller 1998; Stern and Wagner 1999; Müller and Gangl 2003). An influential way of capturing these differences is Allmendinger's typology (1989) based on two fundamental characteristics: (*a*) the standardization of educational provisions, and (*b*) the stratification of educational opportunity. The first dimension concerns the extent to which there is a nationwide uniformity in schooling quality standards, such that educational degrees at various levels provide reliable signals to employers of the degree holders' productive capacity. The second dimension refers to the form of tracking at secondary schooling levels. A high degree of tracking implies that students are separated into vocational and academic tracks upon entering secondary school, and that there is little mobility between tracks. The association between educational qualifications and occupational attainment is expected to be strong in nations with highly standardized and stratified educational systems. In addition to these two dimensions, it is also important to take the degree of vocational specificity into account (Marsden 1986; Maurice, Sellier, and Silvestre 1986): the higher specificity, the stronger the expected association between education and occupation.

In this three-dimensional space, Müller and Shavit (1998) have attempted to locate thirteen OECD nations in a comparative study of school-to-work transitions. At one extreme, with highly standardized, stratified, and vocationally specific educational systems, we find Germany, the Netherlands, and Switzerland. Indeed, Germany and Switzerland are countries with long established apprenticeship systems, in which there are also strong connections between vocational schools and specific employers who provide in-house training and subsequent employment opportunities. (Austria and Denmark would also belong to this category, had they been included in the study.) At the other extreme, with low values on all three dimensions, we find several English-speaking countries: Australia, Britain, Ireland, and, in particular, the United States. Japan is also included here. In the middle ground between these two poles is a heterogeneous group of countries including France, Israel, Italy, Sweden, and Taiwan.

The main hypothesis in the Müller–Shavit study is that the character of the school-to-work transition process is systematically related to this country grouping. This expectation is largely borne out empirically. For instance, the impact of highest educational level attained on occupational status of first job (after leaving full-time education) is strongest in Switzerland, Germany, and the Netherlands and weakest in Britain, Japan, and the United States. Moreover, later empirical studies within the CATEWE project (comparative analysis of transitions from education to work in Europe) show that workers in national labour markets with apprenticeship systems have significantly smoother phases of switching from schooling to employment than workers in other countries, in the sense of facing much lower unemployment risks (see, e.g. Gangl 2001; Raffe and Müller 2002; Müller and Gangl 2003).

Against this background, it is interesting to consider the Swedish case, since it shows that it may be misleading not to expand the simple dichotomy in the production regimes literature between liberal (LME) and coordinated (CME) market economies. As stated above, the educational system in Sweden is of an intermediate character along the dimensions of standardization, stratification, and occupational specificity. In line with this, the empirical association between individual workers' education and occupation is of medium strength in an international context (Müller and Shavit 1998). There are four features of the Swedish school system that are especially important for the link between education and labour market position (Erikson and Jonsson 1998: 372–3). First, the occupational skills taught in vocational education are of a general rather than specific character. Apprenticeships are rare. Second, comprehensive and secondary schooling are highly standardized, with a nationally centralized curriculum. Third, the degree of stratification (tracking) is low. Fourth, there is an absence of educational dead ends, with good opportunities for further education beyond both vocational and academic secondary school, as well as a large system of adult education providing second chances for early school leavers.

Over time, the emphasis on general rather than specific educational content has grown stronger. In fact, five to six decades back Sweden's education system resembled the German apprenticeship model. Since then, the reforms of compulsory and secondary schooling have shifted education towards a system of the US kind (see Nilsson and Svärd 1991; Schröder 2000). The main tendency in secondary schooling is to make vocational and academic tracks increasingly similar in both kind and volume. The most recent reform with this intent was carried out in the 1990s, with an expansion of secondary vocational school from two to three years, bringing it to the level of academic tracks and paving the way for immediate transitions from vocational school to college. This kind of change is in line with international trends, based on conceptions of the 'knowledge society' and an increasingly fluid and mobile working life with growing but less fixed and specific skill demands. The reforms are not without problems, however. Although a large majority (around 98%) of young cohorts in Sweden now continue in school beyond the compulsory level, a significant fraction (about 15%) of students in secondary school leave after one year or less, after having failed to meet the changing requirements. Calls for increasing rather than further reducing the degree of tracking between vocational and academic fields are becoming more frequent, often together with suggestions to introduce apprenticeship opportunities.

Hence, Sweden occupies a middle ground between the German-speaking and English-speaking countries with respect to educational and labour market institutions. In the United States, the loose school-to-work linkages are coupled with an unregulated market with weak insider power and hence low employment barriers, while in Germany the strongly regulated labour market is coupled with an apprenticeship system that significantly eases school-to-work transitions. Sweden combines loose school-to-work linkages of the Anglo-Saxon variety with labour market regulation in the form of high minimum wages (bargained but not legislated) and seniority-based employment protection. This is an unusual combination (possibly shared only with France).

In short, while there are indeed good grounds for thinking that variations in educational institutions may have important implications for skill development, empirical work on this issue suggests that a more refined typology may be needed than that offered by production regime theory.

Outstanding Issues in Need of Empirical Analysis

The discussion above identifies a number of issues in need of further empirical analysis in an internationally comparative context. First, skill demand must be measured directly rather than only implicitly. A consensus is now emerging on how to do this. Below, we will utilize the comparative data from the ESS 2004 that have been designed with explicit skill demand measurement in mind. As will become evident, these data include indicators of the broader process of skill formation, not just schooling but also learning and training outside the education system.

This leads to a second issue for empirical examination: the international variation in how skills are formed and rewarded. As discussed in a previous section, there are several aspects of national education systems that are potentially important for processes of reward attainment in the labour market. The intersection of education and the economy (see Brinton 2005 for a recent overview) is a vast area, however, that is still far from sufficiently well mapped, either theoretically or empirically.

Third, in order to advance the analysis of skill change over time, the connection between social class and skills needs further empirical assessment, given the unavailability of direct skill measures. In particular, cross-national commonalities and variations in this regard have so far not been systematically examined. If a strong connection can be established for several countries, the possibilities to use data on class distributions as a basis for determining the evolution of skill demand would be greatly enhanced.

A fourth important issue, to be dealt with in some empirical detail below, concerns the relation between class and gender as dimensions of stratification. This issue is emerging as a central topic in the discussion of variations across countries in the structure of inequality, with the production regimes literature as a prime example. As spelled out in the introductory chapter of the current volume, a basic distinction in the production regimes model goes between liberal and coordinated market economies (LMEs vs. CMEs). This contrast is similar in many ways to the common economic distinction between unregulated and regulated markets. But rather than supposing that regulation is forced upon employers in CMEs, the production regime argument is that employers support regulation because it fits with the structure of production; in particular, it fits with the character of skills used in the firms. In LMEs, skills are mainly general—usable with many employers and in different jobs—while in CMEs, skills are more specific: to the firm, industry, or occupation. The difference in skill character is supposed to be crucial for the structure of labour market inequality.

The emphasis in the production regime perspective is on class inequality, with the prediction that inequality (in wages and other job conditions) is greater in LMEs, that is, unregulated markets. This prediction is straightforward, and is consistent with the general view of the relation between regulation and distribution. Vocational education and coordinated wage bargaining both reduce class inequality, in skill quantities (the distribution of skills by class) as well as skill prices (the pay-off to skills). So comparing class inequality across different countries is a very weak test of the production regime perspective. What is needed is: (*a*) to look more closely at the character of skill formation in a set of countries (cf. the discussion above); and (*b*) to look at other inequality dimensions than class.

Interestingly, the production regime perspective has recently (Estevez-Abe 2005) been applied to gender inequality. Based on the skill argument, the prediction is that there is a kind of trade-off between class inequality and gender inequality. An emphasis on specific skills reduces class differences but increases gender inequality. The mechanism on the demand side (employers) is statistical discrimination against women. In countries where firm-specific skills are important, women will be more disadvantaged than in general-skill systems, because employers are reluctant to invest in the training of women due to women's higher propensities to leave work for family reasons.

The more important employers' investments in training their employees, the larger the female disadvantage will be. It therefore follows from the production regime model that gender inequality will be larger in CMEs than in LMEs. Another implication is that there will be an interaction effect between class and gender (an 'intersection'). In classes where required skills are higher, the female disadvantage will be larger. So women in the service class will be more disadvantaged, relative to men in the same class, than women in the working class will be. So: firm-specific skill formation reduces class inequality, but at the same time increases gender inequality. Hence, a trade-off.

In what follows, these issues will be dealt with empirically. The first set of analyses are based on micro data from the ESS 2004 (see Appendix of the present volume), while the second set contains analyses of changes in class and gender inequality across recent decades (1975–2004). The cross-sectional micro analyses concern the five countries of Germany, Spain, France, Britain, and Sweden, while the change data on class structures are not available for Spain.

Skills and Wages: Empirical Results

Descriptive Overview

Before we turn to a detailed examination of the specific issues spelled out in the chapter's introduction, it is useful to briefly consider the general pattern of cross-national variation in labour market structures. Table 2.1 shows descriptive statistics for all variables used in the micro analyses based on data from the ESS 2004. In large measure, this pattern confirms established conceptions of the differences in labour market structure across the five countries. We leave skill formation for the next section,

Table 2.1. Descriptive statistics of all variables used

	Germany		Spain		France		UK		Sweden	
	Mean	s.d.	Mean	s.d.	Mean	s.d.	Mean	s.d.	Mean	s.d.
Age	41.9	10.8	37.4	10.7	40.5	10.4	40.1	11.3	42.4	11.8
Female	0.49		0.43		0.50		0.51		0.48	
Service class I	0.20		0.16		0.20		0.22		0.19	
Service class II	0.27		0.24		0.29		0.26		0.28	
Service class total	0.47		0.40		0.49		0.48		0.47	
Routine non-manual	0.25		0.25		0.25		0.27		0.25	
Skilled worker	0.17		0.15		0.11		0.08		0.13	
Unskilled worker	0.12		0.21		0.15		0.17		0.16	
Rest-hotel-trade	0.13		0.13		0.08		0.13		0.07	
Manufacturing	0.24		0.21		0.24		0.16		0.21	
Fixed-term contract	0.10		0.23		0.08		0.10		0.10	
Part-time	0.21		0.10		0.18		0.29		0.15	
Education	13.9	3.1	13.3	4.9	12.9	3.7	12.9	3.1	13.2	3.0
Education, post-compulsory	4.3	3.0	4.5	3.9	3.5	3.2	2.3	2.8	4.8	2.9
Experience	21.1	11.4	15.7	11.4	19.1	11.3	20.2	11.6	21.0	12.1
Seniority (/exp.)	0.63	0.30	0.69	0.30	0.69	0.31	0.48	0.31	0.60	0.32
Educational requirements	2.8	2.6	2.5	3.2	3.6	3.1	1.8	2.5	3.5	2.8
On-the-job initial learning	8.6	13.2	8.0	14.5	13.0	17.7	11.2	15.6	8.8	12.6
On-the-job continuing learning	1.7	0.9	1.5	1.1	1.8	1.1	2.0	1.0	2.1	0.9
Wage/hour (ln)	2.64	0.53	1.99	0.49	2.41	0.50	2.55	0.60	2.69	0.33
N (unweighted)	942		458		704		651		913	
N (contract)	928		445		694		578		909	
N (wage)	595		278		554		522		877	
Response rate, total sample	0.526		0.548		0.436		0.506		0.658	

Note: Employees, aged 19–64 (agricultural sector excluded).

Source: ESS (2004).

and start by looking at the cross-national variation in the distribution of class, industry, contract, seniority, and wages.

On class, it is notable that Britain has the most polarized structure with the largest total proportion of service class I and class VII (unskilled manual workers), that is, the most and the least resourceful (on average) occupational categories. Spain has the least advanced class structure, with the smallest share among the five nations of service class employees (both I and II) and the largest share of unskilled workers. The main reason is surely that Spain is a relatively late economic developer, even if the gap is closing rapidly. In line with this, we see that Spanish employees are several years younger (on average) than employees in the other four countries. (The agricultural sector—which still is large in Spain, with a high mean age of its workforce—is excluded in the sub-sample used here.) Germany is the only country with a majority of its manual workers being in the skilled category (class VI). Britain is the other extreme in this regard, with class VII more than double the size of class VI. We return to the cross-national variation in class structures in the last empirical section below, where changes over the last three decades will be analysed. In that section, we also give a detailed picture of gender segregation by occupational class, including its evolution over time.

Manufacturing industry still employs a much larger share of the workforce than do consumer services (resturants, hotels, and trade), with the exception of Britain where the difference is only three percentage points. France and Germany have the largest manufacturing sectors, and Britain the smallest. According to these data, the consumer services industry is comparatively small in Sweden and France. Fixed-term employment contracts, as measured here, are equally common—about one in ten—in all the countries except Spain where close to a quarter of all workers are employed on a limited-time basis. Part-time employment, on the other hand, is relatively rare in Spain but widespread in Britain. As we will see later, the meaning of these different contract types differs considerably between countries, depending on the institutional configuration of each national labour market.

Two further important stylized facts are reproduced in the descriptive overview in Table 2.1: marked differences across countries in tenure rates and wage dispersion. Britain is an outlier in both respects, with comparatively short employment spells (time spent with each employer) and large wage differentials. To some extent, these two traits are correlated—frequent shifts between firms tend to raise wage differences since the pay-off to such shifts differs more across workers than firm-internal wage trajectories do. But the correlation is limited, as indicated by the pattern across countries. The opposite extremes to Britain in the tenure case are France and Spain, with more than two-thirds (0.69) of an average working life being spent with the current employer compared to less than half (0.48) in Britain. But the opposite to Britain in wage dispersion is Sweden, with only about half the British rate (a log wage standard deviation of 0.33 compared to 0.60). The Swedish tenure rate, however, is only moderately high (0.60); in fact, it is lower than in all the other countries except Britain. The markedly low wage dispersion in Sweden—and the high rate of wage inequality in Britain—obviously has a number of different causes. While some of these causal factors will be explicitly considered in the analyses below, others will only figure implicitly. For example, we look at variations in skill prices (the wage effects of skills) but merely suggest rather than test different explanations of them.

The general pattern described above is by and large well-known from previous findings. Hence, the face validity of the data from the ESS appears to be reasonably high. Against this background, let us now examine in more detail the structure of skills and wages in the five countries, beginning with the process of skill formation.

The Process of Skill Formation

Skill formation is a process, starting in the family (which we abstract from here) well before first school entry and continuing in working life after completed formal education. We look at this process from the viewpoint of the jobs currently held by employees in different countries. The basic idea is to follow a time line: First, to get a certain job, some kind of education is often required. We measure this here by asking how much— if any—schooling beyond the compulsory level is normally required of someone applying for the kind of job that the respondent holds. Second, after entering the job, some amount of training or learning may be necessary before the tasks can be carried out reasonably well. We measure this by asking how long time the initial training or learning typically takes, from the point of job entry. Third, after the initial on-the-job training or learning period is completed, some amount of continuous learning is often required in order to perform at an acceptable level.

These three components—pre-entry education, post-entry initial learning, and continuous learning on the job—together indicate the skill requirements of a job. Importantly, the three parts of the process can be divided between two main arenas where skill formation takes place: the school and the firm. A crucial issue is the relative weight of these arenas in different countries. According to the production regimes perspective, employers play a minor skill formation role in LMEs such as Britain, but a major role in CMEs such as Germany and Sweden. The reason for this difference is that worker skills in CMEs are mainly specific, with employers taking an active interest in their content and formation. By contrast, skills in LMEs tend to be general, and thus mainly formed in schools. In turn, the different emphasis on schools versus firms is believed to be highly consequential for the structure of inequality. While class inequality in skills and wages will be smaller in specific skills systems, gender inequality will tend to be larger in such systems due to statistical discrimination by employers against women.

It should be noted that the distinction between school-based and firm-based learning is not always sharp. In Germany, where apprenticeships play a prominent role in skill formation, around two-thirds of each cohort spend two to three years of human capital accumulation jointly in school and with an employer (Dustmann and Pereira 2005: 24). While apprenticeship periods may be seen as a borderline case between skill formation in schools and in firms, it makes most sense to view them as spells of education rather than jobs: diplomas are not awarded until after apprenticeship completion, much or even most time is spent off the job (in schools or training shops) rather than on the job, and the wages paid by the employer per hour worked are far below the job remuneration rate (see, e.g. Soskice 1994). Although the ESS data do not allow an exact test of this view, we assume that the survey respondents include time spent as apprentices in the category of learning before rather than after job entry. A similar assumption is made by Dustmann and Pereira (2005: 16), who exclude apprenticeship periods from labour market experience.

We begin our empirical examination by asking a simple question: how does the emphasis on school-based versus firm-based skill formation differ across countries? Table 2.2 shows the cross-national variation in the levels of the three components of job skill requirements indicated above. The numbers are relative rates where the average for all countries is set to 100, so numbers above 100 indicate high rates by international comparison and vice versa. (The raw numbers for each country are included in Table 2.1.)

The emphasis in each country on schools versus firms in the skill formation process is revealed by the change in numbers as one moves from the first skill component—requirements of education prior to job

Table 2.2. Skill requirements of jobs in five European countries, ESS 2004

	All	Germany		Spain		France		UK		Sweden	
Pre-entry education	2.8	98	3	87	4	128	1	63	5	124	2
Post-entry learning	9.9	87	4	81	5	131	1	113	2	88	3
Continuing learning	1.8	91	4	84	5	97	3	109	2	119	1

Note: Relative numbers (all countries = 100) and country ranks (1–5). Pre-entry education is measured in years of post-compulsory schooling, post-entry learning in months after job entry until tasks can be carried out reasonably well, continuing learning in index values (0–3) from less to more learning. The second number in each cell is the country's rank (1–5) from highest to lowest on each indicator.

Source: ESS (2004).

entry—to the second and third skill components—initial and continuing learning after job entry. If numbers rise along this route, firms tend to be more important than schools as arenas for skill formation, while schools are more important than firms if the numbers fall. (Note that this is relatively speaking rather than absolutely. Even if one component is more important than the other relative to the situation in other countries, within the country the other component might still have a greater weight; for wages for instance.) Hence, the production regime expectation is that numbers are rising in CME countries and falling in LME countries.

The empirical outcome is close to the opposite of this prediction. The clearest deviant case from the production regime viewpoint is Britain: it ranks lowest of all five countries in school-based skill requirements but close to the top (second in rank) in firm-based skill requirements. And the difference in requirements between these two forms of skill is large— the relative rate almost doubles, from far below to significantly above the international mean, as one moves from school-based to firm-based skills. Although the differences are smaller in magnitude, all other countries have the opposite kind of skill formation process, that is, a higher relative rate of school-based required skills than firm-based required skills. A partial exception is France, where on-the-job initial learning is slightly more important relatively than educational requirements, but the average for initial and continuing on-the-job learning is still below school-based skills in relative rates. Germany is perhaps the theoretically most interesting case besides Britain, as it is usually seen as the exemplar case of a CME. As seen in the table, the difference in relative rates across the three components is not large, but still in the wrong direction from the production regime viewpoint. Firm-based learning thus appears to be relatively unimportant in Germany compared to Britain.

While a crucial part of the story, these incidence rates are not sufficient to decide the issue. In addition, we need an indication of the actual effects of the different skill components. The obvious choice in this regard is wages. It is a reasonable assumption that employers' valuation of different kinds of skills is revealed by the wages attached to them. Table 2.3 shows results from regression analyses of log wages (per hour) on the three components of skill requirements. Both educational requirements and on-the-job initial learning are measured in years, to get comparable scales. (The third component, continuing learning on the job, is measured by ordinal index numbers rather than time, and so the point estimates are less comparable to the other two components.)

In all countries except Britain, the wage increase of one additional year of schooling is larger than the corresponding effect of one year of on-the-job initial learning. Britain has the highest economic pay-off to both kinds of skill (see the strongly significant interaction effects in the pooled regression appearing in the first column), but the difference in wage effects relative to other countries is twice as large in the case of firm-based skills as in the schooling case. This result would seem to clearly support the conclusion from the cross-national variation in incidence rates (Table 2.2). Firm-based skill formation appears to be more rather than less important in the LME case of Britain than in the CME cases of Germany and elsewhere. There is no difference between countries in the wage impact of continuing learning on the job, however. In general, the economic effects of this skill component seem relatively small, perhaps in part due to difficulties of measurement.

The main conclusion of the analysis so far is that the country with the strongest emphasis on general school-based skills—Britain—seems to give a larger role to employers in the overall skill formation process than do countries—such as Germany—where more specific skills are taught in schools. This finding runs directly counter to the production regime claim. But it is not difficult to explain the seemingly anomalous finding. If school-based skills are highly general in kind, specific skills (when needed) have to be learnt elsewhere. The obvious place where such needs are defined is the firm; and so it is only natural that employers are active in bringing the needed skills about. This does not mean that the skills are specific to the firm; the low tenure rates in Britain are one indication that they often are not. Rather, they may be specific to the industry or an occupation. Much recent research indicates that employers in practice are less reluctant to take part in such skill formation than orthodox human capital theory claims (see, e.g. Acemoglu and Pischke 1998). Given the

Table 2.3. Regression of (ln) hourly wages on job skill requirements in five European countries, ESS 2004

	All	Germany	Spain	France	UK	Sweden
Constant	2.184 (39.9)	2.260 (33.2)	1.592 (31.5)	2.138 (42.3)	2.184 (33.9)	2.394 (63.3)
Educational requirements	0.062 (17.6)	0.071 (7.6)	0.065 (9.3)	0.065 (9.7)	0.092 (10.5)	0.052 (12.1)
On-the-job initial learning	0.046 (5.6)	0.054 (2.6)	0.028 (1.4)	0.053 (3.9)	0.112 (6.1)	0.044 (4.2)
On-the-job continuing learning	0.038 (3.8)	0.051 (1.9)	0.102 (5.0)	−0.007 (0.4)	0.033 (1.5)	0.027 (2.1)
Educational requirements* UK	0.031 (3.7)					
On-the-job initial learning* UK	0.067 (3.8)					
On-the-job continuing learning* UK	−0.005 (0.3)					
R^2	0.389	0.183	0.265	0.210	0.302	0.276
N	2,826	595	278	554	522	877

Note: Unstandardized regression coefficients (*t*-values in parentheses). Pooled regression (column 1) includes country dummies (coefficients not shown). For variable definitions, see note to Table 2.2. *denotes interaction effect.

Source: ESS (2004).

shortage of specific skills among British graduates, their employers would seem to have especially large incentives to bring about their formation.

Inequality in Skill Formation and Wages by Class and Gender

We now turn to the variation of skill requirements of jobs by class and gender, and to the role of skills in wage determination. Table 2.4 shows the distribution of educational requirements, that is, the first component along the time axis of skill formation. Immediately apparent is the very strong association between class (in its EGP version) and required education. All class coefficients in the upper panel are highly significant, in all countries. Britain consistently stands out in having lower educational requirements, in all classes except the skilled manual workers. But in all countries, the basic class order in skill requirements is clear. This supports the argument in the introductory overview above that class and skill are tightly connected; or, indeed, that the class dimension of stratification in a fundamental way actually consists of skill differences across jobs. That this pattern comes out so clearly in all five countries, despite their institutional differences, is shown here for the first time. As will be recalled, previous evidence—referred to in the review above—was based on Swedish data only.

In line with the theoretical discussion of the production regime perspective, class should be jointly considered with gender. The lower two panels reveal the combined association between educational requirements, on the one hand, and class and gender together, on the other. As can be seen in the first of the two panels, men in the service class commonly have higher-skilled jobs than service class women. This is true for Germany, Spain, and Britain, while the difference is close to zero in France and actually tends to the opposite in Sweden. An important issue theoretically is to what extent such combination effects of class and gender are additive or interactive. To the exent that they are interactive—that they 'intersect' (cf., e.g., McCall and Orloff 2005)—class stratification is gendered, and vice versa, so that it is not only incomplete but misleading to analyse inequality along one dimension without simultaneously taking the other into account. In the specific case considered here: are the lower educational requirements among female members of the 'salariat' (or service class) than among service class men due entirely to the additive effects of class and gender, or do class effects differ significantly between men and women (or, equivalently, do gender effects differ significantly between classes)? Do we have 'intersections' between class and gender?

Table 2.4. Educational requirements of jobs by class and gender in five European countries, ESS 2004

	Germany	Spain	France	UK	Sweden
Constant (unskilled workers)	0.8 (3.2)	0.4 (1.8)	1.2 (4.9)	0.2 (1.1)	1.3 (6.1)
Service class I	3.8 (12.4)	4.7 (13.4)	5.3 (16.2)	3.2 (12.4)	4.5 (15.8)
Service class II	2.8 (9.4)	3.2 (10.2)	3.1 (10.2)	2.4 (9.4)	3.3 (12.5)
Routine non-manual	1.0 (3.3)	1.5 (4.7)	1.3 (4.1)	0.5 (2.2)	1.0 (3.8)
Skilled manual workers	1.4 (4.2)	1.0 (2.9)	1.0 (2.6)	1.2 (3.4)	1.2 (3.8)
R^2	0.237	0.238	0.326	0.237	0.338
Constant (non-service class, female)	1.6 (9.8)	1.0 (4.8)	2.1 (10.8)	0.7 (4.2)	2.0 (12.2)
Service class, male	2.7 (11.6)	3.6 (11.7)	3.2 (11.7)	2.6 (11.1)	2.9 (12.2)
Service class, female	2.1 (8.3)	2.6 (7.9)	3.1 (10.8)	2.0 (8.9)	3.2 (12.9)
Non-service class, male	0.2 (0.8)	0.4 (1.6)	0.0 (0.0)	0.0 (0.0)	0.0 (0.1)
R^2	0.208	0.206	0.253	0.217	0.301
Service class	2.3 (13.4)	2.9 (13.4)	3.2 (15.6)	2.3 (14.0)	3.1 (17.7)
Female	−0.4 (2.3)	−0.6 (3.0)	−0.1 (0.3)	−0.3 (1.6)	0.1 (0.7)
Service class* female	−0.5 (1.4)	−0.5 (1.2)	−0.1 (0.3)	−0.6 (1.7)	0.3 (0.8)
N	942	458	704	651	913

Note: Unstandardized regression coefficients (*t*-values in parentheses). *Denotes interaction effect.

Source: ESS (2004).

According to the results in the lowest panel of table 2.4, we do not: interaction effects are small and insignificant in all countries. The main effect of class (a simple dichotomy between the service class and others) is very strong and highly significant everywhere. The main effect of gender is negative (for women) and significant in Germany and Spain, negative but not quite significant in Britain, and close to zero in France and Sweden. But even in the cases where the gender effect is significant, it is small relative to the class effect. The message comes across clearly: the schooling component of skill requirements is primarily associated with the class position of the person's job, while gender is a subordinate dimension. And this is true, with only minor variations, regardless of national context.

As we move from school-based skills to firm-based training and learning, the importance of gender should increase markedly. This is the prediction offered by the production regimes model, and would also be in line with common arguments in human capital theory, with statistical discrimination among employers against women as the demand-side mechanism. Table 2.5 provides a parallel account to the educational requirements distribution story of the previous table, but now with on-the-job initial learning as the outcome variable. The results are strikingly different.

Table 2.5. Post-entry learning requirements of jobs by class and gender in five European countries, ESS 2004

	Germany	Spain	France	UK	Sweden
Constant (unskilled workers)	4.5 (3.3)	2.2 (1.9)	5.6 (3.5)	6.7 (5.1)	6.3 (5.5)
Service class I	8.5 (4.8)	9.0 (5.2)	15.6 (7.3)	9.9 (5.6)	5.2 (3.4)
Service class II	5.0 (3.0)	8.2 (5.2)	9.9 (5.0)	8.3 (4.9)	4.6 (3.2)
Routine non-manual	0.0 (0.0)	3.0 (1.9)	0.6 (0.3)	−1.9 (1.1)	−2.5 (1.8)
Skilled manual workers	6.4 (3.5)	11.1 (6.2)	11.4 (4.7)	8.1 (3.4)	6.9 (4.1)
R^2	0.058	0.071	0.114	0.101	0.074
Constant (non-service class, female)	3.8 (4.3)	3.1 (2.9)	5.1 (4.4)	4.6 (4.3)	3.7 (4.2)
Service class, male	9.7 (7.4)	8.7 (5.7)	16.3 (9.7)	14.9 (9.5)	9.2 (5.4)
Service class, female	4.1 (3.0)	6.3 (5.8)	8.4 (4.8)	7.7 (5.0)	5.4 (4.1)
Non-service class, male	5.6 (4.3)	5.4 (3.9)	7.0 (4.0)	4.8 (3.2)	6.0 (4.9)
R^2	0.069	0.043	0.112	0.113	0.068
Service class	4.1 (4.3)	4.5 (4.2)	8.9 (7.1)	8.9 (8.1)	4.3 (4.7)
Female	−5.6 (5.9)	−4.2 (3.9)	−7.4 (5.9)	−6.0 (5.4)	−5.0 (5.5)
Service class* female	0.1 (0.1)	3.1 (1.4)	−0.9 (0.3)	−2.5 (1.1)	2.2 (1.2)
N	942	458	704	651	913

Note: Unstandardized regression coefficients (*t*-values in parentheses). *Denotes interaction effect.
Source: ESS (2004).

It turns out that class has a much weaker but gender a much stronger association with this kind of firm-based skill formation than with educationally based skills. The upper panel shows that the class effects have a strikingly different pattern than in the case of educational requirements. The skilled manual workers—a class heavily dominated by men—have a conspicuously large amount of firm-based learning, in all countries. Their level of firm-based skill requirements is in fact not very different from that of the service class; in some cases it even appears to be higher.

This appearance is partly due to a strong gender effect. The middle panel reveals that, when the class and gender dimensions are considered jointly, men in the service class receive the largest amount of firm-based learning, while women in the service class and men outside it receive roughly comparable amounts.

The lowest panel shows the main and interaction effects of class and gender in a way that provides a test of their significance. The very strong main effect of gender comes clearly across, and—in distinction to the educational requirements case—the main effect of class is about equal in magnitude. So the production regime prediction that women are much disadvantaged in processes of skill formation taking place at the firm instead of in school is clearly supported. But once again, the 'intersection' account does not add anything of explanatory value: there is not a single case among the five countries of a significant interaction effect.

Nor do the countries differ much in the magnitude of the gender and class effects. The strong findings from the analyses in Tables 2.4 and 2.5 are that: (a) gender is closely connected to firm-based skill formation but weakly if at all to school-based skill requirements; and, conversely, (b) that the class position of the person's job is tightly connected to the school-based skills dimension and to a clearly lower degree (although significantly) to firm-based learning. These findings apply to all countries; it is commonality rather than variation that stands out in this respect.

What are the implications of these results for wages? In Table 2.6, wage differences by class and gender are shown, in the same kind of regression framework as in the skills analyses. Two kinds of wage effects are estimated: total effects and the proportion of the total effects that is due to skill-related factors. Here, skills are defined broadly and include both: (a) the supply-side factors of individuals' education (years of post-compulsory schooling) and experience; and (b) the demand-side factors of educational requirements, on-the-job initial learning, and on-the-job continuous learning. Hence, wage gaps by class and by

Table 2.6. Regression analyses of hourly wages (ln) on class and gender in five European countries, ESS 2004

	Germany	Spain	France	UK	Sweden
Constant (unskilled workers)	**2.31**	**1.74**	**2.18**	**2.32**	**2.55**
Service class I					
Total	**0.70**	**0.67**	**0.66**	**0.68**	**0.43**
% skill	**64**	**70**	**77**	**72**	**74**
Service class II					
Total	**0.51**	**0.45**	**0.33**	**0.35**	**0.25**
% skill	**61**	**76**	**94**	**112**	**96**
Routine non-manual					
Total	0.12	0.03	−0.01	−0.12	−0.04
% skill	59	**483**	**−1311**	**−64**	**−213**
Skilled manual workers					
Total	0.15	**0.32**	0.09	**0.20**	0.06
% skill	55	**43**	113	83	**124**
R^2	0.218	0.264	0.259	0.245	0.290
Constant (non-service class, female)	**2.32**	**1.66**	**2.11**	**2.16**	**2.47**
Service class, male					
Total	**0.66**	**0.72**	**0.64**	**0.95**	**0.49**
% skill	**55**	**51**	**51**	**48**	**41**
Service class, female					
Total	**0.47**	**0.48**	**0.41**	**0.40**	**0.29**
% skill	**57**	**51**	**68**	**75**	**73**
Non-service class, male					
Total	**0.19**	**0.30**	**0.17**	**0.26**	**0.13**
% skill	14	7	−2	3	−16
R^2	0.231	0.284	0.245	0.304	0.315
Service class					
Total (nominal)	**0.47**	**0.45**	**0.44**	**0.54**	**0.33**
Percentile	**26**	**27**	**28**	**27**	**29**
% skill	**65**	**67**	**69**	**69**	**66**
% OJIL	**7**	**7**	**15**	**26**	**9**
Female					
Total (nominal)	**−0.19**	**−0.27**	**−0.20**	**−0.40**	**−0.16**
Percentile	**−10**	**−16**	**−11**	**−19**	**−15**
% skill	**30**	**20**	10	**20**	−9
% OJIL	**24**	**11**	**27**	**23**	**21**
Service class* female					
Total	0.00	0.06	−0.06	**−0.28**	−0.07
% skill	0	0	77	**51**	18
% OJIL	25	**35**	10	14	21
N	595	278	554	522	877

Note: Unstandardized regression coefficients (p ≤ .05 in bold) and decomposition by source. *Denotes interaction effect. OJIL = on-the-job initial learning.

Source: ESS (2004).

gender are decomposed into one skill-related part and one part unrelated to (measured) skills. The purpose of this decomposition is to evaluate the role played by skills for economic inequality by class and gender.

The results show a stark contrast between the two dimensions of strati-fication. While most of the class wage gap is 'explained' by skill (again an indication that class is actually a measure of skill), only a minor part (although significant in several cases) of the gender wage gap is skill-related. As can be seen from the upper panel, as much as around 70 per cent of the wage difference between service class I and unskilled workers can be attributed to differences in skill-related factors. This is the case in all countries. For service class II, close to all of the wage effect is skill-related in three of the countries (France, Britain, and Sweden), and most of the effect in the other two.

The lowest panel brings out the contrast between class and gender very clearly: around two thirds of the class wage gap (i.e. the wage difference between the service class—the middle- and upper-white-collar occupational segment—and all others) is connected to skill, whereas only around one fifth or even less of the gender wage gap is skill-related. The class result is remarkably similar across countries, despite a clear cross-national difference in the total gap, with Britain displaying a level of economic class inequality significantly above other countries, and Sweden significantly below. In contrast, the gender wage gap differs clearly across countries both with regard to level and to source. The total gender gap is comparatively large in Britain (with the clearly largest difference of all) and Spain, and comparatively small (but only comparatively) in Germany, France, and Sweden. But the French and Swedish gender wage gaps are not to any significant degree explained by skill differences between women and men, or at least not if skills are measured as a combination of school and firm-based factors.

When wage gaps by class and gender are measured in nominal terms they thus tend to be positively correlated across countries: a large class gap in wages goes together with a large gender gap in wages, and vice versa, with Britain and Sweden as polar cases. But it is also of inter-est to examine the extent to which this cross-national pattern is due to the overall inequality in wages, that is, the general wage structure, of each country. Blau and Kahn (1996) show that most of the inter-national variation in wage differences by gender may be accounted for by the general degree of wage inequality in each national labour market. For instance, they show that female and male workers in the United States are at the same distance from each other in the American percentile distribution of wages as women and men are in the Swedish wage distribution, despite the fact that the nominal gender wage gap is significantly larger in the United States (since the nominal wage difference across percentiles grows with the degree of general wage inequality).

In Table 2.6 the wage gaps by class and gender measured as percentile differences ('standardized' with respect to the overall wage distribution) reveal a different cross-national pattern of inequality compared to the case of nominal wage gaps.[2] The standardized class gap is essentially identical in magnitude in all five countries: the wages of service class employees are on average twenty-six to twenty-nine percentiles above the wages of other employees. (This finding of constancy is intriguing and calls for further analyses which, however, are outside the scope here. But it may be noted that the result is consistent with the strong similarity across countries in the tight connection between class location, wages, and skills.) By contrast, the standardized gender wage gap differs markedly between countries, ranging from a percentile difference between women and men of around ten in Germany and France to almost twenty in Britain. Standardization moves Sweden from a top position (smallest gap) in nominal terms to a middle position, with a wage percentile gender difference of fifteen. Controlling for the overall degree of wage inequality, then, reveals a cross-national correlation between class and gender gaps close to zero.

We saw above that the class wage gap is strongly connected to skills, while the gender wage gap is only weakly skill-driven. This empirical picture changes in a theoretically important way when the firm-based skill component of on-the-job initial learning is considered separately as a wage determinant. It can be seen that gender differences in the incidence of this kind of skill explains a significant part of the wage gap between women and men in all countries. The reason is that this particular skill component—in contrast to others—is strongly biased against females. This finding further supports the claim by the production regime perspective that firm-based skill formation works to the disadvantage of women. But again, cross-national variation in this respect appears to be small. The bias against women in job-based learning seems to be universal, even if—as we have seen—the incidence of such skill formation differs across countries.

[2] See Gornick (1999) and Mandel and Semyonov (2005) for earlier applications of this contrast on gender wage gaps; the application on class wage gaps in the present paper is new in the literature, as far as I know. The general approach is originally due to Juhn, Murphy, and Pierce (1991) who examine racial wage gaps in the United States. It is not obvious whether the nominal or the percentile wage gap is closest to the 'true' gap. Both measures are relevant and answer partly different questions. It is clear, however, that taking both rather than only one of them into account leads to a significant gain in information.

Finally, we may note that there is one significant interaction effect between class and gender on wages. In Britain, the class wage gap is smaller among women than among men. This is in line with the production regime idea that in countries where firm-based skill formation is widespread, women will be disadvantaged, and that this will especially be the case in classes where such skill formation is common. Further, a significant part of this negative interaction is skill-related, supporting the conclusion. But the specific test of the importance of job-based learning contradicts this interpretation, as the effect is not significant. Thus, some further explanation is needed, eluding us for the moment.

Inequality in Skills and Wages by Industry and Contract

Aside from the major stratification dimensions of class and gender, how are skills and wages distributed across other lines of division in the labour market? Specifically, how important are the dimensions of industry and contract? As discussed in the volume's introductory chapter, the industrial division is of interest in the context of large-scale and long-term evolution of the economy: how is the quality of working life affected as the transition to a post-industrial society unfolds? One way to look at this is to compare working conditions in the growing service industries with manufacturing jobs. Although only a partial test of this issue, a simple way to examine this question is to focus on some particular kind of service jobs that arguably can be seen as representative in some sense. We do this here by looking at jobs in consumer services, that is, restaurants, hotels, and retail and wholesale trade. What is the quality of jobs in this sector compared to jobs in manufacturing? The test is tilted against evidence of progress, since consumer services may be seen as the low end of the larger sector of service jobs. So if restaurant jobs—as we call them—turn out not to be of a significantly lower quality than manufacturing jobs, it is an indication that work in post-industrial society might well be an improvement over traditional industrial work.

The contract dimension is of a different kind. We consider two aspects of contract—first, whether employment is on a fixed-term or permanent basis, and, second, whether the job is full-time or part-time. In general, we can view the association between these contract forms and job quality as an indication of labour market institutions. A strong association between fixed-term versus permanent contract and working conditions indicates that insider–outsider relations in the labour market are a significant source of differentiation. Fixed-term contracts may in those cases be seen as solutions to make flexible employment possible in a context generally marked by high entry barriers connected to significant firing costs. In the case of part-time work, labour markets with universal rights should display weak associations with job quality, and vice versa in labour markets with more fragmented rights. Translating these predictions to expectations of country differences, we can suppose, for instance, that Britain has small effects of fixed-term contracts but large effects of part-time work, while Germany or France are more likely to have large effects of fixed-term contracts and Sweden to have small effects of part-time work.

Table 2.7 shows the variation in educational requirements across industries and contract types. The upper panel displays gross associations, with one factor considered at a time, while the lower panel (Panel B) contains

Table 2.7. Educational requirements of jobs by gender, class, industry, and contract in five European countries, ESS 2004

	Germany	Spain	France	UK	Sweden
PANEL A					
Female	−0.6	−0.7	−0.3	−0.2	0.0
	(2.9)	(2.7)	(1.3)	(1.3)	(0.1)
Unskilled workers	−3.8	−4.7	−5.3	−3.2	−4.5
	(12.4)	(13.4)	(16.2)	(12.4)	(15.8)
Restaurants, hotels, and trade	−1.4	−1.2	−1.1	−1.2	−1.0
	(4.5)	(3.0)	(2.5)	(3.7)	(2.5)
Fixed-term contract	−0.6	−1.1	−1.3	0.2	−0.3
	(1.9)	(3.9)	(3.0)	(0.6)	(0.8)
Part-time	−0.7	−0.3	−0.4	−1.1	−1.1
	(3.2)	(0.7)	(1.4)	(5.5)	(3.8)
PANEL B					
Female	−0.3	−1.0	−0.3	−0.2	−0.1
	(−1.6)	(4.5)	(1.3)	(0.8)	(0.6)
Unskilled workers	−3.4	−4.2	−5.0	−3.2	−4.1
	(10.9)	(11.8)	(14.7)	(10.5)	(14.8)
Restaurants, hotels, and trade	−0.7	−1.3	−0.7	−0.9	−0.8
	(2.4)	(3.6)	(1.8)	(2.6)	(2.3)
Fixed-term contract	−0.2	−0.4	−0.3	0.2	0.3
	(0.8)	(1.7)	(0.8)	(0.7)	(0.9)
Part-time	−0.3	0.0	0.0	−0.4	−0.6
	(1.4)	(0.0)	(−0.1)	(1.9)	(2.5)
R^2	0.297	0.311	0.350	0.272	0.442
N	928	445	694	578	909

Note: Unstandardized regression coefficients (*t*-values in parentheses). Upper panel shows gross coefficients, lower panel shows net coefficients (holding other covariates constant). For class (unskilled workers) the reference category is service class I, for industry (restaurants, hotel, retail and wholesale trade) the reference category is manufacturing.

Source: ESS (2004).

net effects, with the different factors plus age considered simultaneously (by multiple regression). Class and gender are included in the analyses, but are not the focus here since they have already been dealt with in the previous section.

We see that restaurant jobs have lower educational requirements than manufacturing jobs in all countries, although the difference tends to diminish somewhat when net effects are estimated. Fixed-term contract jobs and part-time jobs are not significantly less skilled than others in any country when other factors are taken into account, with the exception of Sweden where part-time workers tend to have relatively low-skilled jobs. However, in gross terms, fixed-term contract jobs are significantly less skilled than permanent jobs in Spain and France, while part-time jobs are significantly less skilled than full-time jobs in Britain.

Turning to firm-based skills (see Table 2.8), the pattern of net effects is almost reversed. Industry is not significantly related to this component of skill formation, while fixed-term contract jobs have less on-the-job learning than others in Germany, Spain, and Sweden, and part-time jobs have less firm-based learning than full-time jobs in Germany and Britain. One interpretation is that in the two countries where firm-based learning is most widespread (France and Britain), such skill formation is not contingent upon longer-term employment relationships. The negative part-time effect in Britain is in line with the marginal status of workers on such contracts. The significant contract effects in Germany and Spain indicate the force of an insider–outsider cleavage in those countries. This may also apply to Sweden, while France has net contract effects close to zero.

Wage differentials by industry and contract are shown in Table 2.9. We saw in the previous section that class is clearly distinct from gender as a stratification dimension in that the class wage gap is strongly skill-driven, whereas the gender wage gap must mainly be explained by factors unrelated to (measured) skills. The results in Table 2.9 reveal that class is distinct in the same way relative to industry and contract: for the latter dimensions skills are not the prime driver of wage differentials. In all countries, restaurant jobs are paid significantly lower wages than manufacturing jobs, but in most cases (Spain is a partial exception) this is not primarily due to skill differences. Almost the same goes for wages in fixed-term contract jobs: the gross wage effects are significantly negative in all countries except (in line with expectations) Britain, but differential skills are not the main explanation.

Table 2.8. Post-entry learning requirements of jobs by gender, class, industry, and contract in five European countries, ESS 2004

	Germany	Spain	France	UK	Sweden
PANEL A					
Female	−5.9	−4.2	−8.1	−5.8	−5.1
	(6.1)	(3.9)	(6.3)	(5.1)	(5.6)
Unskilled workers	−8.5	−9.0	−15.6	−9.9	−5.2
	(4.8)	(5.2)	(7.3)	(5.6)	(3.4)
Restaurants, hotels, and trade	−5.6	−3.2	−8.3	−2.8	−3.6
	(3.3)	(1.7)	(3.2)	(1.3)	(1.8)
Fixed-term contract	−4.9	−4.2	−4.6	1.0	−5.8
	(2.9)	(3.2)	(1.9)	(0.5)	(3.8)
Part-time	−6.4	−1.8	−5.0	−7.6	−4.9
	(5.4)	(1.0)	(2.9)	(6.1)	(3.8)
PANEL B					
Female	−3.7	−3.7	−5.7	−4.7	−3.2
	(3.1)	(3.1)	(3.8)	(3.3)	(3.0)
Unskilled workers	−6.0	−8.5	−13.7	−9.1	−5.1
	(3.3)	(4.6)	(6.2)	(−4.5)	(3.2)
Restaurants, hotels, and trade	−1.1	−1.5	−3.6	0.6	0.4
	(0.6)	(0.8)	(1.4)	(0.2)	(0.2)
Fixed-term contract	−3.3	−3.2	−0.6	−0.5	−3.1
	(2.0)	(2.4)	(0.3)	(0.2)	(2.0)
Part-time	−3.6	0.0	−1.5	−3.7	−1.6
	(2.8)	(0.0)	(0.9)	(2.5)	(1.2)
R^2	0.103	0.085	0.142	0.161	0.111
N	928	445	694	578	909

Note: Unstandardized regression coefficients (*t*-values in parentheses). Upper panel shows gross coefficients, lower panel shows net coefficients (holding other covariates constant). For class (unskilled workers) the reference category is service class I, for industry (rest = retail and wholesale trade, restaurants, hotels) the reference category is manufacturing.

Long-term Change in the Structure of Skill Demand

I now turn to an analysis of changes in inequality by class and gender. The data consist of information on the size of different occupational classes (EGP) among women and men from the 1970s to the 1990s (Breen and Luijkx 2004: 74–5) adjusted with OECD statistics on employment rates by gender for the respective time-points and updated with class information from 2003–5 via large national data-sets (the Labour Force Surveys in France and Sweden for 2003 and in Britain for 2004–5, and the German Microcensus for 2004).[3] Change data on Spain are not

---

[3] I thank Karin Halldén (SOFI, Stockholm University) for providing runs on the French and Swedish Labour Force Surveys, Eric Harrison (City University, London) on the British Labour Force Survey, and Heike Wirth (MZES, Mannheim) on the German Microcensus.

Table 2.9. Regression analyses of hourly wages (ln) on gender, class, industry, and contract in five European countries, ESS 2004

	Germany	Spain	France	UK	Sweden
Female					
Total	**−0.22**	**−0.30**	**−0.22**	**−0.39**	**−0.18**
% skill	**35**	**24**	**17**	**17**	−4
Unskilled workers					
Total	**−0.70**	**−0.67**	**−0.66**	**−0.68**	**−0.43**
% skill	**64**	**70**	**77**	**72**	**74**
Restaurants, hotels, and trade					
Total	**−0.40**	**−0.16**	**−0.33**	**−0.51**	**−0.22**
% skill	**37**	**64**	**47**	**33**	**38**
Fixed-term contract					
Total	**−0.45**	**−.027**	**−0.28**	−0.10	**−0.22**
% skill	**36**	**48**	**48**	−40	**29**
Part-time					
Total	**−0.17**	0.11	−0.03	**−0.47**	−0.06
% skill	**54**	−58	69	**45**	**109**
Female					
Total	**−0.18**	**−0.25**	**−0.15**	**−0.32**	**−0.16**
% skill	24	**37**	15	**27**	5
Unskilled workers					
Total	**−0.59**	**−0.56**	**−0.60**	**−0.73**	**−0.45**
% skill	**65**	**76**	**73**	**64**	**64**
Restaurants, hotels, and trade					
Total	**−0.32**	−0.11	**−0.18**	**−0.39**	**−0.18**
% skill	14	**90**	**39**	**35**	**34**
Fixed-term contract					
Total	**−0.35**	**−0.21**	−0.12	−0.10	**−0.11**
% skill	18	22	-22	−40	1
Part-time					
Total	0.02	**0.27**	0.06	−0.11	**0.10**
% skill	−186	−12	−3	**68**	**−38**
R^2	0.346	0.399	0.325	0.399	0.427
N	595	278	554	522	877

Note: Unstandardized regression coefficients ($p \leq 0.05$ in bold) and decomposition by source.
Source: ESS (2004).

available. Four classes among employees are distinguished: I–II (the service class or salariat, i.e. middle- and upper-white-collar occupations), III (lower-white-collar occupations), V–VI (skilled manual workers) and VII (unskilled manual workers); and four time-points: around 1975, 1985, 1995, and 2004.

As in the cross-sectional analyses above, the dimensions of stratification that are in focus in the trend analyses below are class and gender. Based on the theoretical reasoning in the chapter's introduction, and supported by the empirical findings in subsequent sections, class is taken here to indicate—in addition to the manual–non-manual divide—the skill requirements of jobs. By contrast, gender divisions in the labour market are of course conceptually orthogonal to skill, but the empirical relation between them is an important matter for investigation to which we now turn. The general evolution of skill levels and distributions is examined in the following section.

Gender Segregation of the Skill Structure

When assessing gender segregation in the occupational structure, we follow the approach of Charles and Grusky (2004) by distinguishing between horizontal and vertical segregation. I define the horizontal dimension of segregation as the difference between: (*a*) the proportion females of all employees in non-manual occupations (classes I–III); and (*b*) the proportion females of all employees in manual occupations (classes V–VII). Also in line with the Charles and Grusky approach, I define vertical segregation separately for non-manual and manual occupations. In the former case, vertical segregation is defined as the difference between: (*a*) the proportion females of all employees in upper non-manual occupations (class I–II); and (*b*) the proportion females of all employees in lower non-manual occupations (class III). Similarly, in the manual case, vertical segregation is the difference between: (*a*) the female share of class V–VI, and (*b*) the female share of class VII. All differences are expressed in absolute percentage points, with positive numbers meaning that the share of females is larger in (*a*) than in (*b*) as just defined.

According to Charles and Grusky (2004), horizontal gender segregation tends to increase with the development from industrial to post-industrial societies, because jobs in the expanding service sector are disproportionately filled by women. Vertical gender segregation, on the other hand, tends to decrease over time, especially in the non-manual occupational segment. These claims are based on long-term trend data for the United States, Japan, and Switzerland, and on detailed cross-sectional data from the early 1990s for ten countries, including the four nations we consider here. Persistent or growing horizontal segregation is interpreted as deeply rooted expressions of 'gender essentialism', that differences between women and men in the kind of work they carry out are seen as natural and difficult or even undesirable to change. Vertical segregation, on the other hand, is interpreted by Charles and Grusky as expressions of 'male primacy', which is seen by them as more susceptible to change as societies develop, especially among non-manual occupations with strong norms of professionalism and an ideology of equal opportunity.

The broad occupational class data used here are obviously rather crude relative to the detailed breakdowns (sixty-four occupational categories) in the Charles and Grusky analysis. Nonetheless, the simple division between four classes appears to contain much of the essential variance between occupational groups that is of importance for gender segregation. And the big advantage of the data we use here is the possibility to make cross-national comparisons of long-term change.

Table 2.10 shows the evolution of gender segregation (in the sense spelled out above) from the 1970s to around 2004 in Germany, France, Britain, and Sweden. Note that the first three time-points—1975 through 1995—belong to a harmonized set of trend data, while the numbers for the fourth and most recent time-point are based on separate sets of information and are therefore not directly comparable to the earlier numbers. Having said this, the overall impression of the results is that gender segregation of the class structure is rather stable across the several decades that the data span. In line with the Charles and Grusky perspective, however, horizontal segregation appears to have increased somewhat, while vertical segregation seems to have declined (but with no marked difference in change between the service and production segments). There is a certain division between the four countries in these regards. Concentrating on the first three (more comparable) time-points, horizontal segregation has been roughly constant in Britain, increased in Germany and France, and first increased sharply and then declined somewhat in Sweden. Along the vertical dimension, gender segregation has been more or less constant in Germany and France but tended to decline in Britain and Sweden. All in all, then, the pattern of long-term change in gender segregation of the class structure is one of stability, but with some cross-national differences such that women's conditions appear to have improved more in Britain and to some extent in Sweden than in Germany and France.

The General Evolution of Skill Demand

The approach used above to assess segregation may also be applied to the issue of general changes in the level and distribution of skill demand. Substituting the share of all employees for the share of female employees in the same kind of difference estimates as in the assessment of segregation

Table 2.10. Gender segregation of the class structure in four European countries, 1975–2004

	All	Germany	France	UK	Sweden
Horizontal					
1975	28	24	37	27	22
1985	33	26	40	28	39
1995	34	32	42	27	34
2004	32	33	31	24	38
Vertical					
1975	36	36	27	41	41
1985	34	38	27	39	33
1995	32	33	26	36	31
2004	28	33	31	22	28
Average					
1975	32	30	32	34	31
1985	34	32	34	34	36
1995	33	32	34	31	33
2004	30	33	31	23	33
Vertical service					
1975	39	34	33	46	42
1985	38	36	32	44	38
1995	34	33	30	39	32
2004	35	35	38	33	35
Vertical production					
1975	34	38	20	35	40
1985	31	39	22	35	29
1995	30	33	21	34	31
2004	21	30	24	11	21

yields useful indicators of skill demand. Thus, the level of skill demand among service (in the sense of non-manual) occupations may be indicated by the difference between (*a*) the share of employees in class I–II and (*b*) the share of all employees in class III. Let us call this number (the absolute difference in percentage points between *a* and *b*) ss (for 'skill demand in service occupations'; note again that 'service' is used here in the sense of 'non-manual', not in the sense of the 'service *class*' or 'salariat'). Similarly, the level of skill demand among production (manual) occupations may be indicated by the difference between (*a*) the share of employees in class V–VI and (*b*) the share of all employees in class VII. We call this number sp. By combining these two numbers—ss and sp—we get indicators of two phenomena: the overall skill demand level and the overall skill demand distribution (or degree of polarization). The level is indicated by the sum of ss and sp while the distribution is indicated by the difference between ss and sp.

Table 2.11. Skill composition of the class structure in four European countries, 1975–2004

	All	Germany	France	UK	Sweden
Skill level					
1975	6	26	−4	9	−8
1985	12	29	4	19	−5
1995	18	33	8	25	5
2004	3	8	−11	12	3
Skill polarization					
1975	2	2	−5	−2	12
1985	1	3	−8	10	−2
1995	7	6	−8	21	11
2004	4	−2	−3	14	7
Service–production					
1975	2	11	−3	8	−6
1985	19	17	13	21	24
1995	28	28	20	32	33
2004	32	26	32	28	41
Skill service					
1975	4	14	−4	4	2
1985	6	16	−2	15	−3
1995	13	19	0	23	8
2004	3	3	−7	13	5
Skill production					
1975	2	12	1	6	−10
1985	5	13	6	4	−1
1995	5	14	8	2	−3
2004	−1	5	−4	−1	−2

To clarify these definitions, an example may be helpful. Assume that 35 per cent of all employees have occupations in class I–II, 20 per cent in class III, 25 per cent in class V–VI, and the remaining 20 per cent have occupations in class VII. The level of skill demand in service occupations (the component ss in the definition above) is then $35 − 20 = 15$, while the level of skill demand in production occupations (the component sp) is $25 − 20 = 5$. The overall skill demand level, defined above as ss + sp, is then $15 + 5 = 20$, while the distribution of skill demand, defined as ss − sp, is $15 − 5 = 10$. It can be seen that the skill demand level rises with the sum of the proportions in classes I–II and V–VI and falls with the sum of the proportions in classes III and VII. If all employees are in classes I, II, V, and VI, the estimated level of skill demand reaches its maximum possible value, 100; by contrast, if all employees are in classes III and VII, the lowest possible level of skill demand is reached, that is—100. With an even split of all employees between classes I, II, V, and VI, on

Table 2.12. Skill composition of the male class structure in four European countries, 1975–2004

	All	Germany	France	UK	Sweden
Skill level					
1975	35	52	19	43	25
1985	41	57	30	50	29
1995	45	60	35	53	33
2004	30	39	18	32	31
Skill polarization					
1975	3	−1	0	2	12
1985	7	2	−2	16	12
1995	13	5	−2	27	21
2004	18	6	16	27	25
Service–production					
1975	−20	−7	−33	−14	−25
1985	−9	−3	−21	−2	−11
1995	0	2	−16	11	4
2004	5	−3	6	7	11
Skill service					
1975	19	26	10	23	19
1985	24	29	14	33	20
1995	29	33	16	40	27
2004	24	23	17	29	28
Skill production					
1975	16	27	9	20	7
1985	17	28	16	17	9
1995	16	27	19	13	6
2004	6	17	1	2	3

the one hand, and classes III and VII, on the other, the medium level of skill demand results: zero. Similarly, the skill demand distribution (or polarization) expands with the sum of the proportions in classes I–II and VII and contracts with the sum of the proportions in classes III and V–VI. As in the level case, the measure of distribution can take values between plus and minus 100.

Table 2.11 shows the results of these calculations on the basis of the class distribution data for the four countries and four time-points. Again concentrating on the first three (more comparable) time-points, over-all skill demand has increased in all countries. This increase has been rather evenly divided between the service and production occupational segments, coupled with a strong shift everywhere towards service employment. An exception is Britain, which has had a strong upgrading of the service–job structure—much stronger than elsewhere—and a small decline in the skill level of production occupations. The result is a marked

Table 2.13. Skill composition of the female class structure in four European countries, 1975–2004

	All	Germany	France	UK	Sweden
Skill level					
1975	−40	−21	−41	−46	−52
1985	−29	−16	−33	−26	−41
1995	−15	−2	−26	−10	−24
2004	−29	−30	−47	−11	−26
Skill polarization					
1975	−1	8	−14	−10	11
1985	−6	6	−16	2	−17
1995	2	7	−14	13	1
2004	−12	−11	−25	−2	−12
Service–production					
1975	38	43	47	44	19
1985	57	50	61	53	63
1995	63	62	65	59	64
2004	62	60	63	53	73
Skill service					
1975	−21	−6	−28	−28	−20
1985	−18	−5	−25	−12	−29
1995	−7	2	−20	2	−12
2004	−20	−20	−36	−7	−19
Skill production					
1975	−19	−14	−14	−18	−31
1985	−11	−11	−9	−14	−12
1995	−8	−4	−6	−12	−12
2004	−8	−10	−11	−5	−7

polarization of the British class structure, unmatched by developments elsewhere. This is an important finding, in line with the analysis by Goos and Manning (2007) indicating that job polarization has contributed significantly to the rise in wage inequality in Britain. Indeed, they conclude that much of what has often been interpreted in the research literature as increasing wage dispersion within observed skill categories (mainly by education), and seen as rising returns to 'unmeasured individual skills', may in fact be due to the polarization of the job structure. This would shift the theoretical arguments and future empirical research on changes in wage inequality a good deal.

The evolution of skill demand, its level and distribution, is broken down by gender in Tables 2.12–2.14. Tables 2.12 and 2.13 show the skill composition of the male and female class structure, respectively, while Table 2.14 contains the differences between them. The main results are the following: Except in France, the skill demand level among women

Table 2.14. Gender differences (female minus male) in the skill composition of the class structure in four European countries, 1975–2004

	All	Germany	France	UK	Sweden
Skill level					
1975	−75	−73	−60	−89	−77
1985	−71	−73	−63	−76	−69
1995	−60	−62	−61	−63	−56
2004	−59	−69	−65	−43	−57
Skill polarization					
1975	−5	9	−15	−13	−1
1985	−13	4	−14	−14	−28
1995	−11	2	−12	−14	−20
2004	−31	−17	−41	−28	−37
Service–production					
1975	58	51	80	58	44
1985	66	53	82	55	74
1995	62	60	81	48	61
2004	57	63	57	45	63
Skill service					
1975	−40	−32	−37	−51	−39
1985	−42	−35	−39	−45	−49
1995	−36	−30	−36	−38	−38
2004	−45	−43	−53	−36	−47
Skill production					
1975	−35	−41	−23	−38	−38
1985	−29	−39	−24	−31	−21
1995	−25	−32	−24	−24	−18
2004	−14	−26	−12	−7	−10

has risen faster than among men. This is especially the case in Britain and Sweden. Skill polarization has increased strongly in Britain both among men and among women. Germany and Sweden have seen a slight increase in the distribution of skill demand among men, while the male skill distribution has been stable in France. Among women, Britain alone has experienced polarization. In Sweden, the female skill demand distribution has instead narrowed somewhat, while it has hardly changed at all in Germany and France.

Conclusions

The empirical analyses above have produced several important findings that are novel in the research literature on skills and wages. The basis for these findings consists of data with explicit measurement of the skill requirements of jobs, data that have been designed with internationally comparative purposes in mind. Another crucial part of the analysis has been a comparative assessment of the connection between skills and wages, something that also has been difficult to accomplish in previous research. The main findings are as follows.

First, firm-based skill formation seems to be more widespread and more important in Britain than in several other European countries considered here, including Germany and Sweden. This is the opposite of what the production regimes perspective predicts, but is a reasonable result given the general character of British schooling. General schooling thus seems to give employers a larger role in skill formation, not smaller.

Second, in line with the production regime perspective, women are disadvantaged in firm-based skill formation. This is true for all countries, and to a roughly similar extent.

Third, there is no strong indication of an interaction effect between class and gender, such that women's disadvantage relative to men is larger in the service class than in the working class. But there is some tendency in this direction in Britain.

Fourth, nominal wage gaps by class and gender tend to go together rather than trade off. For example, both gaps are relatively large in Britain. But standardized wage gaps (i.e. percentile differences) by class and gender tend to be uncorrelated across countries. Notably, standardized class gaps appear to be identical in magnitude in all considered countries.

Fifth, class and skill are tightly connected in all countries, to a remarkably similar extent. This appears to be a universal trait across labour markets. Class theory should be accordingly revised, since current versions downplay or even ignore the skill character of jobs that seem to be the very basis of class distinctions between employees.

Sixth, most of the class wage gap is due to skill-related factors. In contrast, most of the gender wage gap—in all countries—seems to depend on other factors than skill. But differences between men and women in firm-based (rather than school-based) skill formation accounts for a significant part of the gender wage gap in all countries.

Seventh, class dominates all other considered dimensions of stratification—including industry and contract—with regard to the distribution of skills and wages. Indeed, as argued above, class may be seen as a measure of occupational skill requirements, and is probably linked to wages through productivity. Industry (indicated by the contrast between jobs in consumer services and manufacturing) tends to be significantly related to school-based but not firm-based skill requirements, although the comparatively low wages in consumer services appear to mainly be associated with other factors than skills. Fixed-term contracts carry significant wage penalties in Germany, Spain, and Sweden but not in Britain or France. These penalties are not explained by differences in skill-related factors.

Eighth, the evolution of class structures over time indicates a significant increase in skill demand in all countries. In Germany, Britain, and Sweden, but not in France, this upgrading of the occupational structure has been larger for women than for men. The overall rise in skill demand appears to have been strongest in Britain.

Ninth, the distribution of skill demand has been rather stable in Germany, France, and Sweden. By contrast, Britain is marked by a strong polarization of its job structure, both among men and women. This has probably contributed significantly to the rise in wage inequality.

Tenth, gender segregation of the class structure has changed very little in overall terms. Disaggregation reveals, however, that horizontal segregation has increased somewhat over time, while vertical segregation has declined. Women's occupational attainment has tended to improve more in Britain and Sweden than in Germany and France.

These findings add considerably to our knowledge of the distribution and evolution of skills and wages in Europe. Evidently, current theoretical perspectives on cross-national differences in labour market inequality—such as the production regimes model—are partly in line with the data, but partly not. More research is needed on several issues, one prominent example being the role of employers in skill formation. But perhaps the most urgent task is to make theoretical sense of the pieces of empirical evidence that are now available. Some initial remarks in this direction are offered below.

The trends in skill demand observed above show that Britain has had the most rapid rise among the countries considered, although this rise is entirely confined to white-collar (or service) occupations. This upgrading appears to contradict the early claim (see, e.g., Finegold and Soskice 1988) by proponents of the production regime approach that LMEs such as Britain are locked in a low-skill 'equilibrium' while CMEs such as Germany are high-skill production regimes. As spelled out in the introductory chapter, though, more recent accounts (e.g. Estevez-Abe, Iversen, and Soskice 2001) instead suggest the possibility that upgrading at the high end of the occupational structure is in fact more pronounced in LMEs than in CMEs: '[W]here there is a large pool of workers with advanced and highly portable skills, and where social protection is low, companies enjoy considerable flexibility... [that] allows for high responsiveness to new business opportunities, and facilitates the use of rapid product innovation strategies' (Estevez-Abe, Iversen, and Soskice 2001: 174). In contrast, CMEs 'advantage companies that seek to... continuously upgrade and diversify existing product lines' (Estevez-Abe, Iversen, and Soskice 2001: 174).

Crucially, however, the mechanisms singled out in the production regime approach do not seem to operate in the expected way. Even if general skills dominate British schooling, most of this education occurs at the compulsory level. Accordingly, the British labour market does not seem to have 'a large pool of workers with advanced and highly portable skills', at least not skills based on formal education. Rather, skill formation to a large extent takes place in (or is paid by) firms. It seems likely that these skills—learned on the job—are less portable than skills learned in school. The German labour market, by contrast, appears to be dominated by skills that, while specific to an occupation or an industry, are highly portable across firms. So, although the strong average rise of skill demand in Britain—coupled with polarization—is empirically compatible with predictions from the production regime approach (and squares well with the relatively large increase in wage dispersion in that country), and the relatively stagnant skill demand evolution in Germany may also be in line with expectations in that perspective, the theoretical arguments offered seem rather far off the mark.

This conclusion is reinforced by the case of Sweden, which deviates clearly from both Britain and Germany. In distinction to Britain, skill formation in Sweden to a large extent occurs in schools before labour market entry. In distinction to Germany, continuing learning during working life is widespread, although not quite reaching British levels. Over time, skill demand in Sweden appears to have increased more than in Germany but less than in Britain. Further, the rise in demand is more evenly distributed than in the British case, with no strong trend of polarization. The distinctiveness of the overall Swedish pattern in comparison to other countries would appear to support theoretical approaches that make a clear difference between Nordic and Continental European varieties of CMEs. In this regard, the perspective of employment regimes seems more fruitful than that of production regimes.

In sum, while the empirical findings in the present chapter are complex and cannot be seen as corroborating a single theoretical model, it seems clear that different approaches are not equally supported. Despite the fact that some empirical regularities are remarkably similar across countries—with the tight connection between class and skill as perhaps the most significant example—labour markets under capitalism do appear to come in distinct varieties. In considering the nature of this variation, there are two fairly strong arguments against production regime theory: First, the simple distinction between coordinated and liberal market economies fails to account for the sizeable within-category differences between countries such as Germany and Sweden. Second, the suggested driving mechanisms—in particular the cross-national differences in the character of skill formation—do not seem to operate as predicted. The number of categories argument favours the more elaborate typology of employment regimes. But the mechanism argument is less valid in the employment regime case, because the drivers of variation in this model—that is, conflicts of interest, partisan politics, and bargaining outcomes—have not been explicitly measured and tested, at least not with micro-level data. In addition, the employment regime approach may not be sufficiently clear theoretically on how power struggles, the supply and demand of skills, and wage determination are connected. These tasks—and many others—lie ahead. It seems highly probable that new theoretical perspectives will emerge along the way.

Acknowledgements

Thanks for useful comments go to my co-authors in the present volume, to participants at the LNU project seminar at the Swedish Institute for Social Research (SOFI), Stockholm University, at the Economics Department seminar at Gothenburg University, May 2006, at the EQUALSOC conference at Universitat Pompeu Fabra, Barcelona, September 2006, and to Carl le Grand, Walter Korpi, and Ryszard Szulkin. Jenny Torssander at SOFI assisted in constructing measures of education by collecting time series data on the length of compulsory schooling in European countries. Economic support from the EQUALSOC network of excellence (EU 6th framework programme) and from the Swedish Council for Working Life and Social Research (FAS, grant no. 2004-1908) is gratefully acknowledged.

3

Job-Related Training in Europe:
Do Institutions Matter?

Martina Dieckhoff, Jean-Marie Jungblut, and Philip J. O'Connell

Introduction

The resurgence of interest in recent years in the importance of education and training for economic progress, fuller employment, and social integration coincides with a new emphasis on the need for 'life long learning', both to respond to current changes in the organization and technology of production and service delivery and to counter the socially disruptive effects of increased labour market flexibility. The European Commission, for instance, has emphasized the crucial role of life-long learning in a knowledge-based society. Its Social Agenda describes it as a core factor for the improvement of people's employability, for entrepreneurship, for reducing skill gaps and for developing quality jobs.

Opportunities for continuing training are particularly crucial for low-skilled workers. The fall in demand for low-skilled labour and the shift to more knowledge intensive jobs (Maurin and Thesmar 2003) have left them in a precarious labour market situation—they may be trapped in low-paid jobs with poor employment conditions, or locked into cycles of recurrent unemployment. Likewise, opportunities for training are very important to older workers whose skills obtained through schooling or initial training are likely to have become outmoded. Both groups of workers run the risk of social exclusion, and opportunities for life-long learning are believed to alleviate this risk (Bishop 1997). As well as being an essential policy for social cohesion (European Commission 2000), continuing job-related training is believed to be an important determinate of corporate performance as well as of individual earnings and career development.

There has been a considerable amount of research on the implications of initial education, prior to labour market entry, for both labour market entry and for subsequent career development (see e.g. Allmendinger 1989; Shavit and Müller (eds.) 1998; Ryan 2001, for an overview of the cross-national literature on the transition from school-to-work), but the empirical research on continuing training is much more limited. However, previous studies—often focusing on particular countries—have pointed to some notable features about the opportunities for continuing training.

There is a substantial body of evidence indicating that continuing in-career training is stratified, with the result that those with higher skills, or educational attainment are more likely to participate in training, and in training sponsored by their employers (Lynch 1994; Blundell, Dearden, and Meghir 1996; Bellmann and Düll 1999; Gatter 1999; OECD 1999b; O'Connell 2002). The employed receive more training than the unemployed, who in turn receive more training than those not economically active (O'Connell 1999). Older workers are also less likely to participate in job-related training (Gelderblom and de Koning 2002), as are part-time workers and those on temporary contracts (Arulampalam and Booth 1998). Likewise firm characteristics matter: larger firms and those that pay above average wages are more likely to train their employees than smaller firms (O'Connell 2002).

These patterns of participation would suggest that current allocation principles are in inverse relation to need and training is more likely to exacerbate rather than mitigate existing labour market inequalities. The stratification of continuing training opportunities has often been explained by human capital theory (Becker 1964). The employer is the most common financial sponsor of continuing training, and it seems plausible to assume that an employer's decision to invest in training for his employees is based on expectations about benefits in the form of raised post-training productivity. Based on the assumptions of human capital theory one would predict that an employer believes the training cost of a lower-skilled worker to be higher than for a higher-skilled worker. This is because low educational credentials may signal lower ability, hence suggesting that the lower-skilled worker will require more training hours than higher-skilled counterparts, which in turn would imply higher training costs. Likewise human capital theory might explain why older workers are less likely to receive training than their younger colleagues. Skill investments in younger workers can be recouped for a longer period (Taylor and

Urwin 2001). Moreover, it is often assumed that older workers' skills have already become to some degree outmoded which would increase their training cost. In this chapter we predominantly focus on the skills gap in participation in job-related training, although we recognize that there are other important dimensions to stratification in access to training. The skills gap in participation in continuing job-related training is a near universal pattern: in virtually all European countries, indeed if not all developed industrial or post-industrial societies, the low skilled are less likely to participate in job-related training than those with higher skills (Ok and Tergeist 2003; Bassanini et al. 2005).

Research on the impact of training is also growing. One strand of the literature focuses on firm productivity (e.g. Barrett and O'Connell 2001); while another assesses the effects of training on individual wages (e.g. Pischke 2001; Gerfin 2004). The research on training and firm productivity has shown that different forms of continuing training can have very different effects (Black and Lynch 1997; Barrett and O'Connell 2001). Barrett and O'Connell's (2001) analyses, for example, show a clear positive effect of general training on firm productivity. They could not, however, detect a positive impact of specific continuing training.

Studies assessing wage effects of training have obtained very different results, and the impact of continuing training on wages is still very much debated. An important issue here is whether or not studies have tried to take account of the possibility that there is a selection process into training, such that employees who choose or are co-opted by their employer into training have rather different measured and unmeasured characteristics from those who are not. To the extent that such selection does take place, analyses that ignore it—typically ordinary least squares (OLS) regression analyses—may over-estimate the impact of training on wages. At least part of the effect they show may be due to the different underlying characteristics (for instance with respect to ability or motivation) of employees who receive training and those who do not. Research that has tried to correct for such selection bias has employed a range of techniques. One approach is fixed effects regression analysis that is able to control for unobserved heterogeneity that is constant across time. Another approach often applied is to use a Heckman selection procedure which models the participation in training separately from the effects of training on wages.[1] More recently (as discussed in

---

[1] This technique requires an identifying variable, i.e. a variable that is correlated with training participation, but does not have any independent effect on the outcome

more detail later in the chapter) matching (or propensity score) methods have been used to compare individuals who are as similar as possible. Studies using methods to control for selection effects often arrive at rather different conclusions about the effects of training than those that do not.

Evertsson's OLS (2004) estimates suggest positive effects of continuing in-career training in Sweden. Goux and Maurin (2000) analyse wage returns to employer-provided training for France. While their OLS estimations suggest positive and significant effects, training effects become insignificant and negative once selectivity is controlled for. Booth and Bryan (2005) find significant wage returns for the UK. Their fixed-effects estimates suggest that returns to accredited continuing training are significantly higher than those of non-accredited training. Booth (1993) studies returns to training that has taken place in the first year in a new job using the British National Survey of Graduates and Diplomats (BNSG). Her fixed effects estimates show no wage returns for men, and an increase in wage level of 1 per cent per week of training for women. While most studies have only assessed the impact of training on wage levels, Pischke (2001) estimates fixed effects growth regressions using the German Socio-Economic Panel (GSOEP). His estimates suggest that one year of full-time work-related training does not result in significant wage growth. Finally, Bassanini et al. (2005) assess the effect of training stock on log-hourly wages across a range of European countries using the ECHP and find that their OLS estimates range between 3.7 and 21.6 per cent. When they estimate fixed effects models, however, their coefficients become insignificant for most countries. Generally, their results suggest there might be a negative relationship between training incidence and training returns (Bassanini et al. 2005).

Comparative research on continuing training is still rare. Until very recently it has focused more on similarities across countries than differences. While it frequently points out the common pattern that access to continuing training is highly stratified, attempts to assess the different degrees of this stratification across countries and possible explanations thereof are still scarce. In the recent literature, however, we find an increasing awareness that institutions may play a role in explaining differences in the distribution and impact of training.

---

of interest. The difficulty with this approach is that it is hard to find credible identifying variables.

This strand of research, however, is still very much developing. There is to date little consensus as to which institutions are conducive either to the provision of continuing training or to the quality of training.

Some arguments stress the importance of trade union strength. Booth, Francesconi, and Zoega (2003), provide an overview of the different channels through which unions can affect the provision of continuing training. Unions may directly negotiate better training opportunities for covered workers. This would imply that union-covered workers receive more training and higher training returns relative to uncovered workers. In countries with high union density and where unions effectively represent both high-skilled and low-skilled workers, we could expect that the high-low skilled training gap would be reduced. However, if unions are more effective in representing the interests of the high rather than low skilled in access to training, they could increase the training gap between the low and high skilled.

Another channel through which unions may influence training provision is wage compression (Booth, Francesconi, and Zoega 2003). This argument can take different forms. By flattening wage profiles and reducing wage dispersion unions may undermine workers' incentives to invest in training. In this scenario one would predict a negative correlation between presence of unions and training incidence. Training returns would be expected to be lower for union-covered than non-union covered workers. While wage compression may reduce workers' incentives to invest in training, however, it may provide an incentive for employers to pay for continuing training. Bassanini and Brunello (2003) in an analysis of ECHP data for seven countries, find that the incidence of general training (proxied by off site training) is higher in clusters with a lower differential in the wage growth of trained versus untrained workers. They find no evidence of a relationship between firm-specific training and the training wage premium. Likewise, Almeida-Santos and Mumford (2005) provide evidence for the UK suggesting that higher levels of wage compression are positively related to training incidence and training duration. By contrast, Ericson's analysis of Swedish data (2004) would suggest a weak negative relationship between wage compression and continuing training for male workers in the private sector.

Further information on the importance of labour market institutions comes from Brunello (2001), who finds that countries with higher union density, stronger employment protection, and lower minimum wages (relative to the average wage), tend to show higher incidences of training.[2] His findings further suggest that training is higher in countries with more comprehensive school systems (e.g. Ireland or the UK) than in countries with highly stratified school systems (e.g. Germany) suggesting that continuing training after labour market entry is used to compensate for lack of specialization in initial education.

This brief overview shows that the role of institutions has become a focal point of recent research on continuing training. Their actual importance in understanding cross-country differences in training provision is still very much debated. The aim of the chapter is to compare the incidence, the distribution as well as the impact of continuing vocational training and employer-sponsored continuing vocational training across a number of European countries. In particular we seek to assess whether continuing training alleviates or exacerbates existing inequalities of work–life chances. To answer this we begin by examining the incidence and distribution of continuing training opportunities. We then explore the impact of training participation on wages. Particular emphasis is on differences across countries: Do we find larger inequalities in the allocation of training in some countries than in others? If so, what are the determinants of such differences? If there are differences in the financial returns to training, what are the institutional dynamics behind them?

In developing hypotheses, we draw on the influential schema of skills formation systems developed in the 'production regimes' literature, with its distinction between coordinated and liberal production regimes. The chapter begins by reviewing the implications of this typology, the broad outlines of which were discussed in the introductory chapter of the volume, for the specific issue of training (Soskice 1999; Estevez-Abe, Iversen, and Soskice 2001; Hall and Soskice 2001). While it is valuable in sensitizing us to institutional differences across countries, it is a very broad categorization and we discuss how it might be extended to add to our understanding of cross-national variance in the opportunities for and impact of continuing training. The subsequent empirical part of the chapter focuses on seven countries: Britain, Ireland, Germany, France, Denmark, Finland, and Spain. Britain and Ireland represent examples of the liberal market economics (LMEs) and Germany, Denmark, and Finland of coordinated market economies (CMEs). France and Spain are not easily classifiable in the 'production regime' schema, but are included as examples of what are

---

[2] Brunello's analyses, however, are not limited to continuing training for adult workers, but also include initial vocational training (e.g. apprenticeships) at labour market entry.

often regarded as strong insider–outsider systems (or 'dualistic' employment regimes). The analysis divides into two sections: the first is concerned with the incidence, distribution, and determinants of training; the second assesses the impact of continuing training on wage progression.

The Institutional Context of Continuing Training

Writers from the production regimes perspective (see e.g. Soskice 1999; Estevez-Abe, Iversen, and Soskice 2001; Hall and Soskice 2001*b*) have emphasized how differences in institutional contexts of advanced capitalist economies can help explain the differences in strategies of skill formation found across countries. The critical distinction drawn is between liberal regimes on the one hand and coordinated regimes on the other (Soskice 1999). Coordinated market economies are generally characterized by a significant degree of non-market coordination, direct and indirect, between companies. Unions play a crucial role in the industrial relation systems which tend to be cooperative in nature, and inter-company systems promote standard setting cooperation (Soskice 1999). In LMEs, on the other hand, there is little non-market coordination between companies and industrial relations are characterized by weak unions. The competitive climate in these economies deters cooperation and coordinated standard-setting across companies (Soskice 1999). While LMEs tend to be accompanied by residual welfare states, CMEs tend to be matched with social-democratic or conservative models of welfare with high employment protection.

The framework developed by Estevez-Abe, Iversen, and Soskice (2001) and Soskice (1999) points to the importance of institutions in shaping firms' (and workers') incentives to invest in training. A competitive inter-company system, where it is easy to poach trained workers, discourages employers from providing their workers with portable vocational skills, while cooperative company relations provide an economic climate where such investments are feasible. Liberal market economies tend to encourage 'general skill regimes' where most firms pursue production strategies relying on a small elite of workers with high general skills (i.e. university or other third level qualification) on the one hand and extensive use of un- and semi-skilled workers on the other. Consequently early school-leavers tend to have few valuable career opportunities. In specific skill regimes, on the other hand, production technologies are complex and therefore reliant on a skilled workforce leading to high quality vocational training. This suggests that specific skill systems which tend to be found in coordinated production regimes may offer more equal access to training opportunities than general skill systems in liberal production regimes where access to vocational skills is scarce leading to a polarized skill distribution in the workforce.

An important point to note is that the notion of specific skills in the production regimes literature is used differently than in the human capital theory literature influenced by Becker. Becker (1964) identifies training to be specific when it cannot be transferred to outside firms. By contrast, in the production regimes literature, the emphasis is on industry specific skills, with employers helping to provide skills which are portable, albeit in an institutional context that makes poaching difficult.

The principal emphasis in the work of production regime theorists is on the importance of the broader institutional context for different systems of initial skill formation. Arguably, however, the same factors may also be of importance for understanding differences in continuing training provision across countries.

It is likely that the complex production strategies prevalent in CMEs will require continuous updating of the vocational skills workers obtained at career entry. The high employment protection found in these regimes makes it hard to fire workers, providing an incentive for employers to continuously invest in workers' vocational skills and to distribute training opportunities equitably. Additionally, strong unions in these economies will ensure that the lower-skilled are also provided with continuous training. By contrast, production strategies found in LMEs are likely to predominantly require ongoing training for the small-elite of high-skilled workers resulting not only in relatively low overall incidence rates but also in a high degree of stratification in access to continuing training.

Coordinated and liberal regimes are also likely to have continuing training systems that develop different types of skills. This follows from the general argument about the importance of diversified quality production and specific skills. Further, the two regime types differ in the importance they attribute to collective bargaining in general and this is likely to affect the degree of bargaining about continuing education and training. It can be expected that employers in systems where collective control over continuing training is high are more likely to offer standardized and transferable skills to their employees than in systems where collective control is low. Generally, employers would want the continuing training they provide to primarily serve the firm. In systems where employee representation is weak, companies would mainly invest in firm-specific continuing training, in part to avoid poaching. In systems with high collective control, on the other hand, unions will negotiate the content of training to ensure that the training contains portable elements which would be of value to the worker even outside the current workplace.

The expected difference in the role of collective bargaining is certainly reflected in the practices adopted in the countries under study. In Denmark, Finland, and Germany (our examples of coordinated regimes) collective bargaining plays an important role in the provision of continuing training (Ok and Tergeist 2003). The extent of participation of works councils is also relatively high in these countries (Ok and Tergeist 2003). In contrast, in the UK and Ireland—our examples of liberal regimes—only very few collective agreements on continuing training exist and the role of works councils is negligible (Ok and Tergeist 2003).

While the skill typologies provide very plausible arguments about the logics that underlie different systems of skill creation, they constitute very broad categories that may obscure important differences across countries. In the case of LMEs, the exemplar countries are indeed relatively homogeneous in the broad principles underlying both their skills formation and welfare regimes. Countries within the coordinated category, however, are much more heterogeneous. There exist, for example, substantial differences between Germany and our two Scandinavian countries, Denmark and Finland, which may lead to differences in the organization of continuing training. The former is usually regarded as having a conservative welfare state that primarily protects employees with long job tenure, while the latter are examples of the social-democratic model of welfare that emphasizes a universalistic approach to social protection (Esping-Andersen 1990). Union bargaining coverage is also more extensive in Denmark and Finland (as in other Scandinavian countries, OECD 2004) compared to Germany. Finally, in both Denmark and Finland central-level agreements have considerable importance, while in Germany industry-level wage-setting is predominant (OECD 2004). As discussed in the introduction to this volume, these differences reflect employment systems based on very different principles.

These differences may lead to variations in opportunities for life-long learning in terms both of the volume and distribution of training provision. In Denmark and Finland with their more universalistic ethos, there is stronger emphasis on 'employment-sustaining labour market policies' (DiPrete et al. 1997: 323) which is likely to generate a stronger sense of responsibility for providing citizens with life-long learning opportunities, resulting in a higher volume of continuing training and a potentially more equitable distribution of training opportunities. Germany, on the other hand, with its more dualistic employment and welfare policies, may be more restrictive in its training provision. While in general the strong emphasis on specific skills in the coordinated regimes may provide more incentives (and pressure) for employers to invest in training and reduce polarization of labour market opportunities, we would expect these tendencies to be stronger in the more universalistic Scandinavian context than in Germany.

France and Spain do not fit well into the existing production regime categories. But in these two countries there is evidence of strong internal labour markets (Maurice, Sellier, and Silvestre 1986; Marsden 1990), involving high employment protection for 'insiders' which may lead to a pattern of polarization in labour market opportunities between the 'core' workers and those in 'peripheral' jobs (see DiPrete et al. 2001 for France; Polavieja 2001 for Spain). Access to training in these countries can be expected then to be particularly highly stratified between those in permanent employment and those who are employed on non-standard contracts, that is workers in temporary or part-time employment.

These institutional arguments point to the possibility that there are substantial cross-national differences in the organization of continuing training across countries, potentially leading to differences in the incidence, distribution, and quality of continuing training. The most general expectation would be to find higher continuing training incidence rates in the coordinated economies compared to the liberal ones. Diversified quality production, central to the product market strategies in coordinated economies, requires high-technology vocational skills, which are likely to need general updating. Moreover, collective bargaining on training is relatively common in coordinated economies, and unions can be expected to stipulate high levels of ongoing training provision.

Amongst the coordinated economies, however, we expect those with universalistic employment and welfare models to have somewhat higher continuing training incidences than those with more dualistic regimes, as the provision of life-long learning opportunities in the former countries is considered a central feature of socially responsible employment. These countries are also likely to have higher levels of wage compression, which may affect training provision. This is because wage compression holds down wages of trained workers. Employers who are able to capture returns to training investments are likely to be more readily induced to invest in the training of their workers.

We also expect that the degree of stratification in access to continuing training by education, occupation, and industry would generally be less pronounced in the coordinated economies with high levels of collective control over continuing training compared to the liberal economies where collective control is low as unions can be expected to emphasize equity issues. Similarly, horizontal stratification (i.e. disadvantage of those in temporary and part-time jobs, and female workers) in access to training may be somewhat less pronounced in the Scandinavian countries with more universalistic employment models compared to Germany. We also expect the horizontal axis of polarization to be highly pronounced in France and Spain, given the strong internal labour markets found in these countries.

Further the CMEs, particularly where collective bargaining on training is high, should be more conducive to the provision of high quality training imparting portable qualifications than LMEs where we expect continuing training to be mainly firm-specific. The implications of this for the financial returns to training are debatable. If wage returns are related to the effectiveness of training in terms of skill acquisition, the returns to continuing training may be more pronounced in these countries. In the LMEs where training is more firm-specific, the employer does not have to promote the person trained in order to retain him. As the new skills cannot be resold in the labour market, the worker is without real bargaining power. However, a counter argument is that, since the coordinated economies with strong collective bargaining also will have higher levels of wage compression, they may have particularly low financial returns to training. Where there is wage compression, wages will not generally be a good proxy for the effectiveness of training in terms of skill acquisition and increased productivity. The training quality effect may be cancelled out by the wage compression effect.

The Incidence and Distribution of Continuing Training

In our empirical assessment of these arguments, we look first at the incidence and distribution of training and then, in the following section, turn to examine the issue of the financial returns to training. The analyses are based on the European Community Household Panel (ECHP). The design of the ECHP ensures comparability across countries and over time and is therefore well suited for our comparative research. It is a standardized large-scale longitudinal survey, with annual interviews, carried out under the auspices of Eurostat, the Statistical Office of the European Communities.

As well as a wide range of background variables on characteristics such as occupation, education, and contract status, the data contains detailed information on our explanatory variable of interest—training. The survey asks whether the respondent has participated in any 'education or training' since January of the previous year. The survey then further differentiates between 'vocational training', 'general training', or 'adult education'. The vast majority of training events reported in the ECHP are vocational in nature, and vocational training is more relevant to our research questions than other forms of training. It is also possible to differentiate whether or not training has been funded or organized by the employer. Information on start and end-dates of training allow the researcher not only to determine the exact timing of the training spell, but also to differentiate between short and long training spells. The survey questions do not explicitly indicate whether initial or continuing training is being measured. But to ensure that continuing training and education rather than initial training (e.g. apprenticeships, university education) are measured, we have confined the sample to individuals aged 25 and over. The analyses on training incidence and determinants include individuals aged 25 to 60. Those on training impact, however, are restricted to prime-age workers, so workers aged 55 years or more were not included in the analyses on training outcomes. The sample consists of individuals who were working at least 15 hours a week and who were not self-employed. The analyses exclude apprentices and those on special employment-related schemes.

The first wave of the ECHP was conducted in 1994. Initially, it was planned as a three-wave panel, but has eventually reached eight waves. However, the original ECHP surveys were only continued in Germany and the UK until wave 3. The existing national panels—the German Socio-Economic Panel (GSOEP) and the British Household Panel (BHPS) were then used and harmonized *ex post*. The way continuing training information is collected differs substantially between the original ECHP survey and the GSOEP, which has made data conversion difficult. The GSOEP-based ECHP data excludes many shorter training spells which are recorded in the original ECHP data, which is why the analyses for Germany have to be restricted to the first three waves. For France, we use the survey only from wave two onwards due to problems with the training variable in wave one, leaving us with six waves. We use five waves for

Table 3.1. Continuing vocational training participation

	Vocational training 1994 %	Vocational training 2000 %
Germany	24.6	n.a.^
France	14.9*	7.5
Spain	11.2	14.9
Denmark	44.0	55.7
Finland	57.5+	50.6
UK	22.4	31.8
Ireland	7.7	13.4

Notes: Individuals aged 25 to 60 working at least 15 hours a week, and who were not self-employed. The analyses exclude apprentices and those on special employment-related schemes. Training is since January of the previous year to that of the interview. ^ Data for Germany only available for the years 1993–6. *For France this figure refers to 1995, as the variable specifying type of training has 70% missing cases in the first wave, this is not the case in the following waves. +This estimate refers to 1996 as Finland joined the survey in wave 3.

Sources: ECHP (1994, 2000) (for France 1995, 2000; Finland 1996, 2000).

Finland as it joined the survey in 1996. For the remaining countries we use data from the first seven waves of the ECHP.[3]

Table 3.1 presents the participation rates in adult training for the employed population for 1994 and 2000. It is evident that there were very marked variations between countries in training participation at both time points. The results only partially support the predictions drawn from production regime theory. These suggest that continuing training should be highest in the coordinated regimes. While Finland and Denmark certainly show the highest rates of training in both years, Germany is in an intermediate position (broadly similar in pattern to the UK). The evidence fits better the view that that the inclusiveness or universalism of the employment regime will lead to marked differences between the coordinated economies.

The two countries chosen to represent liberal regimes, the UK and Ireland, also had very different training rates. The UK was in an intermediate position in 1994, and showed a strong increase across the 1990s. (Moreover, the ECHP gives a relatively conservative estimate of training in the UK compared to other sources, see the introductory chapter). Ireland, as predicted, had a particularly low rate of training, although there was also some improvement across time. Training rates were also very low

---

[3] Another reason for using the original ECHP data is that, for confidentiality reasons, the GSOEP-based ECHP excluded all information on sector of industry. However this information is needed to compute the variable with wage-compression and the matched-on figures for union density taken on the industry-level within countries from the ESS.

Table 3.2. Polarization patterns in continuing vocational training participation, 1994

Ratios between	Germany	France*	Spain	Denmark	Finland+	UK	Ireland
Class							
Professionals and Managers/semi-unskilled	4.20	2.96	4.57	1.90	1.94	4.14	4.70
Industry							
Industry/services	0.59	0.85	0.53	0.73	0.82	0.59	0.65
Contract							
Full-/part-time	1.53	1.30	0.77	1.15	1.47	1.99	1.18
Permanent/temporary ~	1.00	0.78	1.41	1.12	1.23	1.01	0.79
Sex							
Male/female	1.10	0.86	0.75	0.91	0.95	1.00	0.80

Notes: Individuals aged 25 to 60 working at least 15 hours a week, and who were not self-employed. The analyses exclude apprentices and those on special employment-related schemes. Training is since January of the previous year to that of the interview. *For France this figure refers to 1995, +This estimate refers to 1996 as Finland joined the survey in wave 3. ~The figures expressing the permanent/temporary workers ratio are based on wave 2.

Source: ECHP (1994) (for France1995; Finland 1996).

in the countries with strong insider–outsider regimes—France and Spain. France, shows a comparatively low rate of training in 1995, which declines further in 2000. In Spain, where there have been dramatic increases in the use of temporary contracts, rates of training were very low in 1994 and increased only modestly by the end of the decade.

How different were training opportunities between different categories of employee? Following the arguments presented in the introductory chapter, we are concerned with differences by class between managerial/ professional employees on the one hand and semi and unskilled employees on the other, between employees in manufacturing and in customer services, between full-time and part-time employees and finally between permanent and temporary workers. Are such differences broadly similar between countries or are there notable differences that can be related to the institutional structures of particular regime types?

There are certainly marked inequalities within countries in relation to occupational class. The ratios in Tables 3.2 and 3.3, which present the patterns for 1994 and 2000, show that there is a clear cleavage in training participation in each of the countries, with professional and managerial workers substantially more likely to participate in training than semi- and unskilled manual workers. In 1994, as expected, the ratio between the two occupational groups is low in the countries characterized by coordinated production regimes with universalistic employment and welfare systems, Denmark and Finland. However, Germany, also an example of coordinated production regime, shows strong occupational

Table 3.3. Polarization patterns in continuing vocational training participation, 2000

Ratios between	Germany	France	Spain	Denmark	Finland	UK	Ireland
Class							
Profesionals and managers/semi-unskilled	—	3.41	3.75	1.65	2.11	2.17	4.66
Industry							
Industry/services	—	0.75	0.47	0.70	0.74	0.78	0.65
Contract							
Full-/part-time	—	2.19	0.81	1.04	1.37	1.19	0.99
Permanent/temporary	—	1.03	1.24	1.09	1.36	0.98	0.73
Sex							
Male/female	—	1.14	0.69	0.86	0.89	0.90	0.86

Notes: Individuals aged 25 to 60 working at least 15 hours a week, and who were not self-employed. The analyses exclude apprentices and those on special employment-related schemes. Training is since January of the previous year to that of the interview.

Source: ECHP (2000).

cleavages in training (and indeed is similar to Spain and more stratified than France—our examples of insider systems). Also, as expected, the two liberal regimes, Ireland and the UK show high levels of polarization in training participation in 1994. But class cleavages in training declined substantially in the UK between 1994 and 2000, giving a ratio at the end of the period close to that of Finland.

With regard to sectoral differences in training participation, we find for 1994 that the coordinated universalistic regimes as well as France show smaller differences than the other countries. By 2000, this picture has changed somewhat. Now it is only Ireland and Spain which really stand out showing a high degree of polarization.

There is little clear impact of regime factors with regard to the other divisions between types of employee. In the UK, Finland, and Germany, examples of rather different production regimes, part-time workers are less likely to train than full-timers. In Spain, part-timers are somewhat more likely to receive training. However, Spain conforms to our expectation that those on temporary or fixed terms contracts are substantially less likely than those on permanent contracts to receive training. In the other countries this cleavage is much weaker, and, indeed, in Ireland and France, temporary workers are more likely to receive training. Finally, gender differences in training are quite muted, although they are greater in Spain, in favour of women, than elsewhere.

Is there any evidence of a tendency to polarization over time? Most of the cleavages found in 1994 are reasonably stable over the period.

The principal exception to this is France, where we can observe increased polarization in training in terms of class, working time, stability of contract, and gender. We also find some decline in class cleavages in access to training between 1994 and 2000 in the UK and Spain.

Who Gets Training? A Multivariate Analysis

The previous section has looked at the differences in opportunities for different types of employee in 'gross' terms, not taking into account that they may vary in terms of other relevant characteristics. A stronger test of the importance of such divisions and whether they vary by regime type requires a multivariate analysis that shows the effect net of other factors. Table 3.4 presents the results of a series of random-effects logit models of training participation for each of our six countries estimated over the 1994–2000 period. The random effects models use the longitudinal information provided by the panel data to control for unobserved heterogeneity. The results show a number of very general patterns regarding training determinants.

As has been argued in Chapter 2, it is important to distinguish the individual's own skill level from the skill level required for the job. The indicator of individual's own skill is educational level. In every country prior educational attainment is associated with participation in continuing vocational training: the higher the level of education, the greater the likelihood of participation in training. This is consistent with previous research (e.g. Bassanini et al. 2005). It confirms the general pattern that those most in need of training—that is the low-skilled—are least likely to receive it.

Class (in this case based upon the International Standard Classification of Occupations (ISCO) measure) is taken as an indicator of the skill requirements of the job. This has a clear effect, even when the educational level of the individual has been taken into account. In every country senior officials, professional and technical workers, as well as clerical and service workers receive more training than those in semi- and unskilled manual occupations. In France and the UK craft workers also receive more training. In contrast to the descriptive analyses presented earlier, where country differences were presented without controls for individual or organizational characteristics, the multivariate analyses suggest strong class effects in all countries, providing little support for the argument that

Table 3.4. Random-effects models for training incidence, 1994–2000 by country

	Germany (1)	France (2)	Ireland (3)	Spain (4)	Finland (5)	Denmark (6)	UK (7)
Sex = female	0.492**	0.883	1.141	1.066	1.057	0.893	1.217**
Secondary education (reference = basic education)	1.503	1.656**	2.702**	2.408**	1.878**	1.723**	1.445**
Tertiary education	2.102*	1.927**	3.379**	3.172**	2.984**	2.097**	1.823**
Age 36–45 (reference = age 25–35)	0.612	0.846	0.769	0.961	1.074	1.086	0.853*
Age 46–60	0.398**	0.512**	0.827	0.720**	1.092	0.998	0.681**
Senior officials, Managers (reference = semi/unskilled man)	4.911**	2.466**	2.438**	3.196**	3.461**	2.257**	2.753**
Professional, technical	5.799**	2.721**	2.356**	2.661**	3.487**	3.020**	2.823**
Clerical and service	3.084**	2.176**	1.666*	1.944**	2.307**	1.700**	1.883**
Craft workers	0.822	1.350*	0.717	1.269	1.321	0.804	1.584**
Part-time (reference full-time)	1.069	0.706**	0.801	1.189	0.753	0.691**	0.654**
Permanent job (reference <5 year contract)	0.762	1.211	1.454**	1.495**	1.670**	1.283**	0.933
Public sector	0.804	1.411**	1.061	1.002	1.158	1.211	1.599**
Tenure <1 year (reference= >10 years)	1.193	1.714**	1.255	0.988	0.687	0.864	1.187
Tenure 2–5 years	0.555*	1.039	1.004	0.855	0.633**	0.967	1.401**
Tenure 5–10 years	0.578	0.891	0.885	0.820*	0.795	0.998	1.124
Firm size < 100 empl. (SME) (reference = 500+ employees)	0.440**	—⊥	0.555*	0.532**	0.609**	0.619**	0.568**
Firm size 100 to 499 employees	0.507*	—	1.233	0.872	0.99	0.961	0.646**
Observations	1,950	15,373	6,420	12,282	4,866	6,498	13,255
Number of scid	990	4,034	1,490	2,970	1,989	1,743	2,948
log-likelihood	−862.37	−5,244.44	−2,042.67	−4,758.68	−2,976.96	−3,978.22	−7,820.6
ρ	0.47	0.33	0.43	0.32	0.36	0.34	0.33

Notes: The estimates are odds-ratios from random-effects logistic regression using panel data for the period 1994–2000, except France 1995–2000, Germany 1994–6, and Finland 1996–2000. Reference categories are male workers with basic education aged 25–35 working full time as operators, assemblers or in elementary occupations in a large company in the private sector with a fixed term contract and tenure of more than ten years. * Significant at 5%; ** significant at 1%. Firm size is not included for France as there were too many missing cases in the public and private sectors.

Source: ECHP (1994–2000).

there would be lower class inequality either in the coordinated economies as a whole, or even in those with more universalistic employment and welfare regimes.

There was also no support for the view that the horizontal axis of polarization would be more pronounced in Spain and France than in the other countries, due to the strong internal labour markets found there and the growth of fixed term contracts for new entrants in Spain. In practice, there seems to be little connection between regime type and the treatment of employees with different contract statuses. Permanent workers did indeed receive more training than their temporary counterparts in Spain (as also in Denmark, Finland, and Ireland), but in France there was no significant difference between permanent and temporary workers. It was anticipated that temporary workers would be less severely disadvantaged in the LMEs, but this only appeared to be the case for the UK. A similar picture emerges for the distinction between full-timers and part-timers. Full-time workers are more likely to receive training than those working part-time in France, Denmark, and the UK—countries in contrasting regime locations. Part-time working made little difference to training opportunities in Germany, Ireland, Spain, and Finland.

Age has also been regarded as a potential source of horizontal polarization with respect to training. It is notable that in general we do find a negative relationship between age and training participation. Older workers (aged 46 to 60) are less likely to receive training in Germany, France, Spain, and the UK, although there was no evidence of age disadvantage in Denmark, Finland, or Ireland.

A factor that appeared to have a major effect on employee training opportunities in all of the countries for which there was adequate data is firm size. Since the variable measuring firm size is missing for most people in the public sector, a dummy variable was created for all public sector workers. For the private-sector firm size is grouped into three categories—small (<100 employees), medium (100–499 employees), and large (>500 employees)—again specified as dummy variables. The reference category was large private-sector firms, so the effect of public-sector refers to the comparison with large private-sector firms, while the effects of firm size refer only to effects within the private sector. In general, we find that the public sector does not differ significantly from large private-sector firms, although in the UK public sector workers are more likely to receive training than those in large private-sector firms. Employees in small private firms are less likely to receive training than their counterparts in large private firms.

We turn next (in Table 3.5) to examine the impact of institutional factors on individual chances of participating in training. In particular, it has been seen that there are arguments that union strength and wage compression are important determinants of training provision. We estimate a series of multilevel models in which we pool the individual-level data for each country and add institutional variables—union

Table 3.5. Multilevel models of participation in continuing vocational training (pooled sample of individuals in seven countries)

	Logit (1)	Random intercept (2)	Random intercept (3)	Random intercept (4)
Female	1.078	1.05	1.068	1.053
Secondary education	1.512**	1.365**	1.444**	1.360**
Tertiary education	1.847**	1.778**	1.857**	1.762**
Age 36–45	0.955	0.957	0.95	0.951
Age 46–60	0.775**	0.791**	0.785**	0.785**
Senior officials/managers	2.999**	3.068**	2.995**	3.106**
Professionals	3.060**	2.970**	2.944**	2.983**
Clerical and service	2.186**	2.078**	2.106**	2.163**
Craft	1.610**	1.694**	1.616**	1.684**
Part-time	0.762**	0.770**	0.755**	0.747**
Permanent	1.577**	1.569**	1.504**	1.535**
Public sector	1.08	1.012	0.99	1.015
Tenure <1 year	0.808*	0.770**	0.753**	0.820*
Tenure 2–5 years	0.97	1.005	0.971	1.033
Tenure 6–10 years	0.923	0.96	0.944	0.979
Private firm, 100 employees	0.527**	0.568**	0.569**	0.570**
Private firm 101–500 employees	0.891	0.919	0.916	0.908
Union density		1.022**		1.023**
Wage compression			1.042**	1.015**
Germany	1.056			
Denmark	4.592**			
Finland	3.338**			
France	0.952			
Ireland	0.479**			
UK	3.442**			
Observations	12,981	12,981	2,981	12,981
pseudo R^2	0.156			
Log-Likelihood	−6,492.07	−6,788.27	−6,799.988	−6,784.672

Notes: * Significant at 5%; ** significant at 1%.

Source: ECHP (1994–2000).

density and wage compression—that vary by economic sector within each country. This represents an analysis of institutional effects at an intermediate level, between the individual level, as in the models presented in Table 3.4, and the national level. Arguably, the impact of union density and wage compression is best measured at this intermediate level.

Equation (1) is a simple pooled logit model specifying all the individual level variables in the country-specific models, as well as a series of dummy variables representing each country with Spain as the reference category. Equations 2–4 are random intercept models that replace the country dummy variables with the sectoral-level institutional variables.

In each of these models we specify a set of individual controls across all seven countries in the sample. These models reflect the general patterns found in the earlier country-specific equations. Those with higher levels of education are more likely to participate in training. Similarly, occupation is important and those in highly skilled occupations are more likely to receive training. Older workers are less likely to participate, as are part-timers and those on temporary contracts. New entrants to jobs, with less than one year tenure, are less likely to receive training than those with longer tenure. Those working in small private-sector firm are less likely to train, and the public sector does not differ from large private-sector firms. These individual effects are consistent with our expectations, with previous research, and with the pattern of effects reported for the country-specific models.

As expected, union density has a positive effect on training (Equation 2). Union density is measured at the sectoral level, so workers in sectors characterized by higher levels of union density are more likely to receive training. Similarly, wage compression has a positive influence on training (Equation 3). The union effect suggests that unions bargain to increase access to training. The wage compression effect, can be explained by employers' need to provide training for low-skilled workers in order to increase productivity in line with wage floors, while for high-skilled workers it may be due to the expectation on the part of employers that they will be more able to capture the returns to training where there are constraints on wage increases of skilled workers (Acemoglu and Pischke 1999b).

In short, the analysis provides strong support for the view that institutions do matter for training opportunities. This is not however with respect to the types of factors emphasized in production regime theory. Rather it supports an emphasis on the role of trade unions (and concomitantly of wage compression) in affecting training chances.

Training Effects on Earnings

How far does training benefit workers in terms of higher pay? And do the financial implications of training vary between countries? It was seen earlier that there were conflicting expectations with respect to the coordinated regime countries. Higher training quality might be expected to lead to a more pronounced wage markup, but wage compression as a result of stronger union influence could reduce the financial returns to training.

As mentioned in the discussion of earlier research, in measuring the impact of training on earnings, there is always the risk that selection bias might alter the results. Individuals with more productive characteristics (such as motivation) might be more likely to receive training while at the same time being more likely to experience higher wage progression in the absence of training. One of the methods increasingly used to control for selection bias is matching. This method is very popular in the evaluation of active labour market policies for the unemployed. The basic idea is that the bias is reduced if one compares the outcomes of individuals who are as similar as possible by matching them. Rosenbaum and Rubin (1983) advocate the propensity score—a single-index variable summarizing the pre-treatment characteristics of each individual. This expresses an individual's a-priori probability of being in the treatment group. The difference in the outcomes of two individuals with the same propensity score, one in the treatment group and the other in the control group, can be interpreted as the 'treatment effect' plus a random element, and averaging over this set of estimates provides the social scientist with the average effect of the treatment on the treated (ATT). An alternative method of matching is based on Mahalanobis metric distances (which can also be applied in combination with propensity scores).

In this study we use the Mahalanobis metric matching[4] estimator in conjunction with the propensity score to adjust for background differences between trained and non-trained workers. It has to be noted, however, that while matching methods are used very frequently when examining special labour market programmes for the unemployed, their application when assessing the impact of continuing training is less straightforward. A general issue is that using matching in a panel setting is not straightforward and the literature on how to bridge matching and panel methods is just developing. The main challenge is how to deal with repeated training participation (cf. Gerfin 2004). If we wanted to assess the true causal effect of training participation in, for example, 1997 on wage levels or wage progression, we should exclude workers who received training in 1996 or 1998 as these training incidences could also influence the outcome we observe in 1998. This would not only cause problems regarding our 'treatment group' (i.e. those receiving training in 1997) but also regarding those in the control group (i.e. those not participating in

---

[4] Mahalanobis matching allows the researcher to match on more than one variable, which gives variables more weight than including them in the propensity score. This is an advantage here as we are working with panel data, and wanted to achieve perfect matches on survey wave.

training in 1997) as this control group would contain workers who did not participate in any training at all as well as those who did participate in training before or/and after the training event that is being evaluated. Excluding these cases, however, is not without problems given the endogeneity of continuing training. We would basically exclude workers with frequent training participation and thereby create a new form of bias. Here, we chose the strategy of conditioning the analyses on workers who were not in training during $T-1$ in order to receive conservative estimates of the causal effect of the training spell in question but are aware of the problems inherent in this.

The longitudinal design of the ECHP allows us to control for (observed) pre-training differences between those workers experiencing training and those who do not experience training within a given time period (T). The following variables are included in the probit model estimating the propensity score (i.e. likelihood of a training spell in survey year T): age, age squared, education, sex, sector (public–private), tenure, tenure squared, log real hourly wages (deflated to 2000 national currency units), occupation at $T-1$ as well as a variable measuring whether the respondent experienced any unemployment during the five years prior to joining the survey. We only count training spells that have started and finished during survey year T and we distinguish between all continuing vocational training and employer-provided vocational training.[5] We only include individuals who were observed in at least three consecutive waves (pre-treatment measures $T-1$, training incidence T, and training outcome $T+1$), with valid observations on all the variables used in the estimation of the average treatment effect of training. By also including previous earnings and previous unemployment experience, we are able to (at least to some degree) achieve matches on unobserved covariates.

The dependent variable in our analysis is the log real hourly earnings at $T+1$. Before turning to our estimations of the average treatment effects, however, we present simple OLS estimates of the training effect. Especially given the problems of applying matching methods in the context of continuing training, we believe that well-specified OLS models should also form a strong basis of our understanding of training effects. Lagged

---

[5] It would have also been interesting to differentiate between on- and off-site training. The ECHP contains a variable which allows to differentiate between off- general and on-site specific vocational training. This information, however, is missing for a number of countries we are analysing. For other countries there exists no category for on-site training. Given the problems with the variable distinguishing between on- and off-site training, we chose to differentiate between the effects of all vocational training, and employer-provided training instead.

Table 3.6. OLS estimates of returns to vocational training

	Vocational training	Employer-provided vocational training
Germany	0.070***	0.075***
France	0.016(*)	0.049***
Spain	0.042**	0.065***
Denmark	−0.006 n.s.	−0.002 n.s.
Finland	0.004 n.s.	0.007 n.s.
UK	0.054***	0.017*
Ireland	0.084***	0.121***

Notes: Each regression includes age, age squared, tenure, tenure squared, education, occupation, sex, a variable measuring previous unemployment, sector (public/private). Significance levels: (*) <0.1; * <0.05; ** <0.01; *** <0.001.
Source: ECHP 1994–2000.

values of the time-varying covariates have been recorded into the data. Only individuals who started and finished training in the previous year are considered to have received training to prevent double-counting of training events. The OLS estimates shown in Table 3.6 suggest significant returns to vocational training in five of our seven countries. A notable finding is that the data suggest that there are no significant training returns in either Denmark or Finland.[6]

In the countries where vocational training returns were significant, the analyses further suggest that returns to training are—with the exception of the UK—substantially higher if training is employer-provided. This gradient seems to be least pronounced in Germany. In sum, the coefficients do not reveal systematic patterns across country clusters, which is contrary to what would be expected in terms of regime theories.

In a next step we present separate analyses for men and women. In view of previous research, it seems likely that we should find gender inequality in returns to training. Previous research suggested men have better promotion opportunities than women with similar qualifications (e.g. Winter-Ebmer and Zweimüller 1997; Granquist and Persson 1999). Booth, Francesconi, and Frank (2003), on the other hand, have shown British women have the same odds to be promoted as men, but that

[6] Our findings differ from results by Bassanini et al. (2005) whose OLS estimates of returns to continuing training, also based on the ECHP data, suggest significant effects in all EU countries under study, including Denmark and Finland. This can be due to a number of reasons. First, whilst our analysis focuses on continuing vocational training, they examine the impact of all continuing training. Second, Bassanini et al. examine the impact of the stock of continuing training, whilst we are interested in the flow of training. Finally, our OLS models include a number of control variables, such as job tenure, occupation, and previous unemployment that are not included in their model.

Table 3.7. OLS estimates of returns to vocational training for men and women

	Vocational training	Employer-provided vocational training
Men		
Germany	0.057***	0.061**
France	0.047***	0.071***
Spain	0.048**	0.074***
Denmark	−0.002 n.s.	−0.012 n.s.
Finland	0.011 n.s.	0.012 n.s.
UK	0.058***	0.018(*)
Ireland	0.098**	0.155***
Women		
Germany	0.084***	0.093***
France	−0.029*	0.012 n.s.
Spain	0.032(*)	0.051*
Denmark	−0.006 n.s.	0.001 n.s.
Finland	−0.004 n.s.	0.000 n.s.
UK	0.045***	0.016 n.s.
Ireland	0.061 n.s.	0.067 n.s.

Notes: Each regression includes age, age squared, tenure, tenure squared, education, occupation, a variable measuring previous unemployment, sector (public/private). Significance levels: (*) <0.1; * <0.05; ** <0.01; *** <0.001.
Source: ECHP (1994–2000).

they are more likely to be 'stuck' at the bottom of the wage scale of the new grade. We may therefore find that women who receive training are rewarded less than their male counterparts.

Our data suggest that indeed in some of our countries male workers' training investments receive greater financial rewards than those of their female counterparts (cf. Table 3.7). In line with our predictions we find particularly notable gender gaps in the insider–outsider systems—in France even more than in Spain. The Irish data also suggests a substantial gender difference. This result should be interpreted with some caution, however, given that the number of Irish women receiving training is rather low (eighty in the case of vocational training; and even less than eighty in the case of employer-funded training). The UK data also suggests a gender gap in returns to training. Interestingly, we find that in Germany female training investment seems to be more highly rewarded than that of male workers.

As discussed earlier, the OLS estimates of returns to training may be biased as they do not account for potential selectivity. Table 3.8 shows the average treatment effects of training once selectivity is controlled through matching to compare individuals who are as similar as possible. We find

Table 3.8. Average treatment effects—training experience and workers' wage level

	Average treatment effect of continuing vocational training on workers' wage level (measured at T+1)	Average treatment effect of employer-provided continuing vocational training on workers' wage level (measured at T+1)
Germany	-4.8×10^{-4} n.s.	0.043 n.s.
France	−0.011 n.s.	0.026 n.s.
Spain	0.044(*)	0.025 n.s.
Denmark	0.020 n.s.	0.029 n.s.
Finland	−0.012 n.s.	0.014 n.s.
UK	0.003 n.s.	0.007 n.s.
Ireland	0.070 n.s.	0.028 n.s.

Notes: Workers aged 25–54. The estimates are based on Mahalanobis metric matching of trained and non-trained workers (using a caliper of 0.001). (*) <0.1, * <0.05, ** <0.01, *** <0.001. The following variables are included in the probit model estimating the propensity score (i.e. likelihood of a training spell in survey year (T): age, age^2, education, sex, sector (public/private), tenure, $tenure^2$, log real hourly wage, occupation at $T-1$ as well as a variable measuring whether the respondent experienced any unemployment during the five years before joining the survey.[8]

Source: ECHP waves (1994–2000).

that in only one of our seven countries does vocational training have a (marginally) significant effect on workers' wage levels: in Spain a worker with a recent continuing training investment has a wage that is 5 per cent higher than that of an otherwise very similar worker who did not receive training. This effect is only significant when all continuing training is measured. In the analyses that assess the impact of training which has been employer-provided the coefficient is not significant anymore. It should be noted that when we conducted separate analyses (which are not presented here) for men and women to assess the average treatment effect of training, we found that male German worker's wages are significantly and positively affected by training participation. Apart from this exception, all training effects in the separate analyses came out insignificant.

Finally, we conducted separate analyses for shorter and longer training spells. If we take the length of training as an indicator of training intensity and quality then one could expect to find more pronounced and significant returns to longer training spells. At the same time, however, previous research has found that less educated workers tend to participate

[8] Number of matched treated (T) and controls (C) in each country; Vocational Training: Germany—T: 217, C: 2,056; France—T: 685; C: 8,187; Spain—T: 608, C: 9,980; Denmark—T: 725, C: 4,022; Finland—T: 225, C: 3,712; UK—T: 1,607, C: 4,927; Ireland—T: 105, C: 3,546. Employer-provided Vocational Training: Germany—T: 193, C: 2080; France—T: 601; C: 8,271; Spain—T: 491, C: 10,097; Denmark—T: 659, C: 4,088; Finland—T: 294, C: 4,406; UK—T: 946, C: 5,588; Ireland—T: 91, C: 3,560.

in longer duration courses, often directed towards learning new skills or a new occupation (Pischke 2001). The returns to such courses are often not immediate, but rather long run (Pischke 2001). In the case of our analyses this would imply that such effects may not yet show. Training spells were considered to be short if they were of less than two weeks duration, and as longer spells if they were of a duration of two weeks and longer. With very few exceptions these analyses also produced insignificant results (not shown here). One exception was Denmark where short employer-funded training spells significantly increased earnings by 4 per cent. Likewise, the estimates for the Spanish data suggest that short vocational training increases earnings by 5.5 per cent.[9] For France, by contrast, we found marginally significant training effects for long employer-funded training which appeared to increase earnings by 9 per cent.

The conclusion that training has little effect on wages when selection effects are taken into account is consistent with previous work on individual countries (e.g. Goux and Maurin 2000 for France; Pischke 2001 for Germany; Leuven and Oosterbeek 2002 for the Netherlands). But the problems of applying matching in the context of continuing training have to be recognized as an important qualification to the results. Finally, we have to consider—as noted by Bassanini (2006)—that wage returns to continuing training are biased, given that the sample is missing all individuals that are no longer in employment. These estimates therefore do not take into account the impact of training on employment prospects and on containing the loss of income associated with unemployment spells.

Conclusions

In this chapter we have sought to explore the determinants and impact of vocational training among employed workers. We have focused on seven European countries and have taken advantage of the differences within and between these countries to examine the influence of labour market institutions on training.

In the context of a virtually universal pattern across all advanced societies in which those who are already well-endowed with human capital, and those in privileged employment situations, are likely to receive more

[9] The results further suggest significant returns to short employer-funded training in Ireland. However, the analyses are based on only fifty matched 'treated' individuals and are therefore rather volatile.

training, we examined the argument that institutional factors in the labour market may play a role in shaping the extent of the training gap between the low and the high skilled, and between different segments of the labour market.

The data show considerable variation between countries in the incidence of training: from a low of 7.5 per cent training participation in France to a high of 55.7 per cent in Denmark in 2000. The descriptive analyses on training incidence show clear evidence of polarization between different types of workers suggesting that training exacerbates existing inequalities of work–life chances. We find little evidence to support a dynamic polarization tendency over time. Most of the cleavages found in the early 1990s appear reasonably stable over time.

Our results from multivariate analyses of training determinants confirm the advantages accruing to those with higher skills or human capital, with positive effects of education at both secondary and tertiary levels in most countries. Occupation is also a very strong predictor of training participation. However, in respect of both education and occupation effects, we did not detect clear patterns that would suggest that stratification was less pronounced in countries with coordinated economies and more collective bargaining on training than in liberal ones.

Our findings from the multilevel analysis of the impact of different institutional factors suggested that workers in sectors characterized by higher levels of union density and lower wage dispersion were more likely to participate in training. This can be understood in terms of the impact of training: wage compression provides incentives for employers to train low-skilled workers, to increase productivity in line with wages, and to train high-skilled workers because employers can expect to capture the returns to training where wage increases are constrained.

Finally, we examined the impact of training on subsequent wages. In line with previous work in this area, we find significant returns to training in the analyses which do not take account of selectivity bias, and no returns once we attempt to correct for selection bias.

In sum, we found no evidence of systematic differences in the distribution of training opportunities and the financial returns to training relating to differences in production systems and employment regimes. We did find, however, strong evidence that the volume of continuing training is by far the highest in the inclusive employment regimes of Denmark and Finland.

4

Task Discretion and Job Quality

Duncan Gallie

Introduction

Task discretion has long been acknowledged by analysts from very diverse theoretical perspectives as critical for people's capacity for self-realization in work, for their personal satisfaction with working life, for their work motivation, and for their commitment to or alienation from their employer. It is generally regarded as one of the most central factors, if not the most central, for the wider quality of working life. Yet there is very little evidence to date about how far the scope for employees to exercise discretion in their work varies between countries. Similarly, we know very little about whether there has been any systematic pattern for differences between specific categories of employee to increase over the period involving greater workforce polarization. This chapter addresses these issues and considers whether there are institutional conditions that affect the level of employee task discretion and the risks of polarization.

The arguments for the importance of task discretion have appealed to quite different underlying explanations. The capacity for self-realization in work can be seen as a natural outcome of processes of childhood and adolescent socialization that seek to enhance autonomy in decision-making (Argyris 1964). It can also be seen as reinforced by the wider normative structure of liberal-democratic Western societies which encourage people to see themselves as equal citizens in the diverse social structural contexts in which they live out their lives (Marshall 1964), a view that is likely to lead to a belief that at work employees should actively participate in decisions rather than be passively subject to managerial authority. The neo-Marxian argument sees individual control over the work task as an essential condition for self-realization, since it provides the conditions for creativity and self-development (Braverman 1974). Finally, more recently, social psychologists have stressed the consequences of task discretion or 'decision latitude' for psychological and physical health. In particular, the 'psychosocial' school has argued that, because of its capacity to mediate work pressure, task discretion (or decision latitude) reduces risks of psychological stress, high blood pressure, and even cardiovascular disease (Karesek and Theorell 1990; Johnson and Johansson 1991; Theorell and Karesek 1996; Theorell 1998; van der Doef and Maes 1999).

There is much less consensus however in predictions of change in task discretion. Theories of trends have been generally closely tied to theories of skill development. There is a general consensus in the literature that those in higher occupational classes, with higher levels of skill, tend to have greater initiative in the way they carry out their jobs compared to those lower in the skill hierarchy. By the same token, changes in task discretion are thought to reflect to a considerable extent trends in the development of skills. For those with a generally optimistic view of the evolution of skills, in which the principal scenario is one of steadily rising skills in an ever more complex and technologically sophisticated economy, the expectation is that job quality will improve significantly over time leading to greater say for individual employees over the work process (Blauner 1964; Piore and Sabel 1984; Zuboff 1988). Very similar assumptions informed more recent theories of the emergence of a new knowledge-based society. Conversely, neo-Marxian theorists, who have a pessimistic view on skill evolution, envisage a long-term decline in job control for those in lower skilled work (Friedmann 1946; Braverman 1974; Wright and Singelmann 1982) resulting in growing polarization between classes in job quality.

There have been similar differences between those who have focused on the significance of sectoral change for the nature of work, in particular the growth of the service sector. For some, service sector work can be seen as offering a release from the constraints of manufacturing industry, in particular the mechanical pacing of work embodied in the Fordian assembly line. Instead work becomes primarily customer-orientated and as such has to allow greater discretion to employees to handle the wide range and low predictability of individual demands and personalities. Others have pointed to the high relative labour costs of service production, the seasonal nature of much work and the dispersion of service workers across a large number of relatively small worksites, to draw a picture of a highly vulnerable sector of the workforce. Such arguments particularly point to the poor work conditions that are thought to prevail in lower skilled private services such as retail and hotels.

Scenarios of change in managerial philosophies of workforce control as a result of product market change also have important implications for task discretion. An optimistic perspective about trends in task discretion has been reinforced by theories of the growth of new forms of managerial policy that emphasize the need to replace constraint with commitment to meet the higher demands that modern competitive economies place on product quality (Walton 1985*a*, 1985*b*). Increased task discretion is introduced as part of a broader bundle of measures designed to enhance employee job involvement and organizational commitment. However, counter to this, has been the view that employers are increasingly adopting strategies that involve dividing the workforce into 'core' and 'periphery' sectors, with very different work conditions, in order to handle the greater volatility of market conditions (Atkinson 1984; Rosenberg 1989; Procter et al. 1994; Cappelli et al. 1997). The division between core and periphery is seen to be crystallized in the distinction between those with standard and those with non-standard contracts. Those in the core have good training opportunities and high levels of job protection, while those in the periphery have few opportunities for skill development and low job security. By extension differences in contract status would be likely to involve differences in the responsibility and initiative that employers would allow to different employees.

Finally, there has been a persisting concern about whether the rise of female employment in most European societies has led to a growing divergence in employment conditions between men and women. A notable feature of the expansion of jobs for women has been that it has taken place within a highly segregated labour market. Research has established the importance of such sex segregation for persisting inequalities of pay (Joshi and Paci 1998). It might plausibly then have significant consequences for other aspects of employment conditions such as task discretion. In addition, female employment has been particularly heavily concentrated in the service sector and women are more likely to be in jobs with non-standard contracts. So polarization with respect to sector and contract may have disproportionately affected women and widened sex divergences in job rewards.

The main theories of job task quality have been universalistic in their assumptions. The key processes that underlie changes in skill and job quality—whether these be market competition or technological change—are held to evolve in broadly similar ways across the advanced societies.

More recently, as was seen in the Introduction, this approach has been challenged by the argument that there are important differences between the advanced societies in skill formation systems and in systems of employment regulation and, if this is correct, they should have important consequences for the nature of work tasks and the opportunities they provide for employee involvement.

What are the main institutional features that could be expected to affect task discretion? In considering the most plausible arguments, it is important to distinguish between factors that might affect the general level of task discretion in the workforce and those that might influence the extent of similarity or divergence of trends between different categories of the workforce. With respect to the average level of task discretion, it is the longer-term strength and political influence of organized labour that is likely to be particularly important. This should be reflected in two factors: the strength of trade union membership and the salience of national policy commitments to work life reform. But a given average level of task discretion is compatible with rather different risks for potentially vulnerable categories of employees. With respect to the risks of polarization, the significant institutional factors should be those that offer significant protection to employees with a weaker position in the labour market. Potentially, three such factors are the structure of collective bargaining, the system of skills formation and the prevalence of an insider–outsider duality in the system of employment protection.

Union Workplace Strength. It is plausible that an important determinant of the general level of task discretion in a country would be the strength of employee representation, in particular at workplace level. Where unions can exercise significant influence in the workplace, they are likely to resist the implementation of tighter systems of employer control of work performance. In general workplace strength will be reflected in union membership density. However, the institutional rights of unions may also be important. (In particular, in France, it has been well established that the institutional privileges accorded to the unions with respect to both national agreements and the activities of the company councils provide much stronger leverage than would be anticipated on the basis of membership figures.) But, where membership falls short of being virtually comprehensive, one would not expect union workplace strength to necessarily reduce risks of polarization. If the non-unionized are those most vulnerable, then unionism may reinforce divergences of experience in the workforce. As mentioned in the Introduction to the volume, there are major differences between the countries in membership strength.

Membership was highest in Sweden (78%), at a medium level in the UK (29%) and Germany (23%), and very low in Spain (16%) and above all in France (8%).

National Policies for Working Life Reform. One would also expect higher levels of task discretion where there are well-resourced national policies for improving the quality of working life. These have tended to adopt a specific focus on the need to regard psychological stress as a significant health risk. Partly as a result of this, job enrichment and job control have typically been a central aspect of such programmes. In practice such policies have been predominantly confined hitherto to the Northern European countries of Denmark, Finland, the Netherlands, Norway, and Sweden (Sandberg et al. 1992; Gustavsen et al. 1996; Gallie 2003). However, other countries have adopted more partial measures. France introduced a major legal initiative in the 1980s in the form of the Lois Auroux which created discussion groups for employees (Eyraud and Tchobanian 1985; Martin 1994; Jefferys 2003). Both France and Germany set up relatively modest ongoing programmes that aimed to stimulate improvements in the quality of working life through advice and financial incentives, although the budgetary resources they received make it unlikely that they had a major impact on work quality outside a limited number of organizations (Fricke 2003; Steiber 2005; van de Velde 2005).

The Structure of Collective Bargaining. The nature of collective bargaining could be expected to be particularly important with respect to risks of polarization. Inclusive centralized systems of collective bargaining should act to establish broadly applicable norms and hence ensure greater equality of treatment by skill, industry, contract type, and sex. The least protective system should be one of highly decentralized bargaining, where employers can take advantage of the market weakness of specific groups to reduce the quality of their employment conditions. The European Commission's (European Commission 2006: 45) index score for the level of coordination of wage bargaining, which takes account both of the basic structure of the system and the coverage rate of agreements, shows Sweden as by far the most highly coordinated, with Spain, Germany, and France in an intermediate position, while Britain has an exceptionally low level of coordination.

Systems of Skill Formation. The risk of polarization may also be affected by the system of skill formation. As discussed in the Introduction an important distinction can be drawn between general skill formation systems on the one hand and occupation or industry-specific skill formation systems on the other. In the first, employers rely primarily on general education for workforce skills. In specific skill formation systems, skills are primarily developed in relationship to occupational norms through formalized inter-employer vocational training programmes. Specific skill formation systems can be either primarily based on vocational training in educational schools or may take the form of a dual system in which training is provided partly through apprenticeships with particular companies and partly through vocational schools.

General skill formation systems are likely to lead to strong differentials between employees with high educational qualifications that employers will be concerned to retain as long-term employees and those with low-level qualifications who are relatively dispensable. In specific skill formation systems, however, employees' skills have a significant degree of independence from particular organizational contexts and this is likely to make it more difficult for employers to alter work posts in a way that would curb employee discretion. Jobs tend to be designed around the externally derived skills of employees rather than around an internal organizational logic (Marsden 1999). This is reinforced by the fact that specific skill formation systems tend to socialize employees into a strong sense of occupational identity (Lane 1987). This gives them a pride in their work, but at the same time a greater reluctance to accept organizational change that would imply a dilution of their status (Finegold and Wagner 1999; Herrigel and Sabel 1999). Of the two types of specific skill systems, it seems likely that the vocational school-based systems will provide the highest level of employee independence, while dual systems will encourage a greater degree of employer control over skill development.

While country systems contain mixes of different skill formation types, Britain and Spain are closest to the 'general' model; Germany is the classic example of the 'dual' specific skill model and France and Sweden of the 'school-based' model. Sweden also combines a strong initial vocational training basis with considerable subsequent opportunities for in-career training.

Employment Regulation. Finally, one could expect polarization to depend upon the degree of formalization of insider–outsider differentials embodied in employment protection regulations. Where employment protection is relatively strong for regular employees, there may be a tendency to compensate through less favourable conditions for those on atypical contracts. The stronger the dualism in employment protection, the more likely it is that wider work and employment conditions will diverge between regular and atypical workers. A detailed indicator of employment protection has been constructed by the OECD (OECD 2004). As was shown in Chapter 1, the countries that stand out as having particularly strict employment protection are Spain and France, followed by Sweden and Germany. However, it is likely that in a country such as Sweden, with high levels of union density, the employment conditions of temporary workers will be better protected than in countries where union strength is aligned primarily upon the core workforce.

Hence our broad expectations about country patterns would be the following:

Sweden has high union density, strong work reform policies, relatively centralized bargaining, and an 'extended' schools-based specific skills formation system. Although it also has a relatively high level of employment protection, non-standard workers should be partly protected by the high level of union coverage and the wider emphasis on reducing differences in conditions of employment between categories of employee. In general, then, one would expect Sweden to be characterized by high task discretion and low polarization.

Spain, in contrast, has low union density, no national work reform policies, industry-level bargaining, a general skills system, and a particularly marked divide between insiders and outsiders. It could be expected then to have low task discretion and a high risk of polarization.

Britain historically has had strong workplace unionism. Although union density has declined substantially in recent decades, it remains relatively strong compared to most Central and Southern European countries. But it has had no significant policies of working life reform. It could be expected then to be in an intermediary position with respect to the prevalence of task discretion. Although it has low dualism in employment protection, its highly decentralized bargaining system and its 'general education' skill development system should provide little protection to vulnerable categories of the workforce. Overall one would expect it to be characterized by a medium level of task discretion, but with significant risks of polarization.

France. French union density is very low, although the institutionalized rights of unions with respect to workplace representation are significant. Through the Lois Auroux, there has been active state intervention in quality of working life issues, although the ongoing programmes to stimulate voluntary reform have been very modest by Swedish standards. Medium levels of bargaining coordination and a relatively high level of employment dualism should give rise to risks of polarization, but a schools-based vocational skills formation system should offer significant protection to those in lower occupational classes. Overall, it could be expected to have a medium level of task discretion, a low risk of class polarization, but a high risk of polarization along contract lines.

Germany. In Germany union density is higher than in France, but it has had no equivalent to the Lois Auroux with respect to legislative intervention for work life reform. Its ongoing work reform programme was of a relatively modest type that was unlikely to have had a significant impact on task discretion. Medium levels of industry coordination and a relatively high level of employment dualism are likely to encourage polarization. But its 'dual system' of specific skills formation should have given significant protection against polarization risks for the less skilled, although less securely than in the case of countries with more strongly schools-based vocational training systems. Overall, like France, it could be expected to have a medium level of task discretion, a low risk of class polarization, and a high risk of polarization by contract status.

The chapter addresses these issues drawing upon both comparative and national data-sets. The comparative data provide a picture of the relative differences in level of task discretion between countries, but the time span for assessing change is short and the sample sizes within countries are inadequate for a reliable analysis of polarization between subgroups. While the national data-sets do not allow comparison of levels between countries, our assumption is that the indicators selected proxy broadly similar aspects of the work situation and allow an analysis of whether there have been trends to polarization in the different countries. The chapter begins by examining the comparative picture of the level of task discretion and then turns to the national data-sets to assess whether there is evidence of polarization within the workforce.

The Level of Task Discretion: A Comparative Overview

To provide a context for the more detailed analysis of the countries that are the focus of analysis, we start by examining their position in relation to other EU-15 countries. The main comparative sources of evidence are the European Foundation's European Surveys on Working

Conditions. There were three surveys covering the decade 1990 to 2000, conducted in 1990, 1995–6, and 2000, respectively. There were substantial modifications in question wording between the first and second surveys of the series that make comparison of task discretion difficult. However, the second and third surveys give us three fully comparable indicators for task discretion. People were asked, 'Are you able, or not, to choose or change: 1) your order of tasks; 2) your methods of work; and 3) your speed or rate of work?'

Although our focus is on a limited number of countries, we begin by showing the picture (Table 4.1) for the full set of countries covered by the survey to give some idea of the relative positions of the countries to be discussed. The data for the two survey years have been aggregated to provide more robust estimates. A first point to note is that there appear to be wide variations in the level of control employees have over their job tasks in different countries. For instance, the proportion of employees who felt they had significant influence over the order of their tasks ranged from 81 per cent in Denmark and Sweden to only 38 per cent in Greece. Country divergence was also very sharp with respect to task methods, ranging from 86 per cent in Sweden to 45 per cent in Greece. It was somewhat less for speed of work: ranging from 81 per cent in the Denmark to 53 per cent in Greece.

Table 4.1. Task discretion: a comparison of EU countries

	Task order	Task methods	Speed of work	Overall task discretion index
Austria	57.9	60.9	69.7	1.88
Belgium	63.9	67.7	66.4	1.98
Denmark	80.6	79.9	80.9	2.42
Finland	77.4	70.5	68.0	2.16
France	66.4	64.3	66.1	1.97
Germany	53.1	67.2	63.2	1.83
Great Britain	70.5	69.0	74.4	2.15
Greece	37.5	44.6	52.7	1.35
Ireland	56.1	58.3	64.8	1.79
Italy	47.0	67.2	70.8	1.85
Luxembourg	60.7	65.4	66.8	1.93
Netherlands	79.8	81.4	80.0	2.41
Portugal	52.2	59.6	61.4	1.73
Spain	51.1	55.8	58.4	1.65
Sweden	80.7	85.5	62.9	2.29
EU total	60.7	67.3	67.6	1.99

Source: European Foundation's European Surveys on Working Conditions (1995 and 2000).

The countries that are the focus of the analysis are at very different points along the spectrum from high to low discretion. Sweden for instance is, with Denmark and the Netherlands, one of the countries with the highest levels of task discretion, while Spain is together with Greece and Portugal one of the countries with an exceptionally low level of task discretion. This can be seen more sharply by examining a summary indicator of the three items in which a score of one is given for each mentioned (Table 4.1, final column). On the overall measure, Sweden emerges in third place among the fifteen countries, while Spain is in fourteenth place. Great Britain, France, and Germany are in an intermediate position (5th, 7th, and 11th respectively).

Universalistic theories of task discretion suggest that such differences are produced by differences in the level of economic development, leading to variations in industry structure and in workforce composition. They might for instance be due to the relative size of occupational categories. The larger the more skilled professional and managerial component of the workforce, the higher one might expect average task discretion. They might also be the result of differences in the relative importance of the service sector or in the prevalence of large-scale establishments (which have often been found to be associated with lower levels of task discretion). Similarly they might reflect differences in the balance between men and women in the workforce. To examine this, countries were compared first in gross terms, not taking account of structural differences, and then in net terms, adding in controls for sex, age, occupational class, industry, and size of establishment. The samples have been combined for the two years, to increase the robustness of estimates and the different countries have been compared with Belgium, which is close to the average on the combined data for 1995 and 2000.

Model 1 of Table 4.2 confirms the wide differences between the countries. Sweden is substantially higher than the reference country Belgium and the difference is statistically very significant. France and Britain are close to the level of Belgium and the differences are non-significant. Finally both Germany and, most notably, Spain have considerably lower levels of task discretion. Can these differences be accounted for in terms of economic structure and workforce composition? The results of Model 2, which takes account of many of the factors that are thought to be important in this respect, suggest that this is not the case. For most countries the coefficients change little and the original pattern of difference between the countries still emerges very clearly after such structural differences have been controlled.

Table 4.2. Relative country differences in task discretion

	Model 1 No controls	Model 2 With controls
Austria	−16**	−0.07 (n.s.)
Belgium	Ref	Ref
Denmark	0.79***	0.75***
Finland	0.20***	0.25***
France	−0.03 (n.s.)	0.06 (n.s.)
Germany	−0.24***	−0.18***
Great Britain	0.07 (n.s.)	0.16**
Greece	−0.91***	−0.92***
Ireland	−0.34***	−0.23***
Italy	−0.24***	−0.24***
Luxembourg	−0.06 (n.s.)	−0.11 (n.s.)
Netherlands	0.62***	0.63***
Portugal	−0.47***	−0.25***
Spain	−0.41***	−0.36***
Sweden	0.36***	0.33***
N	28,726	27,381

Note: Ordered logit regressions. *** = $p < 0.001$; ** = $p < 0.01$. Model 2 controls are sex, age, occupational class, industry, and size of establishment.

Source: European Foundation's European Surveys on Working Conditions (1995 and 2000).

The two institutional factors which were proposed as plausible determinants of the level of task discretion, were the membership strength of trade unions (trade union density) and the salience of national policies for the improvement of work life. If the task discretion scores of the different countries are plotted against trade union density figures, the pattern does indeed broadly correspond to theoretical expectation (Figure 4.1).

The correlation for all the EU-15 countries is 0.53 and it is statistically significant. In particular, Sweden, Germany, and Spain would seem very well accounted for by this relationship. The UK has a relatively higher ranking than might be expected on the basis of its trade union density. But it should be remembered that its level of task discretion was not statistically different from that of Belgium, and were it the same, it would be very close to the pattern for the other countries. Its position may also reflect the historic strength of British workplace unionism in the first three post-war decades, followed by a very sudden decline. The principal surprise is the relative position of France, which has a much higher level of task discretion than would be anticipated on the basis of its union membership strength. While task discretion in France was also not significantly different from Belgium, it is clear this could in no

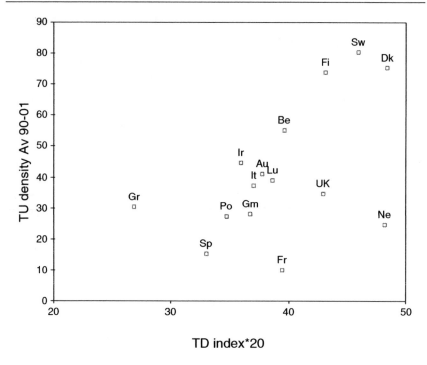

Figure 4.1. Task discretion and trade union density [Correlation 0.526 (sig < 0.05)]

way account for its outlier position. But, as mentioned earlier, there is a consistent literature that points to French unions having a greater impact than could be expected on the basis of their membership strength partly as a result of their ability to exert influence through other workplace institutions such as the Company Councils.

The second institutional factor proposed as a potentially important determinant of the level of task discretion was the strength of national quality of working life policies. These were predominantly developed by the Northern European countries. However, in these countries such an explanation simply reinforces the pattern that emerges from trade union density. The other European country where significant, if more modest, initiatives were taken—partly through legal intervention and partly through financial incentives—was France. In particular, it is arguable that the Lois Auroux introduced in the 1980s may have been a significant factor encouraging greater employee initiative at work. This may also help account for France's relatively high level of task discretion given its low level of unionization.

Convergence or Polarization in Task Discretion?

Our central concern is with the differences in the experiences of particular categories of employee. Have recent decades witnessed a process of polarization—with more vulnerable categories of employee experiencing a deterioration of their situation relative to the more protected? The notion of polarization requires both evidence that a particular category of employee is systematically in a less advantageous position with respect to a given aspect of employment conditions and that this disadvantage has increased over time. In particular, we focus upon four potential lines of polarization. Have experiences diverged between employees in relatively skilled occupations and those in low-skilled work, between employees in the traditional transformative industries (manufacturing, mining, energy, and construction) and those in routine services (retail and hotels) and between those with regular contracts and those with 'non-standard' or 'atypical' contracts? Finally, have differences between male and female employees grown greater or less marked, and if so, how far is this a result of, or independent of, changes in relative positions with respect to skill, industry, and contract status?

Exploration of differences within the workforce places a much greater burden on sample numbers than is the case for analyses of the general trend. The smaller samples of the comparative European surveys are particularly vulnerable in this respect. The sample numbers once the data are disaggregated by year and subcategory of employee could at best provide very tentative estimates of trends over a short five year period. However, for Britain, France, Germany, and Sweden, it is possible to assess trends using the evidence from larger national data-sets. The national data-sets also have the advantage of offering a somewhat longer time window for examining the pattern of change (indeed for Germany and Sweden they offer a picture spanning over two decades). Each survey however provides somewhat different indicators of task discretion and comparisons are only possible within each country. In the case of Spain, we have been obliged to carry out the analyses on the smaller samples of the comparative 'Working Conditions' surveys.

Britain

It is in Britain, with its decentralized bargaining structure and general skills system, that one might expect that employers would have found it

Table 4.3. Britain: employee task discretion, 1992–2001

	1992	1997	2001
% great deal of influence over			
How hard to work	70.7	64.4	50.6
What tasks done	42.4	33.1	30.5
How to do task	56.9	49.7	42.8
Quality standards	69.6	51.1	51.7
Overall task discretion index[a]			
All	2.43	2.25	2.18
Men	2.43	2.26	2.19
Women	2.44	2.24	2.17
N (all employees)	3,408	2,218	3,984

Notes: [a] The task discretion index is computed as the summed average score of the four 'task influence' questions, with a highest score of 3 and a lowest score of 0.

Source: The Employment in Britain Survey (1992) and the Skills Survey (1997 and 2001).

easiest to impose tighter control on those in weaker skill positions, leading to a particularly sharp deterioration in their conditions.

The national data for Britain are drawn from three surveys: the Employment in Britain Survey, carried out in 1992 (Gallie et al. 1998); and the 1997 and 2001 Skills Surveys (Ashton et al. 1999; Felstead, Gallie, and Green 2002). The sample numbers for employees in the three surveys were 3,408, 2,219 and 3,984, respectively.

The surveys were deliberately designed to provide directly comparable indicators. A measure of task discretion was derived from four questions asking people to assess how much personal influence they thought they had over specific aspects of their work: how hard they worked, deciding what tasks they were to do, how the task was done, and the quality standards to which they worked.[1] Employees were most likely to report task discretion with respect to work effort and quality standards (Table 4.3), while employee influence was rather less common over decisions about what tasks were to be done and especially over decisions about how to do the task.

Examining the trend over time, it is notable that there has been not an increase but a reduction in employee task discretion over the period. Between 1992 and 2001 there was a decline in employees' perception of their influence over each of the specific aspects of the work task. For instance, the proportion reporting that they had a great deal of influence

[1] People were asked: 'How much influence do you personally have on...how hard you work; deciding what tasks you are to do; deciding how you are to do the task; deciding the quality standards to which you work?' The possible responses included 'a great deal (of influence)', 'a fair amount', 'not much', or 'none at all'.

Table 4.4. Britain: ratios for task discretion scores

	Ratios			Gross change 1992–2001 sig.	Net change 1992–2001 sig.
	1992	1997	2001		
Class					
Professionals and managers/ semi-unskilled	1.19	1.29	1.27	+	+
Industry					
Industry/retail and hotels	0.99	1.02	0.99	n.s.	n.s.
Contract Status					
Full-time/part-time	1.03	1.09	1.07	+	n.s.
Permanent/temporary workers	1.03	1.04	1.12	+	n.s.
Sex					
Male/female	1.00	1.01	1.00	n.s.	n.s.

Note: Significance of change between 1992 and 2001 is estimated through a regression analysis with year interaction terms: + = greater polarization, sig. at the <0.05 level.

Source: The Employment in Britain Survey (1992) and the Skills Survey (1997, 2001).

over how hard they worked fell from 71 per cent in 1992 to 64 per cent in 1997 to only 51 per cent in 2001. Those with a great deal of influence over choice of task fell from 42 per cent to 31 per cent. The decline was similarly sharp with respect to decisions about how to do the task and the quality of work.

To provide an overall picture, taking account of the full range of responses, a summary index was constructed by giving a score ranging from 0 (no influence at all) to 3 (a great deal of influence) for each item and then taking the average of the summed scores.[2] As can be seen in the last three rows of Table 4.3, the overall index score for task discretion declined from 2.43 in 1992 to 2.25 in 1997 to 2.18 in 2001. The decline in discretion affected both men and women.

Tendencies to polarization can be examined initially through changes in the ratios between the task discretion scores of these different types of employee. Table 4.4 presents the ratios in Britain for each year with respect to the categories for which there has been the strongest theoretical expectation of divergence.

A first point to note is that the ratios point to a growing divergence between the higher skilled and the lower skilled categories. The initial scores (not shown) indicate that task discretion declined for both types of employee, but particularly sharply for the least skilled. A more formal test of polarization over the period can been carried out through a regression analysis in which the data for the years 1992 and 2001 are pooled and

[2] The index was statistically robust, with an overall alpha of 0.78.

the contrast between the higher skilled and lower skilled categories is entered together with a term that captures the year change effect and an interaction term between year and skill level. Two types of analysis were carried out: the first examined the skill effects on their own to examine whether there was a change between the years in gross terms; the second included control variables for sex and for the other potential sources of polarization, in this case industry, part-time work and temporary work. The results are given in the fourth and fifth columns of Table 4.4. They show a greater decline in task discretion among the lower skilled. This was statistically significant and could not be accounted for by changes in either industry or contractual status.

A second potential line of polarization is with respect to *industry sector*. In the traditional industrial sector, technological change may have been conducive to an improvement in work quality. However, in the service sector, given that labour costs tend to be a higher proportion of overall costs, it is possible that employers were more concerned to simplify jobs and to reap the benefits of easy substitutability of labour. This has been thought to be particularly the case in relatively low-skilled service sector industries such as hotels and retail. The data, however, provide little support for this thesis. There was no significant difference between levels of task discretion in the industrial sector of the economy (manufacturing, mining, energy, and construction) and in hotels and retail. There is also no support for the view that divergences grew more pronounced: there was no significant change in relative task discretion scores in retail and hotels compared with industry between 1992 and 2001.

Turning to contract status, is there any evidence that those on non-standard contracts, whether part-timers or temporary workers, experienced a deterioration of job quality over the period relative to those on standard contracts? For part-timers, the comparisons show a marked deterioration over the period as a whole, although most of this occurred over the period 1992 to 1997, with differentials staying relatively stable in the most recent period. Similarly, those on temporary contracts saw a relative decline in task discretion, although in this case the main change occurred in the period between 1997 and 2001. A regression analysis with interaction terms confirmed that the growth of polarization between 1992 and 2001 was statistically significant with respect to both types of non-standard employee. However, this appears to be wholly attributable to compositional shifts with respect to occupation and industry. There was no significant change in relative position once compositional controls had been taken account.

Finally, it can be seen that there is no evidence for Britain that women were systematically disadvantaged compared to men with respect to task discretion. The average level of task discretion for men and women was almost identical and there was little sign of change in this over the 1990s. The lack of any tendency to polarization is confirmed by regression tests: interaction terms with year were not significant whether one takes the models with or without controls (last two columns of Table 4.4).

Britain then did experience polarization over the period with respect to both skill and contract status, but it is only skill polarization that would appear to require further explanation.

France

In France a high level of employment protection should accentuate divisions between those on standard and those on non-standard contracts. But, in terms of its skills formation regime, France is characterized by a schools-based specific skills system that should provide significant protection for those in lower skill positions. Our expectation then is that it is a country with relatively low class, but high contract-based, polarization risks.

French evidence on task discretion is drawn from successive *Enquetes Conditions de travail*—which were conducted as an extension of the regular 'Enquêtes d'Emploi'. These provide a time span of just over a decade—from 1984 to 1998, with surveys in 1984, 1991, and 1998. These were large-scale surveys with sample numbers of 17, 602, 19, 220, and 20, 067, respectively. They provide three principal indicators of task discretion: whether people experience permanent hierarchical surveillance, whether they strictly carry out orders in their job, and whether they sort out unexpected problems. The questions were phrased as follows:

You receive orders, directives, guidance instructions. To perform your work properly, do you: strictly carry out orders; in some cases do things in other ways; most of the time do things in other ways?

When something out of the usual happens when you are at work, is it the case that: most of the time you sort out the problem yourself; you sort out the problem yourself in specific situations that have been defined earlier; you generally call on others (a superior, a colleague or a specialized service)?

Is your rhythm of work imposed by control or permanent (at least daily) surveillance on the part of management?

Table 4.5. France: task discretion, 1984–98

	1984	1991	1998
Does not strictly carry out orders	n.d.	59.0	62.8
Most of the time personally sorts out problems	n.d.	49.6	55.8
Pace of work not imposed by a permanent hierarchical control	82.6	77.5	71.6
Overall task discretion index	n.d.	2.51	2.50

Note: No data available.
Source: Enquetes conditions de travail (1984, 1991, 1998).

The French data provide an ambivalent picture of change over the 1990s (Table 4.5). This reflects distinct trends between the items that focus on work methods and the item that relates to work pace. The first and second items refer primarily to discretion over work methods. They show a clear trend towards greater employee initiative. A higher proportion of people report that they do not adhere strictly to orders about how they carry out their work in 1998 than was the case in 1991 and there was a marked increase in the proportion that sorted out unexpected problems themselves. In contrast the third item, which focuses on control over the pace rather than the methods of work, shows a decline of employee control, which can be traced back even earlier to the mid-1980s. An overall task discretion index, combining the three measures, shows no significant change between 1991 and 1998.[3]

Is there any evidence, however, of polarization? Considering first differences between occupational classes, the evidence suggests not increased divergence but a growing convergence between non-skilled and more highly skilled employees, with a significant reduction in the overall task discretion differential between 1991 and 1998 (Table 4.6). This was statistically significant whether with or without controls. Both professional and managerial employees and non-skilled workers reported rising levels of permanent hierarchical control over work pace across the two time points. Lower skilled workers were more likely to be subject to such control at each point in time, but the relative differences remained virtually identical at the beginning and end of the period. The main factor leading to an improvement in the position of the non-skilled came from the items relating to decisions about work methods. While there was little change in the proportion of managers and professionals who reported that they did not strictly carry out orders, there was a rise among the non-skilled.

[3] The index was the average score across the three items. The first item was scored 1–4, the second 1–3. Since it was dichotomous, positive responses on the third item (pace of work) were given a score of 1 and negative responses a score of 4.

Table 4.6. France: ratios for task discretion scores

	Ratios		Gross change 91–8 sig.	Net change 91–8 sig.
	1991	1998		
Class				
Cadres/semi-unskilled	1.46	1.40	—	-
Industry				
Industry/retail	0.94	0.96	**	**
Contract				
Full-time/part-time	0.99	0.98	n.s.	n.s.
Permanent/temporary	1.10	1.10	n.s.	n.s.
Sex				
Male/female	1.02	1.01	—	n.s.

Note: Significance of change between 1992 and 2001 is estimated through a regression analysis with year interaction terms: — = greater convergence, sig. at the <0.001 level; - = greater convergence, sig. at the <0.05 level; ** = Significant change at the <0.01 level, but not indicating polarization or convergence.

Source: *Enquetes conditions de travail* (1991 and 1998).

Similarly, there was a stronger rise among the non-skilled in the proportion saying that they personally sorted out unexpected problems.

With respect to industry sector, in both time periods employees in retail and hotels had higher task discretion than those in the transformative industries (manufacturing, mining, energy, and construction). Task discretion declined more in retail and hotels than in industry in the 1990s, and this change was significant whether with or without controls. But, since work in retail and hotels was much less controlled at the beginning of the period, and remained so at the end, it is difficult to describe this as polarization.

With respect to contract status, there is no evidence of a relative decline in the position of part-time workers. Part-timers had very similar task discretion scores to full-timers in both years and differentials between part-timers and full-timers remained unchanged over the 1990s. In contrast, temporary workers were more subject to permanent hierarchical control, were more likely to have to strictly carry out orders and were less likely to be able to personally sort out unexpected problems in both 1991 and 1998. But again there was no evidence of polarization in the sense of an increasing difference in conditions between them and more protected employees. Overall, the French employment system seems to have contained any tendencies to polarization in work task conditions rather effectively.

Finally, it is notable that there was a significant improvement in the position of women relative to men. By 1998 there was no discernible difference in average levels of task discretion between male and female French employees. However, the fact that the relative improvement in women's position was no longer statistically significant when controls were introduced indicates that it was entirely attributable to shifts between the two periods in the types of jobs that women occupied.

Germany

Germany also has relatively high employment protection that was likely to favour the 'core' workforce and encourage employers to recoup costs through less favourable treatment of employees on non-standard contracts. However, its skill formation system was of a 'dual system' industry-specific type', and it was expected that this would provide a better protection for the lower skilled than a general skills formation system.

The data are drawn from Surveys on Educational and Vocational Attainment and Careers (BIBB/IAB). To track developments across time, it is best to focus on the evidence for West Germany. This gives the longest series of comparisons over time and it is here that the 'corporatist' German regulative system should be most crystallized and have its greatest impact. There are comparable indicators for 1979, 1985–6, 1991–2, and 1998–9. The sample sizes were substantial: 24,487 in 1979; 23,760 in 1985–6; 21,716 in 1991–2, and 24,536 in 1998–9. The main indicator of job control available on a repeated basis at different time points is a question asking people whether the performance of their work is 'highly regulated in every detail'.

Table 4.7 shows the proportions in the various response categories, together with a summary index derived from a scoring of responses from 0 for 'practically always' to 4 for 'practically never'. There was little change in the proportion with low discretion (those whose jobs were 'practically always' or 'often' highly regulated) between the late 1970s and the mid-1980s. There was, however, a marked reduction in those with very high discretion over this period, leading to a decline in the overall index of job task discretion. Task discretion dropped further between the mid-1980s and the early 1990s, but rose again across the 1990s returning to the level of the mid-1980s by 1998. (The all-German figures for the 1990s show a similar trend, though with a less pronounced increase in task discretion).

In comparing class differentials, the German data allows a contrast between 'higher-level' managerial and professional employees on the one hand and semi and unskilled workers on the other. Whether one takes the overall period from 1979 to 1998 or the period from 1985 to 1998,

Table 4.7. Germany: task discretion, 1979–99, (%) whose work performance is highly regulated and index of job task discretion

| | % | | | |
	1979	1985	1991	1998
Practically always	17.2	16.4	15.8	15.0
Often	14.3	17.6	21.3	18.4
Once in a while	13.8	17.4	17.0	17.4
Rarely	16.9	23.3	24.4	23.7
Practically never	37.9	25.2	21.5	25.5
Means *index of job task discretion*	2.4	2.2	2.1	2.3

Note: The higher the score on the index of job task regulation, the lower the degree of regulation. BIBB/IAB Surveys. Figures for West Germany are for employees (including foreigners except for 1985–6), figures for all-Germany include self-employed.

Source: Surveys on Educational and Vocational Attainment and Careers (BIBB/IAB).

differentials in task discretion between professionals and managers on the one hand and semi and unskilled workers on the other grew greater (Table 4.8). Most of this change occurred between the end of the 1970s and the mid-1980s, although there was a continuation of the process of polarization through to the early 1990s. In contrast to Britain, however, where the 1990s was a period that saw a marked growth of class divergence in levels of task discretion, Germany experienced some degree of equalization. By 1998 the differentials had returned to a figure close to that of the mid-1980s. The detailed task discretion scores show that professionals and managers were steadily losing in task discretion right

Table 4.8. West Germany: ratios for task discretion scores

	1979	1985	1991	1998	Gross change 91–8 sig.	Net change 91–8 sig.
Class						
Professionals and managers/ semi-unskilled	1.59	1.83	2.19	1.88	—	—
Industry						
Industry/retail	0.77	0.80	0.88	0.84	**	**
Contract status						
Full-time/part-time	0.86	0.93	0.96	0.93	n.s.	n.s.
Permanent/temporary	n.d.	1.07	1.05	1.19	+++	+++
Sex						
Male/female	0.96	0.96	1.01	0.96	—	n.s.

Note: Significance of change between 1992 and 2001 is estimated through a regression analysis with year interaction terms: +++ = greater polarization, sig. at the <0.001 level; — = greater convergence sig. at the <0.001 level; ** change significant at the <0.01 level, but not indicative of polarization or convergence.

Source: Surveys on Educational and Vocational Attainment and Careers (BIBB/IAB).

across the period. In contrast, semi and unskilled manual workers experienced declining task discretion from the late 1970s to the early 1990s, but then saw a marked improvement in their situation. Both the initial (gross) regression tests and those controlling for other factors showed that the recent reduction of polarization in the 1990s was statistically significant.

The German case also provides no support for the type of industry sector polarization suggested by the literature. There is no evidence, whatever the period examined, that employees in retail were disadvantaged with respect to task discretion; rather they tended to exercise higher levels of discretion. In the late 1970s work in retail allowed substantially more task discretion than was the case for employees in industry. By the 1990s, the difference between sectors had been reduced, largely because task discretion was eroded more sharply in retail and commerce than in industry. But between 1991 and 1998 the trend reversed, with a growth of the relative advantage of those in retail.

Similarly, there was no evidence in Germany of polarization with respect to the difference between full-time workers and part-time workers. Part-timers were substantially less likely to be in closely regulated jobs than full-timers in the late 1970s, and their relative advantage in this respect remained through to the late 1990s, although the differences between workers with these different types of contract diminished considerably. In the 1990s, however, there was no significant change in the relative position of full-timers and part-timers.

In contrast, in the case of temporary workers, the pattern is consistent with the polarization thesis. The first data available is for the mid-1980s and shows that temporary workers' jobs were more tightly regulated than those of permanent workers. The disadvantage of temporary workers had grown sharper by 1998, primarily reflecting developments in the period 1991 to 1998. The growing polarization between permanent and temporary workers was statistically significant both for the period from the mid-1980s to 1998 and for the 1990s taken separately.

Finally, taking sex differentials, it can be seen that there is no clear evidence that women were at a disadvantage in terms of task autonomy for the greater part of the period. There was a rise in male advantage between the mid-1980s and the early 1990s, but this was reversed in the course of the 1990s. The improvement in women's position in the 1990s was statistically significant, but, as in France, the effect disappeared once other factors were controlled, suggesting that it largely reflected changes in the types of jobs that women were occupying.

Sweden

In Sweden, the expectation is that there would be a relatively high level of containment of pressures for polarization. A high level of centralization of collective bargaining and a skills formation system that combined schools-based specific training with good opportunities for in-career updating of skills should be conducive to an egalitarian approach to employment conditions and to the protection of those more vulnerable in the labour market. Although it had relatively high employment protection, it was thought that this would be offset by the emphasis on the reduction of differentials between employees resulting from high unionization and bargaining centralization.

The Swedish Surveys on Living Conditions (ULF), conducted by Statistics Sweden, provide two indicators of task discretion. They ask respectively how much influence the person had in their job with respect to the 'planning of their own work' and 'work pace'. Respondents were given a choice between 'Great influence', 'Some influence', and 'No influence'. The Swedish surveys provide a long term data series from 1976 to 2002. The results have been averaged over groups of years to give a more robust estimate of trends.

The data (Table 4.9) reveal a clear continuing rise in task discretion with respect to work planning/methods over the entire period from the mid-to-late 1970s to the end of the 1990s. There was a sharp decline over the period in the proportion that had no influence on the planning of their work and a corresponding rise in those who felt they had a high level of influence. The marked increase in employee discretion was primarily before the mid-1990s, with only a small increase for the remainder of the decade. Discretion with respect to control over work pace, however, showed very little change over the period as a whole, with 58 per cent reporting a high level of influence in the second half of the 1970s and 59 per cent at the end of 1990s. Taking the two together, however, the combined job control index still points to an overall continuing increase in discretion throughout the period from the 1970s to the 1990s.

Unlike in Britain, France, and Germany we do not have data in Sweden for the beginning of the 1990s. For the analyses of polarization, we therefore provide a comparison on either side of this period: for the late 1980s and the mid-1990s. Table 4.10 shows the ratios for each period, while Table 4.11 gives the tests of the significance of change from the regressions.

Table 4.9. Sweden: influence on planning of own work and on work pace

	1976–9	1986–7	1994–5	1996–7	1998–2002
Planning of own work					
Great influence	42.5	49.1	57.0	58.1	59.7
Some influence	38.8	37.7	33.9	33.4	31.8
No influence	18.7	13.3	9.2	8.6	8.5
Work pace					
Great influence	57.8	60.8	62.0	62.3	59.2
Some influence	32.0	30.6	29.6	30.0	31.9
No influence	10.2	8.7	8.5	7.7	8.9
Job control index	4.73	4.88	5.01	5.04	5.06

Source: Swedish Surveys on Living Conditions (ULF), Statistics Sweden (1998).

There was no evidence of class polarization over any of the periods from the mid-1970s. Rather, there was a marked decline of class differentials in job control from the late 1970s to the mid-1990s. This change is statistically highly significant whether the comparison is between the mid to late 1970s and the most recent period, or between the mid-1980s and the most recent period. The task discretion scores of managers and professionals declined somewhat after the mid-1980s, whereas there was a marked rise of those of the non-skilled between the mid-1980s and the mid-1990s. This coincided with the most active phase of the quality of work programme, which reached its peak in the early 1990s. The effect still persists when controls are introduced, albeit at a weaker level of significance, indicating that it cannot be attributed to changes in industry or the proportion of employees in different types of contract status. However, from the mid- to late 1990s, the picture is one of stability rather than either convergence or divergence.

Table 4.10. Sweden: ratios for task discretion scores

	1976–9	1986–7	1994–5	1996–7	1998–2002
Class					
Professionals and managers/semi-unskilled	1.31	1.29	1.20	1.20	1.20
Industry					
Industry retail/and hotel	0.97	0.98	1.01	1.00	0.99
Contract status					
Full-time/part-time	1.05	1.06	1.07	1.08	1.07
Permanent/temporary		1.09	1.08	1.08	1.08
Sex					
Male/female	1.05	1.05	1.05	1.05	1.05

Source: Swedish Surveys on Living Conditions (ULF), Statistics Sweden (1998).

Table 4.11. Sweden: change in task discretion index

	Gross change 1986–7 to 1998–2002	Net change 1986–7 to 1998–2002	Net change 1994–5 to 1998–2002	Net change 1994–5 to 1998–2002
Class				
Professionals and managers/semi-unskilled	—	-	n.s.	n.s.
Industry				
Industry/retail and hotels	n.s.	n.s.	*	*
Contract status				
Full-time/part-time	n.s.	n.s.	n.s.	n.s.
Permanent/temporary	n.s.	n.s.	n.s.	n.s.
Sex				
Male/female	n.s.	n.s.	n.s.	n.s.

Notes: Significance of change between 1992 and 2001 is estimated through a regression analysis with year interaction terms: — = greater convergence, sig at the <0.001 level; - = greater convergence, sig. at the < 0.05 level; * = change sig at the 0.05 level, but not indicative of polarization.

Sources: Swedish Surveys on Living Conditions (ULF), Statistics Sweden (1998).

With respect to the difference between employees in the retail and hotel industries and those in manufacturing, there was much less difference in the first place between these industries in Sweden than in other countries and change in terms of relative position was very small over the entire time period. There was some tendency for the relative position of those in transformative industries (manufacturing, mining, energy, and construction) to improve over the period between the mid-to-late 1970s and the early 1990s, after which the trend reversed. Overall, job control differentials between employees in the different economic sectors did not change significantly from the mid-1970s to the most recent period. But, taking just the 1990s, there was a significant improvement in the relative position of employees in retail and hotels. However, since this improvement made the work situation of those in retail better than that for employees in industry, it cannot be regarded as either polarization or convergence in terms of the initial arguments.

There is also no evidence of polarization by contract status in Sweden from the later 1980s. Between the 1970s and mid-1980s, the increase in task discretion among full-timers was stronger than for part-timers, leading to a growing differential by contract status. But from the mid-1980s the differential between full-timers and part-timers remained very stable. There was also no evidence of polarization between permanent and temporary employees. Whether the comparison is with the mid-1980s or with the mid-1990s, the relative position of temporary workers was unchanged. Finally, there was a markedly consistent pattern with respect to sex differentials: men were a little more likely to be in jobs in which they could exercise task discretion, but the differences remained unchanged over the period as a whole.

In short, the evidence is indeed consistent with the view that the Swedish system provided relatively strong protection against polarization. It was the only country in which there was a long-term trend towards the improvement in the situation of the lower skilled, particularly between the 1970s and early 1990s. There was no evidence of polarization with respect to industry sector, contract status, or sex.

Spain

In Spain the expectation is that the institutional structure of employment regulation would provide weak protection to vulnerable categories of employees, due to its combination of a 'general' skill formation system and a strong dualism in terms of employment regulation. Spain is the country that saw the most marked expansion of temporary work, reaching approximately a third of its workforce.

Our evidence in this case must be regarded as particularly tentative as we rely on further analysis of the data available in the comparative European Foundation data-sets which provide relatively small sample numbers when disaggregated by employee skill, industry, or contract category. The overall sample of employees was 729 in 1995 and 1,080 in 2000. However, for Spain, the sample numbers for the subcategory of employee which in most countries is usually the most problematic in comparative surveys— that of temporary workers—are reasonably satisfactory (N = 288 in 1995, 332 in 2000), due to the very extensive utilization of workers on short-terms contracts.

Taking first the general trends, it is clear from Table 4.12 that task discretion declined in Spain between 1995 and 2000. This was true both for control over work methods and for control over work speed. The pattern for Spain over this period closely resembles that for Britain.

Turning to the experiences of different categories of employee, the first point to note is that there was polarization with respect to skill: the change in the ratios for the task discretion scores indicates a divergence between professional and managerial employees and those in the low-skilled in elementary occupations (Table 4.13). This was polarization in its strongest form, with the task discretion of higher-level employees rising and that of low-skilled employees falling. A regression test showed that the increased relative disadvantage of the low skilled was statistically

Table 4.12. Spain: task discretion measures

	1995	2000
Can choose or change		
Order of work tasks	51.8	50.6
Methods of work	59.2	53.5
Speed or rate of work	60.5	57.0
Task discretion index	1.71	1.61

Note: For details of the task discretion index see p. 114.

highly significant. Moreover it remained significant when controls were introduced, so it could not be accounted for by compositional changes with respect to industry or the contract status of employees.

As in other countries, the work situation of employees in retail/hotels did not emerge as a significant source of disadvantage when compared to employees in manufacturing. In both years retail and hotel workers could exercise greater, not less, discretion in their jobs than those in the transformative industries and this became true to a greater extent over the years as a result of a marked decline in discretion in manufacturing (while the situation for retail and hotel workers remained unchanged). While there was significant change over the period, it cannot be regarded as either polarization or convergence.

There was no consistent pattern of disadvantage for those commonly classified together as workers with atypical contracts. Part-time employees had greater task discretion than full-time employees, while workers on

Table 4.13. Spain: ratios for task discretion index scores

	1995	2000	Gross change 1994–7 to 1998–2002	Net change 1994–7 to 1998–2002
Class				
Professionals and managers/semi-unskilled	1.14	1.92	+++	+++
Industry				
Industry/retail and hotels	0.92	0.74	n.s.	*
Contract status				
Full-time/part-time	0.77	0.77	n.s.	n.s.
Permanent/temporary	1.16	1.21	n.s.	n.s.
Sex				
Male/female	0.87	0.79	***	n.s.

Notes: Significance of change between 1992 and 2001 is estimated through a regression analysis with year interaction terms: +++ = greater polarization, sig. at the <0.001 level; + = greater polarization, sig. at <0.05 level; *** = change sig. at the 0.001 level, but not indicative of polarization or convergence.

Source: European Foundation's European Surveys on Work Conditions.

temporary contracts had lower discretion than those on regular contracts. However, in both cases, the notable finding with respect to the pattern over time was its stability: in neither case was there a statistically significant change between 1995 and 2000.

Consistent with the pattern for part-time work, there was no evidence that women in Spain were in a disadvantageous position with respect to task discretion. The evidence for the period 1995 to 2000 shows that women's jobs offered higher, not lower, levels of discretion than men's. Moreover, women's relative advantage increased over the period: while the level of task discretion in men's job declined, there was little change for women's jobs. But the improvement in women's conditions appears to be primarily related to changes in the types of jobs women occupied, with the effect disappearing once other aspects of workforce structure were taken into account.

The only major source of polarization in Spain over the period was then between employees of different skill levels. This might seem surprising given the emphasis on the significance of temporary work as a factor enhancing the labour market vulnerability of less protected groups. However, a major expansion of temporary work may have implications that go beyond the work conditions of temporary workers themselves. It may also give employers greater leverage on regular employees, whose position can be undermined by a cheaper and more disposable source of labour.

Overview of Polarization Trends

The broad pattern of the results for the 1990s is summarized in Table 4.14. It is notable that there was evidence in none of the countries for two of the potential lines of polarization. In no country were employees in retail and hotels significantly disadvantaged with respect to task discretion compared to those in the industrial sector and in France, West Germany, and Spain their position was markedly better. The only country in which there was a relative deterioration in their situation was France, but their conditions remained markedly better than those of employees in the traditional transformative industries. Second, there was no evidence that women's position grew worse relative to that of men. But equally the evidence for convergence is slight. In two of the countries in which they were relatively disadvantaged—France and West Germany—their position improved, while in the third (Sweden) it remained unchanged. However, in those countries in which it improved,

Table 4.14. Comparison of net polarization tendencies

	Class	Sector	Contract-part-time	Contract-temporary	Sex
France	−	ND	ND	=	=
Germany	---	ND	ND	+++	=
Great Britain	+++	ND	=	=	N.D.
Spain	+	ND	ND	=	N.D.
Sweden	− / =	ND	=	=	=

Notes: For Sweden the first sign relates to the period late 1980s to 1998–2002; the second from 1994–5 to 1990s. ND = No disadvantage. + polarization, − convergence, and = no change.

this was largely accountable for by the types of jobs women were in, with the effect disappearing when occupational and industry factors had been controlled.

However, in other respects, there were marked differences between countries in the nature of the trends. There was indeed evidence of polarization in the case of Germany, Spain, and, most particularly, in Britain. Britain stands out in that there was polarization on three of five of the lines of employee differentiation that were examined (class, part-time work, and temporary work). There was polarization by occupational class in Spain and temporary workers saw a relative deterioration of their position in Germany. While the divergence of employees by contract status in Britain was largely accountable for by compositional changes in the types of jobs they were in, class divergences remained unaffected by taking account of other changes in employment structure. Similarly, the relative deterioration of the position of the non-skilled in Spain and of temporary workers in Germany could not be attributed to compositional changes.

Overall, the least protective systems were those of Britain and Spain, where the only significant trends involved polarization. Germany represents an intermediate case in which a tendency to class convergence was offset by polarization between permanent and temporary workers. The two countries that were most successful in containing polarization were Sweden and France. In neither country was there evidence of increased divergence and in both there was some indication of increased class convergence. Indeed in Sweden there was evidence of a sustained convergence between occupational classes from the 1970s.

How far are these differences in pattern related to institutional differences? Three institutional mechanisms were initially postulated as potentially providing protection for weaker labour market groups: the level of coordination of bargaining, low dualism in the system of employment regulation, and a 'specific' system of skill formation. With respect to collective bargaining, the high level of coordination in Sweden and the very low level in Britain certainly would fit well the very different patterns in those countries with respect to occupational class. But Spain also had a relatively high level of bargaining coordination and this was a country that saw sharp divergence over time between those in different occupational class positions. The view that the degree of dualism in systems of employment regulation may be important for the divergence of experience of standard and non-standard workers is consistent with the pattern in Germany, where there was polarization between permanent and temporary workers. However, it is doubtful whether this can be attributed to the strictness of employment regulation per se, since there was no evidence of a particularly sharp deterioration in the position of temporary workers in either France or Spain, which had even stricter employment protection.

The pattern fits better the view that the nature of the skill formation system is important for class polarization risks. The two countries where there was evidence of polarization between the higher skilled and lower-skilled employees—Britain and Spain—had general skills systems. The two societies that were most successful in containing polarization were those with schools-based specific training systems.

Conclusions

Available evidence on the level and pattern of change in task discretion is clearly such that conclusions need to be tentative. Although there was substantial improvement in the availability of comparative data in the 1990s, the sample sizes are still generally inadequate for detailed breakdown by different categories of employee. While national data-sets provide much better sample numbers (and often rather more extensive evidence over time), they can be at best viewed as providing only approximate comparability.

The analysis of the comparative data focused primarily on the differences in the level of task discretion between the five countries—Britain, France, Germany, Sweden, and Spain—that have been taken as exemplars of different types of institutional arrangement. It was evident that across European countries as a whole there was a very wide range of difference in the initiative that employees could exercise whether with respect to work methods or the control of work pace. Very little of this could be accounted for by broad differences in economic structure—such as the relative size of different skill categories, the size of different economic sectors, the prevalence of different sizes of establishments, or the degree of feminization of the workforce.

The high level of task discretion in Sweden (as with the other Nordic countries) more plausibly reflects an exceptionally strong trade union movement, with an inclusive membership and the capacity to protect its members' conditions within the workplace. This is likely to have been reinforced by a particularly active government commitment to the improvement of working conditions conceived broadly to include the organization of tasks. The relative positions of Germany and Spain (and less clearly of Britain) also relate to differences in the membership strength of their trade unions. The case that definitely does not fit with an explanation in terms of union density is that of France, which has an exceptionally low level of union density but an intermediate position with respect to task discretion. However, the capacity of the French unions to pull above their weight because of their institutionalized position both with respect to industry-level bargaining and company-level representation has often been noted in the literature. France was, moreover, a country in which the state had actively intervened to introduce a programme of enhanced employee participation.

There was also a major difference between countries with respect to the tendencies to polarization. Polarization processes were most evident in Britain where there was a growing divergence in the 1990s between the more skilled and less skilled sectors of the workforce, between full-timers and part-timers and between regular and temporary employees. For the very short time period for which there is evidence for Spain, there was marked polarization in the second half of the 1990s by skill level, but not by industry sector or by contract status. In Germany, there was evidence of a significant deterioration in the relative position of temporary workers. In contrast, in Sweden, France, and Germany, there was evidence of a convergence between class categories. Although some of these differences could be accounted for by compositional change, this was not the case for polarization between class categories in Britain and Spain, for convergence between classes in Sweden, France, and Germany, and for the deteriorating position of temporary workers in Germany. This suggests that different country institutions may have offered different levels of protection to more vulnerable employees.

The disadvantage of temporary workers in Germany is consistent with the view that countries with specific skills systems would have a particularly strong divide between employees that were in a position to acquire such skills and those who were not. But the fact that this did not turn out to be the case in France and Sweden suggests this is not a sufficient explanation. A further understanding of the distinctiveness of the German pattern is likely to require more detailed analysis of the origins of temporary workers in the different societies and of their prior training. It may be that the dual system of vocational training places sharper boundaries between permanent and temporary workers than schools-based training, as a result of a stronger specialization of skills. The 1990s in former West Germany was also a period when there was significant migration of workers in the aftermath of the unification of Germany, and these may initially have found temporary employment. It is plausible that issues of the evaluation of the qualifications of former East German workers may have played a role in the level of responsibility they were given at work.

The institutional factor that best accounts for the risk of polarization with respect to class is the nature of the skill formation system. The countries with general skill formation systems experienced significant polarization, whereas those with schools-based specific skills training provided the strongest protection to potentially vulnerable categories of the workforce. Where employees were largely dependent on their employer for the development of their technical skills, and there were few external norms about how jobs should be organized, it was easier for employers to restructure work in a way that enhanced their control. It was in those countries where the training system provided employees with a technical expertise that was substantially independent from their employers that they were best placed to protect the decision-making scope of their jobs.

In short, there is no evidence of general processes affecting either the overall level or the extent of polarization in task discretion in West European societies. Rather there have been distinct national developments, which are plausibly related to differences in institutional patterns. In particular, the strength of trade unionism is associated with the level of task discretion across the EU-15 countries as a whole, while national policies to enhance the quality of working life may help account both for the distinctiveness of the Nordic countries and for the high position of France relative to the strength of its trade union movement. In general differentials between different categories of employees remained relatively stable over time. The main exception was with respect to class, where the trends were quite different between countries. Of the different potential explanations that have been examined, it is the nature of the skills formation system that offers the most satisfactory account of these divergent trends.

5

Work and Family in Conflict? The Impact of Work Demands on Family Life

Stefani Scherer and Nadia Steiber

Introduction

The conflicting demands of work and family life have come to the fore in contemporary debates on the quality of work life and its relation to quality of life issues more generally. The main trigger for this has been changing female labour market behaviour: the massive influx of women into the labour market in recent decades, their increasing aspirations for careers and financial independence, falling fertility rates, and the consequent changes in household composition and household employment patterns. This has been reinforced by other factors. First, there is concern that the spread of flexible and potentially 'unsocial' work hours leaves less scope for 'quality' family time. At the same time, however, flexible work arrangements are promoted as a way to augment women's continuous labour market presence by providing work schedules that ease the combination of work and family duties. Second, there are indications that the pressures of work have been intensifying in recent decades (Gallie et al. 1998; Green 2001; Green and McIntosh 2001; Burchell, Lapido, and Wilkinson 2002; Ladipo and Wilkinson 2002). Factors such as accelerated technological change and the consequent heightened demand on workers to keep up with skill requirements (Gallie 2005), advances in information and communication technology and its implications for the need for constant availability can be sources of increased time pressure at work (Green and McIntosh 2001; Green 2001). Furthermore, although there has not been a general increase in working time (Evans Lippoldt, and Marianna 2001), in some countries there have been rising numbers of people working very long hours, along with a simultaneous spread of part-time work (OECD 1998; Bosch 1999; Evans, Lippoldt, and Marianna 2001; Green 2001; Jacobs 2003; Kodz et al. 2003). The problem of work hours polarization is accentuated by the fact that paid work hours have been concentrated among fewer households, giving rise to an increasing number of workless households along with an increase in the share of dual-earner couples (Gregg and Wadsworth 1996; Gregg, Hansen, and Wadsworth 2000; Green 2001). As a result, so the argument runs, the demands of work have begun to dominate life, creating acute problems of work–life imbalance.

These developments entail the need to address the challenge of the work–life balance as a contemporary policy issue. The reconciliation of work and family life has been incorporated into the European Employment Strategy (2002). Member states are called upon to facilitate the conciliation of work and family life through the implementation of 'family-friendly' policies, including the promotion of flexible work time arrangements, adequate care facilities, parental leave provisions, and the improvement of part-time employees' working conditions. Recent EU-Directives have laid down guidelines on working time, parental leave and part-time workers' rights. In most EU-member states increased efforts have been made to promote 'family-friendly' measures as part of recent legislation. However, reconciliation policies remain extremely uneven across European welfare states (among others, e.g. Gornick, Meyers, and Ross 1998; Stier and Lewin-Epstein 2001; Gornick and Meyers 2003; Mandel and Semyonov 2006).

Not only has the question of how to reconcile work and family gained importance on the political agenda, problems associated with the work–family interface are also central issues in current academic debate. There has been substantial research on the interference between work and family responsibilities. The first studies that empirically assessed the sources of work–family conflict date back to the late 1970s, when the theory of inter-role conflict was developed. These studies already dealt with time- and strain-based pressures resulting from long working hours, high physical and psychological work demands, and work schedules incompatible with family responsibilities (for an overview, see Greenhaus and Beutell 1985). However, the extent to which work demands impact on family life is heavily dependent on contextual factors: first, how paid work is organized in the *household context*; and second, how the interface between paid work and family life is organized in different *societal contexts*. To date, few studies on work–family conflict have systematically addressed these issues. In the main, research has tended to be qualitative (an exception is Duxbury, Higgins, and Lee 1994) and there is surprisingly little comparative research into the determinants of work–family conflict in different policy contexts (for recent exceptions, see Crompton and Lyonette 2005; van der Lippe, Jager, and Kops 2006).[1] What has been lacking is an *integrative perspective* which examines potential risk factors arising from both the work and family domains in the context of different societies.

This study takes a first step in this direction. Based on comparative survey evidence, it examines the difficulty of reconciling work and family demands in six European countries, looks at divergence in experiences among different sectors of the workforce, different family types and household employment patterns, and gauges the extent to which such experiences are mediated by different institutional structures. It considers the extent to which successful conciliation between paid work and family life may be facilitated by 'family-friendly' social and employment policy and explores alternative explanations of cross-country variations, focusing on national variations in the system of employment regulation. Finally, it examines whether there are general trends towards higher or lower levels of work–family conflict. As in previous chapters, the hypothesis of increasing divergence of experiences in the workforce is tested.

Theoretical Background and Hypotheses

It is common practice to distinguish between two types of work–family conflict: work-to-family conflict (WFC) and family-to-work conflict (FWC). Whereas the former occurs when paid work interferes with family responsibilities, the latter arises when family-related responsibilities constrain work activities. Although these phenomena are correlated, it is generally argued that they are distinct constructs—conceptually and empirically (Gutek, Searle, and Klepa 1991; Frone, Russel, and Cooper 1992a; Duxbury, Higgins, and Lee 1994; Netemeyer, McMurrian, and Boles 1996; Frone, Yardley, and Markel 1997). While acknowledging the bidirectional nature of work–family conflict, this study focuses on the analysis of work-to-family conflict (henceforth WFC). Previous research has shown that this form of conflict is more common than FWC because family boundaries are more permeable than are work boundaries (Frone,

---

[1] The psychology literature comprises a small number of cross-cultural comparative studies focusing on the relationship between collectivistic and individualistic values with work–family roles (e.g. Aryee et al. 1999; Hill et al. 2004). These studies are not directly relevant to the present study, however.

Russel, and Cooper 1992*b*; Kinnunen and Mauno 1998; Roehling, Moen, and Batt 2003). Furthermore, previous research suggests that WFC is more strongly affected by work variables (e.g. work hours and stress) than is FWC (Byron 2005), and is more strongly related to job satisfaction (Kossek and Ozeki 1998).

The focus of the analysis is on time- and energy-based conflict between work- and family-related responsibilities. It is based on the assumption that human energy is limited, so that individuals who take on multiple time- and energy-demanding roles will experience conflict. From this perspective we develop our hypotheses about the individual-level determinants of WFC, focusing on working hours, work stress, and time autonomy—in the work domain—and on household composition, household employment patterns and household income—in the family domain (see following section). Section 'The Potential Impact of Institutional Structure' puts forward our hypotheses concerning the impact and mediating effects of the structural context. Our hypotheses on trends in the incidence of WFC over time (between 1996 and 2001) are then presented in section 'Change over Historical Time' together with the results. The empirical analysis is based on prime aged individuals, who live in a cohabiting union with a partner. The work–family interface differs in important ways for single people, and in particular for single parents, and therefore warrants a separate analysis.

Potential Sources of Work–Family Conflict at the Individual and Household Level

The determinants of the work–life balance are located in work and home contexts. On the one hand, the level of conflict between work and family life depends on the demands of paid work in terms of time and intensity. The scheduling of work may support the work–life balance when employees are able to set their own work hours, or it may drastically curtail employees' possibilities to reconcile their work and family responsibilities through a work culture that demands long and irregular hours. On the other hand, the level of WFC will depend on the amount of time commitments and obligations outside work. Here, demands are likely to increase with the number of children or elderly relatives in need of care. Furthermore, family culture and its expectations regarding the time considered necessary to maintain a functioning and fulfilling family life is likely to have an impact on the incidence of WFC. This may affect the allocation of family duties, such as care for the children, and views on whether these should be undertaken by family members or may be contracted out.

WORK DEMANDS

The point of departure for our analysis is the expectation that the risk of experiencing conflict increases, the greater the amount of time spent in paid work (Greenhaus and Beutell 1985; Gutek, Searle, and Klepa 1991; Dex and Bond 2005). The level of WFC should thus rise with the number of work hours performed. This may give rise to important cross-country differences in the incidence of WFC, because national working-time regimes differ greatly across Europe (see section 'The Potential Impact of Institutional Structure'). Furthermore, given that not only time but also energy is limited, we would also expect WFC to increase with higher levels of work stress (Greenhaus and Beutell 1985; Kelloway, Gottlieb, and Barham 1999). Finally, the question of whether the trend towards the increased flexibilization of labour markets across Europe has positive or negative implications for the successful combination of work and family roles has attracted growing scholarly attention (Duxbury, Higgins, and Lee 1994; Parasuraman and Simmers 2001; Crompton 2002; White et al. 2003; Cousins and Tang 2004; Fagan 2004; Haas and Wallace 2004). The findings of an increasing number of studies suggest that flexibility can be both a source of conflict between paid work and family life, and a means to reduce it, depending on the kind of flexibility provided. Typically, a distinction is drawn between forms of flexibility that take account of employees' needs and give them the freedom to vary their work time so as to accommodate their paid work lives with their out-of-work commitments, and forms of flexibility that mainly benefit employers and leave little scope for employees to decide on when and how many hours they work (Fagan 2004). In this regard, the literature suggests that the amount of time-based conflict between work and family should decrease as the *amount of control over one's working time* increases (Pleck, Stains, and Lang 1980; Duxbury, Higgins, and Lee 1994; White et al. 2003; Fagan 2004). Employees who have significant control over their working time and its organization (e.g. those able to change their work schedule or to take time off for personal matters) should be less likely to experience WFC than those whose working times are mostly determined by their employers. However, the counter-hypothesis is that those employees who are given more control over organizing their time *in* work also tend to spend longer hours *at* work (e.g. Taylor 2002; Fagan 2004). Because of the work demands involved in higher-status jobs, employees with autonomous

Table 5.1. Mean work hours and work stress by occupation, sector, and employment status

	Men		Women	
	Work hours	Work stress	Work hours	Work stress
Legislators, senior officials, and managers	47.6	6.4	40.7	6.2
Professionals	42.5	6.3	36.0	6.2
Technicians and associate professionals	41.2	5.7	34.4	6.0
Clerks	38.5	5.7	32.2	5.6
Service and sales workers	42.1	5.5	31.9	5.3
Craft and related trades workers	42.8	5.4	37.5	5.6
Machine operators and assemblers	42.3	5.4	35.3	4.9
Elementary workers	40.7	5.0	29.6	5.1
Public sector	40.0	5.6	34.0	6.0
Private sector	43.7	5.8	34.0	5.6
Self-employed	48.8	5.9	38.4	5.5
Dependently employed	41.9	5.7	33.7	5.7

Source: ISSP (2002) (omitted: skilled agricultural and fishery workers).

time flexibility are not necessarily able to organize their work and family lives any better than those who do not have this autonomy. In fact, there are indications that the high degrees of time flexibility typically found among employees in higher positions and among the self-employed do come along with higher levels of WFC (Parasuraman and Simmers 2001; Grönlund 2004), because employers often presume a willingness of their higher-level employees to adjust their working times primarily to the organization's needs, and only secondarily to their own needs.[2]

The incidence of the three work-domain factors hypothesized to cause WFC, namely long working hours, work stress, and a low level of autonomous flexibility with respect to the work schedule, are unequally distributed across the labour force. As Table 5.1 shows, the higher an employee is in the occupational hierarchy, the greater his/her work stress tends to be. Women's working hours tend to monotonically increase with occupational category, with by far the longest hours being worked by those in the highest ISCO category. Among men, by contrast, this relation is not linear. Comparatively long hours are worked in the two highest ISCO categories and among the self-employed, but also by craft and related trades workers, machine operators, and assemblers. The shortest hours are worked by clerks and elementary workers.

---

[2] The literature also stresses the importance of family-friendly policies at company level (Berg et al. 2004).

Given this, we would expect WFC to be more common among workers in the highest occupational classes than among elementary workers. However, workers in higher-status occupations (and the self-employed) are more likely to enjoy autonomous time flexibility (Fagan 2004). For this reason, occupational differences in the experience of WFC may be less pronounced than expected given the differences in work hours and work stress.[3] Furthermore, one would expect problems of work–family integration to be particularly pronounced in the private sector, where work hours tend to be longer and work stress higher, at least among men, compared to the more closely protected public sector (see Table 5.1). However, also women may find public employment beneficial in terms of work–family reconciliation because public-sector organizations are more likely to employ family-friendly policies (Dex and Smith 2002). Another potential line of divergence in the experience of WFC relates to the type of contract. Given that permanent workers tend to enjoy stronger employment protection than their counterparts on temporary contracts (OECD 2002), we may expect them to have more bargaining power, and therefore to be more likely to be in a work arrangement that enables the reconciliation of work and family life. However, the position of temporary workers relative to their more securely employed counterparts varies substantially across national contexts (Arrowsmith 2006).[4]

FAMILY DEMANDS

Experiences of time pressure are closely bound up with the family context. The time strategies of individuals will crucially depend on the time and financial *demands* of the family, as well as on the *resources* provided by other household members, again in terms of both money and time. Because time allocation takes place at the household level (Jacobs and Gerson 2001; Clarkberg and Merola 2003), considerations about the work–family interface must go beyond the single individual's situation. The analysis will therefore take account of the household composition and the gender division of paid and unpaid labour in coupled households. First, it is likely that the presence of children increases family demands in terms of time and financial resources: indeed, previous research suggests that parents tend to experience higher levels of WFC (Voydanoff 1988;

---

[3] Owing to a lack of data, it is not possible to test for the effect of time autonomy at the individual level.

[4] The impact of the contractual situation on WFC can only be assessed with the data used for analysis of trends over time (Eurobarometer), because data used for the core analysis (the ISSP 2002 Gender Roles Module) provides no information on the type of contract.

Man's labour market involvement	Woman's labour market involvement			
	FT (>40 hours)	FT (30–40 hours)	PT (<30 hours)	OLF (0 hours)
FT (>40 hours)	Dual high	Prog. neo-traditional	Strong neo-traditional	Strong male breadwinner
FT (30–40 hours)	Fem. breadwinner	Dual moderate	Mod. neo-traditional	Mod. male breadwinner
PT (<30 hours)	Fem. breadwinner	Fem. breadwinner	Low involvement	Low involvement
OLF (0 hours)	Fem. breadwinner	Fem. breadwinner	Low involvement	

Figure 5.1. Definition of household employment patterns

Kinnunen and Mauno 1998). Second, it is also important to investigate the effect of a differential division of paid labour among couples. By combining the hours of paid work performed by the woman and the man, and distinguishing for each partner among inactivity (0 hours), part-time (less than 30 hours[5]), moderate full-time (30–40 hours), and long full-time (more than 40 hours) employment, we obtain nine *household employment patterns* (see Figure 5.1).

These types can be defined as *dual high commitment households*, in which both partners work more than 40 hours, *dual moderate commitment households,* in which both partners work between 30 and 40 hours; *male breadwinner households* in which the man works full-time and the woman is out of the labour force; *neo-traditional households*, in which the man works full-time and his female partner part-time; and *female breadwinner households*, in which the woman works full-time and longer hours than her partner. The residual category is termed *dual low involvement*, defined as households in which neither of the partners works more than part-time hours. Male breadwinner households are further subdivided depending on the extent of full-time involvement of the male partner (*strong* version when the man works more than 40 hours and *moderate* version when he works between 30 and 40 hours). Neo-traditional households are divided into three sub-types: *strong* (the man works long full-time hours and the woman works part-time, *moderate* (the man works between 30 and 40 hours and the woman works part-time) and *progressive* (both partners work full-time but only the man works more than 40 hours).

Based on the assumption that the level of WFC increases with the amount of time spent in paid work, one may generally expect to find the highest level of WFC among women/men in households where they work particularly long hours, with the level of conflict further increasing with the number of hours their partners work. We would thus expect WFC to be highest in *dual high commitment* households, in which both

[5] The definition of part-time work is the one used by the OECD (Van Bastelaer et al. 1997).

partners have a limited amount of time available for family matters. When there is nobody to rely on to do the unpaid household and care work in the home, the employed will experience levels of time stress higher than those of their counterparts in family arrangements in which one of the partners is not in the labour force or works significantly reduced hours. We do not generally expect WFC to be highest among dual-earners, however. Instead, in households where both partners have a *moderate commitment* to paid work, we expect lower levels of WFC than in dual-earner households where the man works long full-time hours. Those who choose this 'family-friendly' mode of paid work-sharing between partners are also more likely to have gender role attitudes in favour of a more equal sharing of unpaid care work.

However, work behaviour should be viewed in the context of life-course and gender dynamics. Although we assume the same pattern for both sexes, we nevertheless expect women to experience higher levels of conflict because they still bear the bulk of family responsibilities (Gutek, Searle, and Klepa 1991; Frone, Russel, and Cooper 1992*b*; Duxbury, Higgins, and Lee 1994)—even in households in which both partners work the same number of hours. For most men, the dual-income situation differs fundamentally from the experiences of their female partners, to whom the 'second shift' tends to be allocated (Hochschild 1989). Hence, possible differences between the sexes in the experience of WFC may to some extent be explained by the respective differences in the time spent doing household work. Those who are engaged in paid work while doing more than their fair share of the household chores should experience higher levels of WFC than do those who do little extra work in the home in addition to paid employment.

Finally, it can be expected that the reduction in the resource 'time' can to some extent be off-set by augmented financial resources. Because a higher family income increases the ability to buy services from the market, it may reduce the time demands on the family and thus lead to lower levels of WFC. However, the effect of household income may be mediated by cultural and attitudinal factors. The purchase of services on the market is not equally common and socially accepted in all European countries. Moreover, it is likely that differential expectations with regard to the 'ideal' organization of family life impact on the incidence of WFC. All else equal, those who believe that maternal employment is detrimental to child and family well-being, should experience higher levels of conflict.

The Potential Impact of Institutional Structures

There is reason to believe that variations in social and labour market policy among countries affect the degree to which participation in paid employment interferes with family life. In what follows, we present some hypotheses about institutional effects, first discussing cross-country differences in reconciliation policies, and then turning to national systems of employment regulation.

WELFARE STATE REGIMES—STATE INTERVENTION AND RECONCILIATION MEASURES

Countries differ in the extent to which the state supports the reconciliation of work and family life. Especially in the Nordic countries (here exemplified by Sweden), there has been a concerted effort to facilitate the combination of participation in paid employment with family life. A range of 'family-friendly' policies have been introduced, including the provision of high-quality and affordable care services for children of all ages, and parental rights such as generously paid parental leave and entitlement to reduce daily working time when children are young or ill. It was suggested in the introductory chapter in the volume that such provision could be seen as an integral part of an 'inclusive' employment regime. In liberal countries such as Britain, as well as in most continental European countries including Germany and the Netherlands, by contrast, fewer efforts are made to facilitate the balance between work and family life. Parental rights are less extensive than in the Nordic countries, and owing to a lack of public support for care work, parents must find their own individualized solutions to the problem of combining work and family life (Platenga 2002; Visser 2002). As a result, part-time work is the dominant strategy with which women combine work and family responsibilities. France, however, is an exception, for its childcare policy is much closer to the Nordic than the Continental European model, while female labour-market participation tends to be on a full- rather than a part-time basis. Finally, Southern Europe has the worst of both worlds: the provision of public care facilities for small children is scarce, while at the same time part-time options are largely unavailable, leaving women with the choice between staying out of the labour market or working full-time.

The importance of welfare state interventions for female labour supply is well established in the literature (Stier and Lewin-Epstein 2001; Gornick and Meyers 2003; Uunk, Kalmijn, and Muffels 2005; Mandel and

Semyonov 2006). It is frequently argued that the provision of adequate care facilities eases the successful combination of work and family life. We may therefore expect a policy context designed to facilitate the conciliation of work and family life to result in less WFC than does a less family-friendly policy context (Cousins and Tang 2004). However, there is a plausible counter-hypothesis: a social policy context designed to enhance the combination of paid employment with family life represents a gender ideology where both men and women are expected to combine paid employment with family responsibilities, while a 'family-unfriendly' policy context creates disincentives for female labour-market participation and hence tends to reduce work demands for women in terms of hours (higher female part-time rate) but also job content (in these countries, female part-timers tend to be concentrated in low-pay, low-demand jobs). Where traditional solutions to the problem of combining paid work and unpaid care work prevail, WFC may thus be less common not only among women but also among men, given that their female partners tend to act as home-makers.

It therefore still has to be demonstrated that 'family-friendly' policies indeed have an effect in reducing WFC, taking account of cross-country differences in female labour-market participation patterns. In countries such as Sweden, most women work, and not just those who find it particularly easy to combine work and family (e.g. the childless). This may produce higher overall levels of WFC in countries with higher maternal employment rates. The empirical analysis will have to take account of the fact that working women may differ in crucial ways from those out of the labour force, and that the manner in which women are selected or self-select into the workforce may differ greatly across countries.

SYSTEMS OF EMPLOYMENT REGULATION

Like the welfare state via family policy, the system of employment regulation may have an impact on the extent to which work and family responsibilities can be successfully integrated. As argued by Berg and colleagues (2004), in countries characterized by weak collective bargaining institutions and scant labour market regulation, employers have more power to shape employees' working time. Accordingly, in liberal market economics (LMEs), working time has until recently not been regulated at all, with the consequence that working hours in full-time employment tend to be very long (e.g. the UK). Conversely, countries where collective bargaining is more strongly developed have witnessed a more marked decline in the standard work week over the last decades (e.g. the

Netherlands, Germany, Sweden, and France, but less so in Spain despite high bargaining coverage: see Table 5.2 for an overview). Countries also differ in the prevalence of part-time work. Where the availability of this employment option is limited, as in Spain (see Table 5.2), working mothers tend to have full-time work commitments which—in the absence of an adequate childcare infrastructure—makes it very difficult to combine care responsibilities with employment.

Furthermore, national systems of employment regulation differ in the extent to which workers enjoy autonomy in the timing of their work hours. While in some countries policies introduced since the 1980s have mainly sought to increase the power of employers to demand greater flexibility from their employees, in others explicit attempts have been made to promote the power of employees to determine their working times in a flexible manner (Fagan 2004; Haas and Wallace 2004; Fagan, Hegewisch, and Pilinger 2006). The more strictly regulated labour markets and strong collective bargaining institutions typically found in Continental Europe should increase the power of employees to negotiate work schedules geared to their needs. However while collective negotiation plausibly increases *collective control* over working time, the extent to which *individual control* over working time has developed also varies a good deal among countries (Berg et al. 2004). In some but not all European countries, employees have been given individual rights to demand reduced work hours or alternative work schedules from their employers. To the extent that this is the case, we would expect employees to exercise more control over their working time.

The Netherlands provide a good example of an employment system that gives employees a high level of time autonomy (e.g. Wilthagen, Tros, and van Lieshout 2003). Opportunities for a new type of part-time work have expanded since the 1980s and, more recently, the Adjustment of Hours Act has facilitated individual reductions in weekly working time. Today, a 36-hour standard work week and a flexible approach to working hours are widespread, with employers being formally obliged to take account of employees' obligations in relation to care work when scheduling their hours (Fagan, Hegewisch, and Pilinger 2006). Also Sweden provides workers, and in particular working parents, with a high level of autonomous time flexibility. Parental leave regulations grant workers the right to reduce their work hours around child birth and then later increase them again. Indeed, the regulations allow for reduced hours schedules until a child's eighth birthday (Fagan and Hebson 2004). Regulations of this kind, in combination with consultation rights through labour unions,

Table 5.2. Cross-national differences and institutional background

Country	Childcare coverage (1)		Parental leave (2)	WSII (3)	Female employment rate (4)	Female part-time rate (4)	Mean work hours (5)		Household work (hours/week) (6)		Individual time autonomy	% temporary workers (7)		Work stress (8)	
	0–3	3–6					m	f	m	f		m	f	m	f
UK	2	60	25	27	66	28	43	31	7	13	Polarized	6	8	6.2	6.5
Netherlands	6	71	11	27	66	49	37	25	6	15	High	11	17	5.6	5.8
Sweden	48	80	118	100	71	25	39	34	8	13	High	12	17	5.9	6.6
Germany (W)	2	60	49	20	59	43	41	32	6	20	Medium	13	13	6.4	6.5
Germany (E)	16	87	—	—	58	24	—	—	7	15	—	—	16	6.4	6.4
France	29	99	50	50	57	17	40	34	5	11	Low	14	16	6.0	6.1
Spain	5	84	50	43	48	8	42	37	9	29	Low	31	35	5.1	5.3

Note: When no value is reported for East Germany, the value for West Germany refers to Germany as a whole.

Sources: (1) For Sweden, France, Spain, and the Netherlands: Kamerman (2000); for the Netherlands (0–3): OECD Employment Outlook (2001); for Germany: Engelbrecht and Jungkunst (2001). (2) Gauthier, A.H. and Bortnik, A. (2001): Comparative Maternity, Parental, and Childcare Database, Version 2 (University of Calgary). (3) Mandel, and Semyonov (2006). WSII is an additive index of welfare policies (0–100) based on a combination of the size of the public sector, maternity leave (number of fully paid weeks), and % of children aged between 0–6 in public childcare. (4) European Commission (2006b), for most countries; for Germany: data from Matysiak and Steinmetz (2006). (5) Fagan (2004); except Germany: data from the European Labour Force Survey (2001). (6) ISSP (2002), authors' own calculation of the mean hours of weekly household work among those living in couple households (including 'zero' hours). (7) European Labour Force Survey, share of employees in temporary jobs in 2000. (8) ISSP (2002), authors' own calculation of average work stress in the working population aged 20–60.

give Swedish workers a significant degree of control over their working time (Berg et al. 2004). In Germany, working time flexibility has been on the agenda since the late 1980s. Today, working time policy is used as a means to help workers balance their work and family responsibilities. In 2001, German employees in companies with more than fifteen employees received an individual right to demand a contractual reduction in working time from their employer. This right applies to employees irrespective of their parental status and employers have to agree to the demand unless they can present business reasons for a refusal (Burri, Opitz, and Veldman 2003). Additionally, parental leave legislation grants new parents the right to a temporary reduction of working hours to between 15 and 30 hours per week for two years, after which parents are entitled to return to full-time work with equivalent pay and status (Fagan and Hebson 2004). Although flexibility in starting and ending daily work is not as common in Germany as in other countries, the widespread introduction of working time accounts, which allow workers to accrue paid time off for working excess hours, have contributed to increased time flexibility (Promberger 2001; Riedmann 2006).[6] The fact that such agreements are negotiated at workplace level ensures that employees benefit from such regulations.

In other countries, 'flexibility' reforms have been primarily to the benefit of employers. In the UK, a right for parents with young children to request reduced or flexible hours only came into force in April 2003. But still today, the average British worker fares worse than his/her German, Swedish, or Dutch counterparts by having to work longer full-time hours and having less personal flexibility within these hours (Fagan, Hegewisch, and Pilinger 2006), although flexibility in starting and ending times seems to be on the increase. However, whether employees in the UK have the bargaining power to gain some control over their working time depends closely on their position within the labour market. Owing to the lack of collective agreements, only those workers with valuable skills tend to have the power to negotiate working time options that fit their individual needs, and this produces a polarization within the workforce with regard to the ability to define work schedules autonomously (e.g. Fagan 2004). This contrasts with Sweden, Germany, and the Netherlands, where time flexibility is embedded in collective bargaining and social partner negotiations. Finally, France and Spain serve as examples of employment

[6] In 2000, about 80 per cent of German companies in the private sector offered some form of working time account to their employees, and there is evidence that some employees make extensive use of their working time accounts to alter their weekly work schedules or take time off to deal with personal or family issues (Promberger 2001).

regulation systems in which collective control over working time (duration) is combined with comparatively weak individual control over it. Especially in Spain, the law gives employers discretionary powers to regulate the distribution of working time (Berg et al. 2004), which has resulted in the widespread introduction of irregular working hours, shift work, and weekend work (Artiles 2005). Indeed, Spain has experienced a rapid shift from one of the most rigid employment protection systems to a highly flexible labour market with large numbers of temporary employees (see Table 5.2). France enacted a law reducing the standard working week from 39 to 35 hours in 1998. The purpose of this legislation was to increase employment, but also to promote a trade-off between fewer weekly work hours and greater employer flexibility in scheduling work. In sum, employee autonomy in deciding on the number and scheduling of work hours appears to be most marked in the Netherlands and Sweden, followed by Germany; but less so in the UK, where time autonomy tends to be lower for the majority of the workforce, and also in France, and especially Spain, where we find strong collective but a rather low level of individual time autonomy (for an overview, see Table 5.2).

COUNTRY DIFFERENCES

Owing to national differences among working time regimes, the availability of part-time employment, and the availability of individual control over work schedules, as well as among the levels of state support for maternal/paternal employment, one would expect to find country differences in the incidence rate of WFC. Among women, it is possible that WFC is higher in countries where more mothers engage in paid work (e.g. in Sweden as opposed to West Germany or Spain) since women who have a particularly difficult domestic situation may nonetheless remain in employment. Taking account of the level of labour force participation, however, the highest WFC incidence rates among women are likely to be found where women tend to work full- rather than part-time (e.g. in Spain as opposed to the Netherlands). Among men, the highest levels of WFC may be expected where they tend to work long full-time hours while they cannot rely on a female provider to do all the unpaid work in the home, and thus in countries with many dual-career households. However, long working times and high female participation do not tend to go together at country level. For instance, in Sweden there are many dual-earner households while the standard work week in full-time employment is of moderate length. In the UK and Spain, by contrast, full-time hours tend to be longer but fewer women engage in full-time work.

We may expect the factors important for the incidence of WFC at the individual level (e.g. work hours, work stress, the presence of children, and employment situation of the partner) to go a long way towards explaining national differences in the incidence of WFC. However, if the experience of WFC is mediated by national contexts, we may still find some country-differences when these factors are taken into account. First, if it is true that WFC can be ameliorated by state policies intended to facilitate the combination of work and family, we may expect Swedish couples to experience less conflict than their counterparts in less supportive welfare regimes. Second, we may expect to find higher levels of WFC in Spain and France as these countries offer the lowest variety of flexible working time options such as part-time opportunities. This may decrease the likelihood that Spanish or French employees find a work schedule that fits their needs. Also individual time autonomy in full-time employment tends to be less developed in these countries than in Sweden or the Netherlands.

National contexts may also have a mediating effect on how WFC is distributed across the labour force. For instance, the number of paid work hours performed should have a stronger negative effect in countries where employees have a low level of individual time autonomy (Spain and France). The presence of children is likely to have a stronger effect on WFC in countries with a high level of female labour market participation and hence many mothers in the sample (e.g. Sweden, when no control for sample composition). However, the effect of increased care demands on mothers may be ameliorated when there is an adequate childcare infrastructure. Moreover, in countries such as the UK, where workers in higher occupational classes have more power to individually negotiate their work schedules, we may expect to find a marked divergence across occupational groups. Finally, in countries such as Spain, where two-tier labour markets have been established, we may expect to find a polarisa-tion according to type of contract.

Data and Methods

For the core analysis, we draw on the 2002 ISSP Gender Role Module, which apart from measures of WFC, provides measures of work stress, respondents' and their partners' weekly work hours, family composition and income, gender role attitudes, educational attainment, and occupa-tional status. In addition to the 'core' countries focused on in this volume, namely France, Germany, Great Britain, Spain, and Sweden, we include the Netherlands, which is of theoretical interest in regard to work–family compatibility issues given the development into a part-time economy and the accompanying steep rise in female labour market participation in recent decades. Moreover, in the analysis we further differentiate between the western and eastern part of Germany, because the 'New Länder' still differ in important ways from the 'Old Länder' (e.g. labour market conditions or childcare provision).

WFC conflict is assessed by two items using a 4-point scale (several times a week, several times a month, once or twice, and never). Respondents were asked how often each of the following had happened to them in the past three months: 1) 'I have come home from work too tired to do the chores which need to be done', 2) 'It has been difficult for me to fulfil my family responsibilities because of the amount of time I spent on my job'. The two items correlate highly (Cronbach's α: 0.82), which allows for the construction of an additive index. However, given that they are very differently distributed, with worries about neglecting one's family responsibilities being far less prevalent than the neglect of household chores due to exhaustion, we decided to assign a greater weight to the former.[7] Neither incidence rates of WFC nor country differences in this respect are substantially affected by this procedure. Finally, we dichotomise the resulting measure of WFC, defining a *high level of WFC* as a situation in which respondents report that, in the past three months, they felt too tired to do the chores which needed to be done at home several times a week *and* found it difficult to fulfil family responsibilities at least several times a month.

The ISSP data provide rich information on individuals' work and household context, but they not allow for an analysis of change over time. Therefore, to assess trends in WFC, we use two Eurobarometer surveys from the years 1996 and 2001. These measure WFC on a 5-point scale (always, often, sometimes, hardly ever, and never) asking respondents how often they: (*a*) feel too tired after work to enjoy the things they would like to do at home; and (*b*) find their job prevents them from giving the time they want to their partner or family. These two items are combined to form an index ranging from 1 to 10 and then recoded into a dummy variable in which values smaller than or equal to 3 are taken to represent a high level of WFC (i.e. respondents experienced WFC always or often).[8]

[7] We combined the answer categories 'once or twice' or 'never' in Q1 and 'several times a week' and 'several times a month' in Q2, so that the resulting three-category variables showed almost identical distributions.

[8] This measure differs from the one provided in the ISSP. Here the focus is on incompatibilities between employment and unpaid work in the home, on the one hand, and the time desired to dedicate to things 'one would like to do at home' and to 'family leisure', on the

Since it is plausible that WFC is differently determined for women and men (e.g. the presence of children might be more strongly related to WFC for women), we compute separate sex-specific models. On comparing the incidence of WFC between different countries, the problem arises that the level of WFC can by definition only be measured for persons in paid work. However, as countries vary considerably with regard to female labour market participation, and thus with regard to the female population potentially exposed to WFC, the need to account for sample selection effects arises. As a consequence of different female participation rates, we may well be dealing with differently selected groups of women across countries. Self-selection should play a lesser role in countries where the great majority of women are in paid work. In countries with low female participation rates, however, the female sample may represent a self-selective sub-sample of the female population that differs in characteristics that not only structure women's participation decisions but are also potentially relevant determinants of WFC. For instance, the sample of employed women might have a greater ability to combine their work and family roles (Bratberg, Dahl, and Risa 2002). From this perspective we might find lower levels of WFC in countries where female participation is low, owing to the fact that the women who are employed are those who find it less difficult to combine paid work with out-of-work responsibilities (e.g. childless women). We control for such selectivity processes by applying a two-step Heckman procedure (Heckman 1979). We simultaneously estimate the two equations of: (*a*) labour market participation; and (*b*) the incidence of WFC for the working population. The labour market participation equation controls for age, the level of education and the presence of children of different ages in the household. The selection effect is expected to be of little relevance for men because male participation rates are (about equally) high in all countries.

Country Differences and the Determinants of WFC: Empirical Patterns

The presentation of the empirical results is organized as follows. First, we set out the cross-country differences in the incidence of WFC and explore to which extent such differences are attributable to differently selected

other. In the ISSP measure, by contrast, the conflict is between employment and time needed and desired for family life both for *unpaid work and leisure* purposes.

samples of working populations. Then, we investigate the work and family-related factors affecting the incidence of conflict. This is followed by an investigation of the determinants of cross-country differences, focusing on the composition of the workforce but also on institutional factors. The last part of the analysis is devoted to trends in WFC over historical time.

Country Differences and the Selectivity Problem

On average, in the six countries considered, about 12 per cent of male and female workers living in couple households report a high level of WFC, that is, feel too tired to do the chores which needed to be done at home several times a week *and* find it difficult to fulfil family responsibilities at least several times a month. WFC rates vary between 6 per cent (East German men) and 19 per cent (Spanish women, see Table 5.3).

Investigating country differences, taking West Germany as the reference country for comparison, shows significantly higher WFC incidence rates for Spanish and Swedish women, but significantly lower rates for Dutch women (see Table 5.4). However, as mentioned, there may be a methodological problem arising from the fact that the countries differ considerably with regard to female labour market participation rates, and thus sample composition. The assumption is that, in countries with low female participation, we may find a more 'positively' selected sub-sample of women in the labour force showing greater capacity for combining work and family duties than in countries where the vast majority of women work. Participation rates are comparatively highest in Sweden, France, and Great Britain (Table 5.2). However, in most countries, with the notable exception of Sweden, female participation rates drastically fall with the presence of young children. Participation rates of mothers range from 36 per cent in Spain and 37 per cent in the Netherlands to 61 per cent in France and 85 per cent in Sweden (OECD 2005). We might therefore suppose that the relatively high incidence of WFC in Sweden

Table 5.3. Share of working population reporting high levels of WFC

	Germany (W)	Germany (E)	Sweden	Netherlands	UK	France	Spain
High WFC men	11%	6%	14%	12%	13%	15%	15%
High WFC women	9%	8%	15%	7%	12%	13%	19%

Table 5.4. Country differences and the selectivity problem

	Normal probit model		Probit with sample selection	
	Men	Women	Men	Women
EQ1: WFC				
Germany (W) ref.				
Germany (E)	−0.37	−0.07	−0.37	−0.11
Netherlands	−0.01	**−0.38**°	0.01	**−0.41***
Sweden	0.13	**0.28**°	0.14	0.26
UK	0.11	0.09	0.11	0.08
France	0.16	0.11	0.15	0.08
Spain	0.17	**0.43***	0.17	**0.41***
_cons	−1.21***	−1.32***	−1.20***	−1.09***
EQ2: working				
Above lowest formal qualification (reference below)			0.45***	0.37***
Upper-secondary education			0.56***	0.54***
Above upper-secondary level			0.79***	0.87***
Small child (reference no child)			−0.11	−0.54***
Older child			0.02	−0.08
Age			0.33***	0.12***
Age squared			−0.004***	−0.001***
_cons			−5.26***	−1.86***
/athrho			−0.03	−0.34*
ρ			−0.03	−0.33
LR				
test of correlation between the 2 equations			indep	dep*
Number of observations in EQ 1	1,952	2,010	1,744	1,798

Notes: Sample—Cohabiting couples aged 20–60. *** $p < 0.001$; ** $p < 0.01$; * $p < 0.05$; ° $p < 0.1$.

is due to the fact that more women/mothers participate in the labour market.

As shown in Table 5.4, the results of the models controlling for sample selection confirm that selectivity exists for women (the participation equation is correlated with the WFC equation of interest). As a result, controlling for selection bias, the coefficient for Swedish women is no longer significant when compared to their West German counterparts. The difference between West Germany and Spain, by contrast, remains. Hence, we can conclude that the relatively high WFC rates in Sweden are to some extent due to differently selected subpopulations of working women, while this does not seem to be the case for Spain. Also the relatively low level of WFC in the Netherlands compared to West Germany persists when we control for sample selection. To sum up, the results indicate significantly higher levels of WFC for women in Spain and considerably lower levels of WFC for women in the Netherlands.

Table 5.5. Gender differences in WFC: effect of being female on WFC

	Germany (W)	Germany (E)	Sweden	Netherlands	UK	France	Spain
Traditional probit model	−0.11	0.19	0.05	**−0.50****	−0.12	−0.15	0.15
...Controlling for work time	0.09	0.53	0.16	−0.20	0.23	0.19	**0.38****
Model with selection correction	−0.11	0.08	0.05	**−0.43****	−0.13	−0.16	0.17
...Controlling for work time	0.04	0.22	0.11	−0.16	**0.27**°	**0.25**°	**0.40****
...And time spent for household work	−0.04	0.79	0.02	−0.11	0.22	0.19	**0.30****

Notes: Separate probit models, coefficient of gender dummy. *** $p < 0.001$; ** $p < 0.01$; * $p < 0.05$; ° $p < 0.1$.

Individual, Work, and Household Level Determinants of WFC

We expected women to experience higher levels of WFC because the bulk of unpaid work and care responsibilities still tends to fall upon them—irrespectively of whether or not they are in paid employment. However, on comparing incidence rates for women and men, gender differences either fail to reach statistical significance or men report higher levels of WFC (in the Netherlands). This can, however, be explained by gender differences in the number of paid work hours. Women tend to work fewer hours, albeit with considerable variation among European countries. Once the number of paid work hours is controlled for, we find a significantly higher level of WFC for women in Great Britain, France, and Spain. The higher level of WFC among women than among men in Britain and France is likely to reflect a situation in which women spend more time on household work than men, given that the gender difference in the level of WFC fails statistical significance in these countries once this factor is taken into account (see Table 5.5). Controlling in addition for occupation, supervisory duties, and sector of activity, does not reveal further gender differences (not shown).

The impact of the different variables hypothesized to affect the severity of WFC is examined in Tables 5.6 and 5.7 through a series of probit regression models. As we found confirmation for a selection process for women and cannot be sure about its consequences on the effects of the other variables, the following analyses of the main individual and household level determinants of WFC are based on selectivity corrected models (although for reasons of space the selection equations are not

Table 5.6. Women's WFC, probit models with selection correction

Women	Model 1	Model 2	Model 3	Model 4	Model 5	Model 6
Germany (W)	ref	ref	ref	ref	ref	ref
Germany (E)	−0.51°	−0.12	−0.27	−0.05	−0.44	−0.42
Netherlands	−0.01	−0.37°	−0.17	**−0.40***	0.01	0.02
Sweden	0.13	0.25	0.21	**0.37***	0.17	0.18
UK	0.08	0.08	0.13	0.13	0.14	0.19
France	0.18	0.12	0.17	0.15	0.23	0.20
Spain	**0.60*****	**0.48****	0.33°	**0.40***	**0.58****	**0.55****
Work hours fewer than 20	**−0.77****					−0.83**
Work hours 20 < 30	−0.11					−0.16
Work hours 30 < 35	0.07					0.02
Work hours 35 < 40	ref					ref
Work hours 40 < 45	**0.25***					**0.29***
Work hours 45 or more	**0.49*****					**0.47****
Work stress	**0.26*****				**0.26*****	**0.25*****
Higher class occupation		**0.22***			0.13	0.09
Intermediate class occupation		ref			ref	ref
Lower class occupation		0.00			0.02	0.03
Self-employed		0.03			−0.09	−0.05
Public sector		0.04			0.02	0.03
Supervisor		0.15°			0.00	−0.04
Household types						
Man Woman						
>40 hrs >40 hrs			ref		ref	
>40 hrs 30–40 hrs			**−0.36****		**−0.37****	
>40 hrs <30			**−0.55*****		**−0.45****	
30–40 hrs 30–40 hrs			**−0.53*****		**−0.42***	
30–40 hrs <30 hrs			**−1.05*****		**−0.94****	
Female breadwinner[a]			−0.02		−0.11	
Low involvement[b]			**−0.97*****		**−0.76***	
Partner's working hours						
Not working						0.10
< 30 hrs						0.09
30–40 hrs						ref
> 40 hrs						0.00
Presence of children: none				ref	ref	ref
Small child				0.13	**0.24***	**0.31****
Older child				0.00	0.08	0.08
Low household income				0.20	**0.38***	**0.42***
Medium household income				ref	ref	ref
High household income				0.16°	−0.03	0.00
Dual housekeeper				ref	ref	ref
Female housekeeper				**0.16***	0.14	0.15
Male housekeeper				0.20	0.19	0.13
Pro compatibility				**−0.13*****	**−0.12*****	**−0.13*****
_cons	−3.11***	−1.24***	−1.00***	−0.82***	−2.48***	−2.63***
N (all)	2,701	2,720	2,783	2,753	2,617	2,612
N (those in employment)	1,716	1,735	1,798	1,768	1,632	1,620
/athrho	0.06	−0.33°	−0.08	−0.63***	−0.25	−0.41°
ρ	0.06	−0.32	−0.08	−0.56	−0.24	−0.39
Test	indep	indep	indep	dep*	indep	dep

Notes: Sample—Cohabiting couples aged 20–60 in the labour force. Selection equation not reported. [a] The woman works full-time (30 hours or more) and longer hours than her partner. [b] Neither of the partners works more than part-time. *** $p < 0.001$; ** $p < 0.01$; * $p < 0.05$; ° $p < 0.1$.

Table 5.7. Men's WFC, probit models with selection correction

Men	Model 1	Men	Model 2	Model 3	Model 4	Model 5	Model 6
Germany (W)	ref		ref	ref	ref	ref	ref
Germany (E)	−0.39		−0.35	−0.35	−0.42	−0.39	−0.41
Netherlands	0.31°		0.07	0.08	0.00	0.26	0.21
Sweden	0.35*		0.18	0.18	0.13	0.32°	0.33°
UK	0.12		0.15	0.13	0.07	0.20	0.07
France	0.35*		0.20	0.28°	0.17	0.42*	0.30°
Spain	0.51***		0.22	0.17	0.13	0.45**	0.37*
Work hours fewer than 20	−0.21						−0.16
Work hours 20 < 30	0.41						0.49
Work hours 30 < 35	−0.19						−0.21
Work hours 35 < 40	ref						ref
Work hours 40 < 45	0.08						0.04
Work hours 45 or more	0.32*						0.25°
Work stress	0.25***					0.25***	0.26***
Higher class occupation			−0.01			−0.15	−0.19°
Intermediate class occupation			ref			ref	ref
Lower class occupation			−0.35			−0.23	−0.27
Self-employed			0.17			0.10	0.02
Public sector			−0.21*			−0.13	−0.11
Supervisor			0.22**			0.12	0.10
Household types							
Man		Woman					
>40 hrs		>40 hrs		ref		ref	
>40 hrs		30–40 hrs		0.01		0.01	
>40 hrs		<30		0.16		0.01	
>40 hrs		0		0.19°		0.12	
30–40 hrs		30–40 hrs		−0.35°		−0.19	
30–40 hrs		<30		−0.13		0.06	
30–40 hrs		0		−0.49*		−0.29	
Female breadwinner[a]				−0.16		0.16	
Low involvement[b]				−0.11		0.27	
Partner's working hours							
Not working							0.29*
<30 hrs							0.15
30–40 hrs							ref
>40 hrs							0.00
Presence of children: none					ref	ref	ref
Small child					0.17	0.09	0.07
Older child					0.07	0.04	0.04
Low household income					0.11	0.14	0.12
Medium household income					ref	ref	ref
High household income					0.08	−0.03	−0.03
Dual housekeeper					ref	ref	ref
Female housekeeper					0.31***	0.24**	0.22*
Male housekeeper					0.40**	0.34*	0.33*
Pro compatibility					0.02	0.03	0.05
_cons	−3.21***		−1.34***	−1.26***	−1.54***	−3.32***	−3.54***
N (all)	1,931		1,967	1,989	1,959	1,885	1,857
N (those in employment)	1,686		1,722	1,744	1,714	1,640	1,612
/athrho	0.33		−0.02	−0.06	0.02	0.06	0.09
ρ	0.31		−0.02	−0.06	0.02	0.06	0.09
Test	indep		indep	indep	indep	indep	indep

Notes: Sample—Cohabiting couples aged 20–60 in the labour force. [a] The woman works full-time (30 hours or more) and longer hours than her partner. [b] Neither of the partners works more than part-time. *** $p < 0.001$; ** $p < 0.01$; * $p < 0.05$; ° $p < 0.1$.

reported). Women and men are often thought to differ with respect to the mechanisms influencing the incidence of WFC and are for this reason investigated separately. Besides the complete models that test all of the main factors hypothesized to shape the work–family interface (Models 5 and 6), we present partial models focusing on different sub-sets of predictors (Models 1–4).

We hypothesized that there are two main work-related factors causing WFC, namely long *working hours*[9] *and a high level of work stress*.[10] This receives empirical support (Model 1). The longer the hours of paid work that women perform the more likely they are to experience time strains with their families—independently of other work or family characteristics (Models 5 and 6). For men, a significant increase in WFC is only found for those working more than 45 hours a week. Women thus appear to be more sensitive to their own work hours in respect of their difficulties in combining work and family life than men.[11] This is attributable to the well-established fact that it is still women who, independently of their employment status, undertake the main share of care and household work (e.g. Sørensen 2001; Gershuny and Sullivan 2003). The results also show that workers in jobs that involve higher levels of *work stress* are more likely to experience WFC. This is the case for both sexes, independently of the number of paid work hours performed or the qualification level of the occupation (Models 5 and 6).

The two main work-related factors causing WFC—long working hours and a high level of work stress—are unequally distributed across the labour force. For women, they tend to be highest in the highest *occupational categories*.[12] Accordingly, women in more highly skilled occupational classes[13] are more at risk of WFC. For men, long working hours are more evenly spread across the workforce and hence there is no clear effect of occupational level. However, men are more prone to WFC when

[9] Working hours base on individuals' reported usual working hours.

[10] *Work stress* was assessed by an additive index consisting of two items. Respondents were asked if they (strongly) agreed or (strongly) disagreed that 'There are so many things to do at work, I often run out of time before I get them all done' and 'My job is rarely stressful'.

[11] The gender difference in the strength of the effect of work hours on the level of WFC is significant at the 95% security level (interaction effect of continuous measure of working hours with sex, not shown).

[12] Among men, however, only work stress is linearly related to occupational position, while the relation with respect to work hours is less straightforward (see Table 5.1).

[13] Respondents' occupational statuses were measured using the ISCO qualification, grouped into three categories: highly skilled (ISCO 1 and 2), medium skilled (ISCO 3–8), and low- or unskilled (ISCO 9).

they have *supervisory functions* and when they work in the private sector (Model 2). All of these effects are due to longer work hours and higher levels of work stress in such jobs (Model 5). Moreover, once work hours and work stress are controlled for, male workers in professional or managerial occupations (ISCO 1 and 2) tend to report lower levels of WFC than their counterparts in lesser skilled occupations (Model 6). This may be due to a higher level of time autonomy enjoyed by those in higher skilled occupations.

Arguably, it is not just individual working hours but also the way paid work is divided between the sexes in couple households that is important in explaining different levels of WFC. On investigating the effect of the *household employment pattern* (Model 3), we find that, compared to the dual high commitment pattern (both partners work more than 40 hours per week), women in most other types of couple households (except when they act as female breadwinners) are less likely to report WFC, with the moderate neo-traditional pattern seemingly representing the ideal situation for women in terms of work–family compatibility (i.e. when the man works less than 40 hours and the woman works fewer than 30 hours per week). Interestingly, there are no differences between the dual moderate commitment (where both partners work between 30 and 40 hours) and the neo-traditional models (where the man works more than 40 hours and the woman less than 30). This suggests that for women, an increase in their own work hours may be compensated by reduced work hours of their partners. For women, these effects of household structure remain significant when controlling for work and family characteristics (Model 5).[14] For men, on the other hand, there are no significant effects once account is taken of work stress (Model 5). Model 6 suggests that men, whose partners are out of the labour force, are more likely to face WFC than their counterparts with full-time working partners. Given that the effect of men's own work hours becomes marginally significant when account is taken of women's employment status, it seems likely that single breadwinners face a specifically strong need to work long full-time hours.

Besides the time and energy constraints imposed by the employment situation, the amount of WFC should also depend on how demanding family life is. The *presence of children* in a household increases such

[14] Interestingly, on looking at the effect of the partner's work hours, controlling for own work hours, rather than at household employment patterns (Model 6), no significant effects emerge. This suggests that it is the specific combination of partners' working hours, rather than the spouse's work demands, that makes the difference.

161

demands in terms of time and financial resources.[15] At first sight, however, the presence of children seems not to affect the incidence of WFC
(Model 4). This, however, is because mothers of small children tend to
work fewer hours. Once work hours are taken into account, a different
picture emerges. Mothers, but not fathers, of small children are more
likely to experience WFC than their childless counterparts, or those with
grown-up children (Model 5). To investigate the effect of the *distribution
of household tasks* between partners we control for whether the female
partner or the male partner takes the major share of household tasks or
whether the partners share such tasks equally. We find that both women
and men tend to be more prone to WFC when *they* do the main share
of household work than when household duties are equally shared with
or mainly done by the partner. However, a more equitable division of
household work does not seem to have an alleviating effect for women,
once the gender division of paid work is controlled for (Model 5).[16] A
higher *household income*[17] may provide the resources to 'outsource' some
household work to the market and in this way may help to avert WFC.
This contention receives empirical support for women (Models 5 and
6). Women in low-income households are at greater risk of experiencing
WFC, net of working hours. Finally, as the assessment of WFC is highly
subjective, *attitudinal factors* are expected to play a key role. In fact,
employed women who believe that preschool children suffer when the
mother goes out to work do tend to experience higher levels of WFC
(Model 5, negative effect of attitude 'pro compatibility'), although there
are no such effects for men.

Investigating Country Differences: Micro and Macro Determinants?

As outlined above, the reasons for cross-country differences in the experience of WFC may also be located at the institutional level. Our initial expectation, however, is that the factors that are important for the

[15] Also elderly care duties are of growing importance in an aging society. Unfortunately, we
cannot control for this with the ISSP. To our knowledge, this aspect has been largely ignored
by empirical research.

[16] The models were also run with an indicator of the time that respondents spend on
household work (in weekly hours). For women but not for men we find the amount of
household work performed to positively correlate with WFC, also once we control for the
number of paid work hours and the level of work stress (not shown).

[17] Comparing absolute income across countries on the basis of ISSP data is not possible
because the respective questions differed greatly. We therefore use a relative measure of the
household income distinguishing the categories: below or equal 80%, 81%–130%, and more
than 130%.

incidence of WFC at the individual level also help to explain country differences. The diverse distribution of the main explanatory variables, such as work hours, work stress, or the presence of children among the workforce is likely to account for most of the observed differences in the level of WFC across countries. Our earlier analysis (Table 5.4) revealed significantly higher levels of WFC for Spanish women and lower levels for Dutch women. The comparatively low levels of WFC among women in the Netherlands are due to their high propensity to work part-time. Accordingly, this effect disappears once work hours are controlled for. The high levels of WFC for Spanish women, by contrast, cannot be explained by work- and household-related factors (see Table 5.6, Models 5 and 6).[18] No significant country differences were initially found for men. Once we control for the couples' work and family situation, however, higher levels of WFC among Spanish men (p < 0.01) and to some extent French and Swedish men (p < 0.1) than among their West German counterparts become apparent (Table 5.7, Models 5 and 6). The different distributions of work and family characteristics across countries can thus only partly account for country differences in the average level of WFC. The distinctiveness of Spain, France, and Sweden remains. The question, therefore, is whether institutional differences may add to the explanation of different WFC incidence rates across countries.

We investigate whether *state efforts to facilitate the combination of work and family* life and higher levels of (individual) *time autonomy* can help to prevent WFC (see section 'The Potential Impact of Institutional Structure'). To place our results about nationally measured macro indicators on a more solid empirical base, we enlarge the sample to include Austria, Denmark, Finland, Portugal, the Flemish part of Belgium[19], and Norway. As to reconciliation policies, Mandel and Semyonov (2006) have proposed an index measure of the amount of state intervention for the reconciliation of work and family duties (*Welfare State Intervention Index*, in short: WSII). The index is based on three aspects related to female labour market participation: the length of paid maternity leave, the amount of public childcare, and the size of the public sector. The WSII is in line with Esping-Andersen's welfare state typology in that it allocates high values to social-democratic regimes and the comparatively lowest values to liberal ones. For a measure of time autonomy (with the data at hand, its effect cannot

[18] Also the high amount of time that Spanish women tend to spend on household work (see Table 5.2) cannot explain the high level of WFC found in this country.
[19] For some reason, the ISSP only covers the Flemish part of Belgium.

be tested at the individual level) we draw on the Third European Working Conditions Survey, which asked respondents whether or not they can influence their working hours (Q 26.4). For a measure of average time autonomy in a country, we use the share of employees that answered affirmatively to this question. Both measures were recoded to range from zero to three, the latter indicating strong state intervention and high autonomy, respectively.

As shown in Table 5.8, greater time autonomy indeed appears to be conducive to work–family life balance, especially among women (Model 1). This is in line with the literature and suggests that having discretion over one's work schedules mitigates the potential negative effect of increased work demands on the quality of family life (Staines and Pleck 1986; Christensen and Staines 1990; Clark 2001; Tausig and Fenwick 2001; Batt and Valcour 2003). The lack of individual time autonomy in Spain and France thus goes some way in explaining why workers in these countries tend to experience higher levels of WFC than elsewhere. Moreover, a high level of time autonomy appears to mediate the effect of long working hours for women: long hours have a less negative effect on work–life balance when women enjoy discretion in setting their work schedules (Model 2).

More developed reconciliation policies (WSII), by contrast, seem to come along with greater rather than lower levels of WFC for both women and men, regardless of job and family characteristics (Model 1). Thus, while state intervention helps to augment women's labour supply, and in this sense can be argued to facilitate the reconciliation of employment with motherhood, it does not seem to help preventing WFC among those in paid work.[20] Moreover, contrary to what one might expect, a high level of state intervention does not mediate the effect of the presence of small children for women (Model 3). Interestingly, however, Model 4 shows that working hours tend to have a weaker effect on women's experience of WFC in countries that score high on the WSII index. As one might expect, this effect becomes somewhat stronger when the analysis is restricted to mothers (not shown).

In sum, we find WFC to be lower when employees enjoy higher levels of time autonomy but to be more commonly experienced where the state actively encourages maternal employment through the provision

[20] Especially the coverage of childcare facilities for small children is often thought to help parents with combining their work and family duties. However, we find that higher coverage for small children is associated with higher WFC, and so are generous parental leave systems (not shown).

Table 5.8. WFC, probit models with selection correction

	Male				Female			
	Model 1	Model 2	Model 3	Model 4	Model 1	Model 2	Model 3	Model 4
Work stress	0.23***	0.23***	0.25***	0.25***	0.25***	0.23***	0.24***	0.24***
Work hrs[a]	0.11***	0.01	0.10***	0.03	0.19***	0.39***	0.20***	0.31***
Work hrs spouse[a]	-0.08***	-0.06***	-0.08***	-0.09***	-0.02	-0.03	-0.01	-0.01
Small child	0.10	0.13	0.19	0.12	0.11	0.17*	0.10	0.07
Older child	0.09	0.08	0.31**	0.06	0.02	0.06	0.00	0.01
Low household income	0.08	0.07	0.08	0.08	0.41*	0.38*	0.36*	0.36*
High household income	0.05	0.02	0.03	0.04	0.11	0.08	0.06	0.05
Time autonomy (TA)	-0.09*	-0.11			-0.22***	0.23		
TA × work hrs		0.02				-0.10*		
WSII	0.17***		0.22***	-0.14	0.17***		0.07	0.46**
WSII × work hrs			-0.07	0.06°				-0.11**
WSII × small child			-0.21**				-0.03	
WSII × older child							0.01	
_cons	-3.05***	-2.83**	-3.38***	-2.86***	-3.28***	-3.83***	-3.52***	-3.92***
N	2,562	2,672	2,865	2,865	2,697	2,835	2,975	2,975

Notes: Sample: Cohabiting couples aged 20–60. Selection equation not reported. Country coverage: UK, NL, SE, FR, ES, DE, NO, PT, AT, NO, SF, and BE (FL). [a] Work hours are divided by ten. *** p < 0.001; ** p < 0.01; * p < 0.05; ° p < 0.1.

of childcare facilities, generous parental leave schemes and employment opportunities in the public sector. However, caution is warranted when interpreting these results as a high level of state intervention in support of maternal employment, as measured by the WSII index, comes along with other correlated aspects that may be the real triggers of observed effects.[21]

Nevertheless, and most interesting for our concerns, the importance of working hours (as the crucial factor leading to WFC) appears to be moderated by the institutional context, at least for women. Where individual time autonomy is higher, and where the state actively intervenes with reconciliation policies, longer working hours are less of a problem in the aim to achieve a successful balance between work and family responsibilities.

Change over Historical Time

The final part of our analysis investigates principal trends over time. Drawing on the diverse arguments about the factors affecting WFC, there are a number of competing hypotheses about the trends over time. One expectation is that the level of WFC has risen since the mid-1990s because the demands of work have increased: working hours are increasingly anti-social, the predictability and security of hours is declining, and the pace and intensity of work is increasing. However, the empirical evidence is mixed. For instance, while there is research emphasizing developments towards an increase in work intensity and work-related stress (e.g. Green and McIntosh 2001), a recent study suggests that in the second part of the 1990s work pressure has, rather than increased, actually remained stable in the EU (Gallie 2005). If this is the case, we would not necessarily expect WFC to have increased owing to heightened work demands. Furthermore, WFC may have risen because of women's increased participation in employment resulting in a rising number of dual-earner households and hence increasing pressure between the demands of paid work and family life. However, recent efforts to implement more family-friendly policies in countries such as Britain and the Netherlands might have helped to alleviate combination pressure and hence counteracted potential negative effects. Declining incidence rates of WFC may also be expected in France (introduction of the 35-hours week) and in Britain where working hours

---

[21] For instance, high levels of WSII are observed in countries, where we find high female employment rates and large female-dominated public sectors.

Table 5.9. Weekly work hours and odds of having a work stress, change between 1996 and 2001

	Weekly work hours (a)		Work stress (b)			
	Male 2001 vs. 1996	Female 2001 vs. 1996	Male		Female	
			2001 vs. 1996	N	2001 vs. 1996	N
UK	98	102	−1.07***	406	−0.41	362
Germany (W)	100	95	**0.15**	433	−0.20	302
Germany (E)	99	99	**−0.52****	380	−0.37	310
France	96	97	0.04	545	0.05	406
Spain	100	99	0.10	393	−0.26	213
Sweden	99	102	−0.34	504	0.19	452
Netherlands	97	98	**−0.73*****	410	0.29	354

Notes: Respondents were asked how often they found their work stressful: always, often, sometimes, hardly ever, or never. Control for age, presence of partner, presence of child aged <5, age at which finished education, and employment status (employee vs. self-employed). *** $p < 0.001$; ** $p < 0.01$.

Sources: (a) LFS (1996, 2001), base = 1996 (set as 100); (b) Eurobarometar 44.3 and 56.1.

have decreased for male workers following the implementation of the EU Working Time Directive in 1998 (see Table 5.9). Finally, although the secular increase in non-standard employment may have contributed to increased levels of insecurity, there are also arguments that increased flexibility and the rise in part-time work may indeed be of advantage with respect to work–family compatibility.

For the empirical assessment of the trend in WFC over time, we use two Eurobarometer surveys from the years 1996 and 2001. WFC is measured as a dummy variable, created from two questions in the survey. It indicates whether or not respondents *often feel too tired after work to enjoy the things they would like to do at home and also often find that their job prevents them from giving the time they want to their partner or family* (for details see section 'Data and Methods'). Although this measure of WFC produces somewhat higher incidence rates than the ISSP measure, it yields a similar picture of country differences. When compared to West Germany, WFC is less common among Dutch workers, while Spanish and French workers, East German men and Swedish women are more at risk of experiencing WFC (see Table 5.10).

Using the pooled data from the EB 44.3 and EB 56.1, we assess whether there were significant changes in the experience of WFC between 1996 and 2001. Controlling for age, cohabitation status, the presence of a child aged below five, workers' skill level (occupational status), and employment status (self- or dependently employed), we find (see Table 5.10) that rather than an increase in WFC there has been a relatively stable pattern

Table 5.10. Logistic regression analysis, change in the incidence of WFC between 2001 and 1996

	Male workers				Female workers			
	1996–2001 high WFC (a)		Trend		1996–2001 high WFC (a)		Trend	
	%	sig.	Standard controls (b)	Plus control for work hours (c)	%	sig.	Standard controls (b)	Plus control for work hours (c)
Germany (W)	21	ref	n.s.	n.s.	20	ref	n.s.	n.s.
Netherlands	15	*	n.s.	n.s.	11	***	n.s.	n.s.
Germany (E)	29	*	n.s.	n.s.	23		n.s.	n.s.
UK	27		–	–	23		n.s.	n.s.
Spain	29	**	n.s.	n.s.	28	*	–	–
France	32	***	-	n.s.	32	***	n.s.	–
Sweden	24		n.s.	n.s.	28	**	n.s.	n.s.

Notes: Sample—employees and self-employed aged 20–60. (a) Incidence of WFC calculated from pooled data for 1996 and 2001 (% experiencing high levels of WFC). Differences between countries in the incidence of high WFC with reference to West Germany (baseline): *** p < 0.001; ** p < 0.01; * p < 0.05. (b) Analysis of trend with logistic regression analysis, dependent variable is a dummy indicating the presence of a high level of WFC. Controls for age, presence of partner, presence of a child aged below 5, sector of activity (public or private), occupation (*unskilled:* plant and machine operators and elementary occupations; *medium-high skilled:* service workers, craft and related trades workers; *high-skilled:* managers and professionals), and employment status (employee vs. self-employed): – decline at p < 0.01; -decline at p < 0.05; n.s. not significant, i.e. no change. (c) Additional control for weekly work hours: - decline at p < 0.05; n.s. not significant, i.e. no change.

Source: Pooled data from Eurobarometer Surveys EB 44.3 and EB 56.1.

for most countries between 1996 and 2001 and even a decline in some countries (France, Britain for men, and Spain for women). There is no indication of an increase in the incidence of WFC in any of the countries considered. The decline in terms of WFC for French men is rendered insignificant once we control for weekly hours of paid work, while for their British counterparts this is not the case. This suggests that in France the reduction in average work hours in the period between 1996 and 2001 was the major reason for the alleviation of WFC among men over the period. In Britain, the reasons were more diverse and possibly included a decline in work stress over the late 1990s (see Table 5.9). Among women, WFC has declined in Spain and France. In France, however, this is only the case when we control for weekly work hours, which have slightly decreased (see Table 5.9).

In a next step, we investigate whether there have been *trends of polarization* in the experience of WFC during the late 1990s. The question is whether WFC has declined for some segments of the labour force, while for others it has remained stable or increased. For this purpose, we run logistic regression analyses based on pooled data for 1996 and 2001. In more detail, we test for divergence in the experience of WFC across occupational lines, between the public and private sector,[22] between the self-employed and the dependently employed, between part- and full-time workers, and finally, between workers with children aged below five and their counterparts with no or older children.[23] In all models, we control for age, the presence of a partner and the country. We run separate models for women (Table 5.11*a*) and men (Table 5.11*b*).

Due to sample size restrictions the analysis cannot be performed on a single country basis. Instead, it is carried out once for the EU-15 plus Norway, and then for five country clusters, which more or less align with welfare state typologies commonly found in the literature (Esping-Andersen 1990; Lewis 1992; Gornick, Meyers, and Ross 1997). We distinguish between the Nordic countries (Sweden, Denmark, and Finland representing the social democratic welfare states that are especially supportive of maternal employment), Southern Europe (Spain, Italy, Greece, and Portugal representing the familistic regime), Anglo-Saxon countries (Great Britain and Ireland representing the liberal welfare state), Continental European countries with little state support of maternal

---

[22] The data at hand do not allow testing for differences across industries.
[23] We enter a term that captures the overall change effect (dummy for the year 2001) and a set of interaction terms between the year 2001 and the mentioned covariates.

Table 5.11a. Regression test of polarization in WFC across the workforce, women

Women	EU-15 plus Norway	Nordic countries (a)	Southern Europe (b)	France and Belgium	Continental Europe (c)	UK and Ireland
Year 2001	**-0.78*****	**-1.05****	-0.66	**-0.97***	**-1.03***	-0.41
Child < age 5	0.25°	0.23	0.31	0.13	0.33	0.17
ISCO 1–3 (high skill)	ref	ref	ref	ref	ref	ref
ISCO 4 (clerks)	**-0.50*****	-0.27	-0.33	-0.22	**-0.98****	-0.64
ISCO 5 and 7 (medium-low)	-0.01	-0.07	0.57°	-0.04	0.00	-0.82
ISCO 8 and 9 (low skill)	0.12	0.24	**0.94***	0.14	-0.14	**-0.83***
Temporary contract	-0.25	-0.42	-0.67°	0.10	0.26	0.16
Public	**-0.23***	-0.28	-0.49°	-0.49°	0.07	0.10
Self-employed	0.06	-0.25	0.06	0.32	-0.26	-0.58
Part-time worker	**-1.42*****	**0.76***	**-1.46*****	**-1.59*****	**-1.64*****	**-1.45*****
Year 2001*child < age 5	0.15	0.28	0.28	0.06	0.50	-0.17
Year 2001*ISCO 1–3	ref	ref	ref	ref	ref	ref
Year 2001*ISCO 4	0.24	0.07	0.18	0.26	0.73	-0.60
Year 2001*ISCO 5 and 7	-0.04	0.02	-0.50	0.34	-0.23	0.36
Year 2001*ISCO 8 and 9	-0.30	-0.60	**-1.35***	-0.15	0.74	-0.32
Year 2001*temporary	0.39	0.45	0.95°	0.50	-0.78	—
Year 2001*public	**0.38***	**0.85*****	-0.06	**0.84***	0.09	0.28
Year 2001*self-employed	0.16	1.04°	-0.05	-0.27	—	0.97
Year 2001*part-time	**0.55****	0.40	**0.93***	0.84	0.56	0.42
R²	0.11	0.06	0.13	0.14	0.15	0.17
N	4,435	1,133	821	622	844	604

Table 5.11b. Regression test of polarization in WFC across the workforce, men

Men	EU-15 plus Norway	Nordic countries (a)	Southern Europe (b)	France and Belgium	Continental Europe (c)	UK and Ireland
Year 2001	-0.34*	-0.33	-0.28	-0.08	-0.88**	-0.92*
Child < age 5	0.31**	0.30	0.22	0.93***	-0.24	0.46°
ISCO 1–3 (high skill)	ref	ref	ref	ref	ref	ref
ISCO 4 (clerks)	-0.32*	-0.32	-0.16	0.00	-0.77**	—
ISCO 5 and 7 (medium-low)	-0.15	-0.38	-0.45°	0.26	0.00	-0.09
ISCO 8 and 9 (low skill)	-0.02	0.05	-0.21	0.29	-0.06	-0.35
Temporary contract	-0.15	-1.25**	-0.09	-0.32	0.57	-0.21
Public	-0.21*	-0.02	-0.62**	-0.39	-0.12	-0.45
Self-employed	0.43***	0.64*	0.39°	0.82*	0.11	-0.36
Part-time worker	-0.14	0.09	0.33	-0.30	—	-0.36
Year 2001*child < age 5	-0.13	-0.22	0.17	-0.22	0.06	
Year 2001*ISCO 1–3	ref	ref	ref	ref	ref	ref
Year 2001*ISCO 4	0.14	0.52	-0.80°	0.10	1.24*	0.30
Year 2001*ISCO 5 and 7	0.06	0.16	0.19	-0.42	0.44	1.03*
Year 2001*ISCO 8 and 9	-0.04	-0.04	-0.10	-0.72	-0.27	
Year 2001*temporary	0.06	0.20	0.45	0.52	—	
Year 2001*public	-0.06	0.39	0.02	0.13	0.05	-0.16
Year 2001*self-employed	-0.25	-0.17	-0.20	-1.24*	0.64	-0.46
Year 2001*part-time	-0.27	—	-0.17	—	—	-0.41
R^2	0.07	0.07	0.11	0.12	0.09	0.10
N	5,602	1,229	1,251	779	1,078	737

Notes: Sample—employees and self-employed aged 20 to 60. *** $p < 0.001$; ** $p < 0.01$; * $p < 0.05$; ° $p < 0.1$. (a) includes Sweden, Finland, and Denmark; (b) includes Spain, Italy, Greece, and Portugal; (c) includes West Germany, Austria, and the Netherlands. In all models, we controlled for age, presence of partner, and country of residence.

Source: Pooled data from EB 44.3 and EB 56.1.

employment (Germany, Austria, and the Netherlands), and finally, the Francophone countries (France and Belgium) with stronger welfare state intervention in support of maternal employment than typically found in Continental Europe.

First, the aim is to determine whether it is those in higher or those in lower occupational classes who have experienced a decline in the incidence of WFC. Given that WFC does not relate in linear way to occupational level, we carry out a test of polarization trends across the workforce by comparing the experience of four occupational groups.[24] As can be seen from Table 5.11a, the way WFC is stratified across occupational groups differs between country clusters. For instance, while in Southern Europe women's risk of experiencing WFC tends to decrease with occupational attainment, the converse is the case in the liberal countries. In Continental Europe, the incidence of WFC tends to be lowest among women in clerical occupations. These differences all remain significant when we additionally control for weekly hours of paid work (not shown). In terms of trends over time, the analysis shows that, in Southern Europe, WFC declined more markedly among workers in low-skill occupations (ISCO 8 and 9) than among those in professional or managerial occupations (ISCO 1–3). For men, two significant trend effects emerged (see Table 5.11b). First, in Continental Europe, workers in clerical occupations tend to be least at risk of experiencing WFC. However, this advantage is mainly due to lower weekly hours of work and seems to have disappeared by 2001. Second, in the liberal countries, WFC appears to have declined less strongly among those in low-skilled occupations than among those in professional and managerial occupations.

Workers employed in the *public sector* tend to be less at risk of experiencing WFC than their counterparts employed in the private sector, especially among Southern European men for whom this effect remains highly significant even when we control for weekly hours of paid work (result not shown). The advantage of public sector employees may stem from the greater scope for the regulation of working conditions in public employment and the lower exposure to market pressure. In terms of polarization trends over the late 1990s, we find that women's experience of WFC has declined faster in the private than in the public sector. However,

---

[24] We distinguish between managerial and professional occupations (ISCO 1–3), clerical workers (ISCO 4), service and sales, craft and trades related workers (ISCO 5 and 7) and low status occupations (ISCO 8 and 9). We omit ISCO 6 (skilled agricultural and fishery workers).

as revealed in Table 5.11a, this is mainly the case in the Nordic countries, France and Belgium, where WFC remained stable in the public but significantly decreased in the private sector. Indeed, in the Nordic countries, the strong improvement in the private sector resulted in a higher risk of experiencing WFC in the public than in the private sector by 2001[25], even when controlling for work hours and occupational status (not shown).

If it is correct that persons on *temporary contracts* have less control over their working conditions and work schedules than more securely employed workers (Paoli and Merllié 2001), we would expect the incidence of WFC to be higher among temporary workers than among their counterparts with contracts of unlimited duration. Contrary to this expectation, however, we find no differences according to type of contract.[26] But there are regional differences with Nordic men on temporary contracts seemingly less at risk of experiencing WFC than their permanently employed counterparts (a finding that remains even when controlling for weekly hours of work, results not shown). In terms of polarization trends, there is some evidence that, among Southern European women, there was a reversing trend from a more favourable situation among temporary workers in 1996 to a growing disadvantage in WFC.

As we already know from the previous analysis, female *part-time* workers tend to be less at risk of experiencing WFC than their counterparts in full-time employment.[27] This effect is least pronounced in the Nordic countries, where female part-timers tend to put in comparatively long hours (Table 5.11a). A separate analysis showed that, interestingly, female part-timers tend to experience lower levels of WFC even when we control for working hours (not shown). This suggests that apart from the obvious difference in working hours part-time workers differ in important ways from their full-time employed counterparts (e.g. lower work demands or career aspirations and more time flexibility among female part-timers even in the same occupation). Among male part-timers, by contrast, we find higher levels of WFC when compared to full-timers once controlled for work hours

[25] In Sweden, Finland, and Denmark taken together, the share of women with a high level of WFC amounted to 23% in the public sector both in 1996 and 2001. In the private sector, this share declined from 30% to 17%.

[26] We compared those in permanent jobs (either self-employed or dependently employed) with temporary workers (employees either in seasonal, temporary or casual jobs, or under contract for a fixed time period).

[27] Part-time work was defined as working less than 30 hours per week.

(not shown). In terms of polarization trends, it appears that between 1996 and 2001 the situation improved more strongly for female full-timers than for their counterparts in part-time work, especially in Southern Europe.

Among men, but not among women, *self-employment* tends to correlate with higher levels of WFC in the Nordic countries, France, and Belgium (see Table 5.11*b*). This effect is mainly driven by differences in average working hours between the self-employed and their dependently employed counterparts and for this reason is rendered insignificant once working hours are controlled for (not shown). In terms of changes over time, we find that in France and Belgium the situation improved more strongly for self-employed men than for dependent employees, irrespective of whether or not we control for work hours.

Finally, we look at trends in the experience of WFC comparing workers with a child aged below five and their counterparts without small children. In the EU-15 plus Norway, we find the presence of children to be associated with higher levels of WFC, both among women and men. However, contrary to what might be expected given the focus of policy in many countries to improve the combinability of paid work with caring responsibilities, the decline in WFC over the late 1990s in some of the countries under consideration (i.e. among French workers, Spanish women, and British men), does not seem to have mainly occurred among parents.

In sum, while among Southern European women, unskilled workers have experienced the most pronounced decline in WFC, among men from the Anglo-Saxon countries, WFC appears to have more strongly declined among those in professional and managerial occupations than among low-skilled workers. The Nordic countries, which stand out as those with the largest public sector in which women are over-represented, display an interesting trend: while in the mid-1990s, WFC incidence rates were lower in the public than in the private sector, by 2001 public sector employees seemed to encounter more difficulties in combining their work and family roles. Notably, this reversing trend stems from the improved situation among private sector employees and is thus not the effect of public sector reforms aimed at making public services more efficient. In Southern Europe, the initially more favourable situation of women on temporary contracts has diminished during the 1990s. Finally, comparing parents and childless workers has revealed no significant differences in *trends* in WFC, suggesting that improvements in the policy context for working parents are unlikely to be among the factors that contributed to a decline in WFC.

Summary and Conclusions

Reconciliation of work and family life is an essential part of the European Employment Strategy and the need to improve the 'work–life balance' has been explicitly promoted as an objective of the EU Social Policy Agenda. Member states are called upon to implement 'family-friendly' policies. The type of arrangements that are advocated to improve work–family compatibility—which in terms of policy goals essentially means to increase maternal employment rates while promoting fertility—include adequate childcare services, parental and other family leave schemes and a variety of measures to enable people to adjust their working hours (e.g. opportunities for part-time work and in particular the right for workers to request an adjustment between full-time and part-time hours in their existing job, flexi-time and other forms of 'time accounts'). The strong emphasis by the EU on policies to support work–life balance has given a major impetus to the introduction of such measures across Europe. However, marked national differences still exist in the extent that reconciliation policies help women to be continuously employed over the life course. The Nordic countries are most successful in this regard: they have the most comprehensive public childcare services and statutory family leave provisions that enable employment to be more readily combined with parenthood than in other countries. Both female employment and fertility rates are at a comparatively high level. At the other extreme, there are the Mediterranean countries with very low female employment rates and one of the lowest fertility rates in Europe.

Female employment and fertility rates tell only part of the story, however. An important component of a successful combination of work and family life is employees' evaluation of the compatibility of the two roles and the amount of conflict that may arise between the demands of the two spheres. This chapter has sought to investigate the trends and determinants of this in six European countries, namely Germany, the Netherlands, Sweden, France, Spain, and Great Britain.

Overall, work–family conflict (WFC) showed to be a rather stable phenomenon, although with some cases of decline in the later 1990s. Our results confirmed the major importance of the micro level determinants for the incidence of WFC in all of the European countries investigated. Assessing institutional effects on individual and overall levels of WFC is more complex, in part because of the high inter-correlation of different institutional factors. Since WFC is a subjective measure, it is also likely to be subject to socially and culturally shaped aspirations and expectations with regard to both work and family life.

Long working hours and a high level of work stress are core risk factors for the onset of WFC, for both women and men. It is largely these two factors that shape the underlying mechanisms generating divergent experiences of WFC across the labour force. They account for the findings that women in the highest status occupations tend to report the highest levels of WFC, while men tend to report higher levels of WFC when they have supervisory functions and lower levels of conflict when they are public rather than private sector employees. Apart from individuals' work situation, the level of WFC depends also on the household context. Women turned out to be least affected by WFC when they work part-time while their partner works moderate full-time hours. Men, by contrast, are most at risk of experiencing WFC when their partners are out of the labour force, as they need to compensate for their partners' economic inactivity by working particularly long hours. The huge impact of working hours on the compatibility of work and family underlines the importance of EU-wide regulations to limit working hours. Another key factor in the incidence of WFC is the presence of small children, especially among women. There is also some evidence for the importance of the gender division of unpaid labour in couple households suggesting that work–family balance may be enhanced by the promotion of a more equal sharing of family responsibilities between women and men. A higher household income and thus an increased ability of the household to buy services from the market is of help for women. Finally, the correlation between the level of WFC and beliefs in mothers' role and responsibility as primary care-givers reveals the role played by normative attitudes in shaping women's experience of the compatibility of work and family responsibilities.

We found considerable variation in the incidence of WFC across countries. Cross-country differences for women are chiefly due to differences in the individual work situations. The highest levels were found among

Spanish and Swedish women, whereas it was relatively low among Dutch women. The high level among Swedish women was due to their higher labour market participation (a sample selection effect), while the lower level in the Netherlands was primarily caused by shorter working hours. Spain, however, emerged as an interesting case, where the high levels of WFC cannot be adequately explained by the distribution of individual-level characteristics such as working hours or parental status among the female workforce. Among men, we initially found no significant country differences. Once account was taken of work and family characteristics, however, we find higher levels of WFC among Spanish, French, and Swedish men. Hence, the question emerged of whether institutional differences add something to the explanation of the different incidence rates across countries.

We investigated the effects of two institutional aspects: the amount of state intervention in terms of family policies and childcare provisions, and the overall level of working-time autonomy in the single countries. The findings suggest that the amount of state intervention to ease reconciliation, though important for the level of female labour market participation, does not help working parents to combine their work and family lives without conflict. On the contrary, 'family-friendly' policies seem to come along with heightened levels of WFC. Although the analyses controlled for individuals' employment situation, we cannot exclude the possibility that this is due to differences in work content or career involvement: it may be that pressures of work are less likely to interfere with family life in countries that do not support women's continuous involvement in full-time career jobs.

Welfare policy measures were found to have an effect for the consequences of working time: the higher the levels of welfare state intervention, the less the amount of WFC among individuals working long hours. This suggests that reconciliation policies could make a difference for those individuals deeply engaged in work commitments. The level of autonomy enjoyed by employees in setting work hours was also found to be important in reducing WFC. In countries with low levels of individual time autonomy, WFC tends to be more common. Moreover, time autonomy seems to mitigate the effects of long working hours for women.

Yet, we have to be cautious in interpreting specific institutional effects. Not only are they based on a small sample of countries but there is a very high correlation between different institutional policies. However, the results do point to the general conclusion that, where female participation rates are high, there tend to be institutional structures that mitigate the effect of female full-time work on work–family balance. A lack of individual time autonomy may also be an important factor in the explanation of why Spanish workers tend to have more problems with combining the demands of work with their family responsibilities than their counterparts in other European countries.

6

Job Insecurity

Serge Paugam and Ying Zhou

Introduction

The 1980s and 1990s saw a marked increase in the number of employees who perceived their employment as insecure (OECD 1997*b*). For many analysts this was seen as an inherent structural trend in the development of advanced capitalist economies. It reflected both the accelerating rate of change that accompanied the spread of new computer technologies and the growing need for flexibility in an increasingly volatile international economy. By the end of the 1990s the implications of job insecurity for employee well-being became a central theme of both public debate and empirical research.

A wide range of studies have highlighted the very negative consequences of job insecurity for employees' physical and mental well-being. The picture they provide is very similar to that of earlier research on unemployment. As employment provides individuals with income, social contact, opportunities for self-actualization and a more structured life, and these have been shown to be strongly related to psychological well-being (Warr 1987), it is predictable that a threat of losing work may lead to psychological distress among employees. Stress theorists also emphasize that the feelings of uncertainty and ambiguity which result from a lack of control over potentially stressful events have a detrimental impact on individuals' well-being (Lazarus and Folkman 1984). Physical health complaints, mental distress and work–life balance problems tend to increase with the level of insecurity experienced on the job (Jick 1985; Ashford, Lee, and Bobko 1989; Hartley et al. 1991; Barling and Kelloway 1996). Indeed, research has shown that a perceived threat concerning the continued existence of employment can inflict as much stress upon individuals as job loss itself (Latack and Dozier 1986; Dekker and Schaufeli 1995).

Sociological analysis has also underlined the importance of job security for wider social integration. As Durkheim argued (Durkheim 1930), in modern societies with a strongly developed division of labour, the integration of individuals in the social system to a great extent takes place through the world of work. Loss of work comes then with the menace of the rupture of key social ties, social marginalization, and potential social exclusion.

However, the risk that job loss will lead to social marginalization is likely to depend crucially on how job insecurity relates to other job characteristics. Developing an argument already to some degree present in Durkheim's analyses, Paugam (2000) stressed the importance of distinguishing the employment relationship from the work relationship as two separate dimensions of a job. It is the way these interrelate that is crucial for employee's effective risks with respect to social integration. Where an unfavourable employment relationship—characterized by sharp job insecurity—is reinforced by a poor work relationship—in which job tasks are routine and do not provide opportunities for skill development—then the risks of job loss resulting in social marginalization are much greater than where insecurity is associated with high quality work tasks which provide the employee with updated skills that facilitate job change.

The assumption has tended to be that these two dimensions of jobs are very closely related. The pattern is thought to be one of cumulative advantage or cumulative disadvantage in job rewards, with job insecurity inextricably associated with poor quality job tasks. Labour market segmentation theory—which did much to give a central place to the issue of job insecurity in discussions of the quality of work—emphasized the polarized nature of the job structure between a primary sector of relatively skilled, well-protected 'core' workforce who hold regular work contracts and a secondary sector composed of low-skill, less protected employees who hold 'non-standard' or 'atypical' forms of work contracts. But an examination of the issue of whether there has been polarization between categories of employees, that has formed a core theme of the book, requires empirical examination of how far disadvantages in work and employment conditions map on to each other and of whether the pattern varies between different sectors of the workforce.

If job insecurity is generally associated with poor job task quality, is the strength of the association mediated by the institutional environment of different societies? The main line of societal differentiation that would be expected given the institutional regime types discussed in the introduction to the book is that 'inclusive' employment systems could be expected to lead to a much weaker relationship between job insecurity and poor quality job tasks. Hence the Nordic societies should stand out rather clearly from the others. In part this would reflect the greater attention to quality of work–life issues for those in less skilled work. But this could be reinforced by the fact that the generous provision of parental leave may increase the number of temporary positions among higher skilled employees, given high demands for cover for people on leave. Production regime theory, which emphasizes primarily the influence of skill formation systems, would lead us to expect that the main line of difference should be between the coordinated market economies (CMEs) and the liberal market economies (LMEs). In countries that have focused on the development of specific skills, one would expect employers to be concerned to retain their employees in order to be able to recoup their training investment. If this is the case, Germany could be expected to be broadly similar in pattern to the Nordic societies and there should be notable differences between the experiences of men and women (since it has been argued that women in these countries are less likely to train in specific skills).

In addressing these issues, the chapter examines in turn the following:

1. Is job security broadly similar across different categories of the workforce or is there evidence of polarization between a highly protected core and peripheral workers (whether defined in terms of low skill, sex, consumer services, part-time work, or temporary work)?

2. Is the general pattern one of a cumulative disadvantage, in which those in insecure jobs are also in poor jobs in terms of other criteria, or are there quite distinct dimensions of job quality with insecurity associated with jobs of varying quality on other dimensions?

3. Do countries differ in the extent to which job insecurity is associated with poor job quality on other dimensions? If so, does this correspond with what might be expected from the regime typologies? Most particularly, are the Nordic countries particularly distinctive in the extent to which job insecurity is dissociated from job quality in general or is there evidence of a broadly similar pattern between countries that have been classified as coordinated market economies?

Measures and Data

There has been little consensus about the best way of measuring job insecurity. The OECD (OECD 1997) has placed considerable emphasis on job tenure as a measure and the analysis of changes in job tenure has tended to suggest that there has been little change over time within countries. However, there are considerable differences in levels between countries, with particularly short tenure in the United Kingdom, followed by Denmark, the Netherlands, and Ireland and with the longest tenure being in the Southern European countries (with the exception of Spain) and in Belgium and Sweden (Auer and Cazes 2003). The main problem with relying on tenure as an indicator of job security is that it fails to distinguish whether job quits are voluntary or coerced. Paradoxically, job security may appear to be increasing during periods of high unemployment because fewer people wish to take the risk of leaving their employer, while it may appear to decrease when the labour market recovers as people feel more confident of their chances in the labour market. Finally, as the OECD noted there is a disturbing discrepancy between trends in insecurity measured by tenure rates and trends measured through employees' own assessment of their security.

Much of the more recent concern with job insecurity has focused on the growth of temporary work. The more apocalyptic scenarios of labour market change have envisaged a drastic shift from the model of long-term employment contracts towards a reliance on short-term contracts that leave employees in a permanent state of insecurity. But in practice, the forms of temporary work are quite diverse and their implications for experiences of insecurity are a matter for examination rather than assumption. They may indeed be a mechanism for managing short-term fluctuations in demand, providing jobs with little future. But it may also be the case that employers are increasingly using temporary jobs as entry ports, providing the opportunity to assess the potential of new recruits without risking major dismissal costs. In this form, a significant proportion of temporary workers may be effectively at the beginning of some type of career ladder, and this should reduce the insecurity experienced in such jobs. Further, focusing primarily on short-term contracts leads to the neglect of insecurity in other sectors of the workforce, in the much larger sector of jobs that are often, but rarely accurately, described as 'permanent'. If the extent of use of temporary contracts reflects specific institutional conditions, such as the ease with which labour market regulations allow employers to dismiss their normal employees, then focusing uniquely on

Table 6.1. Trends in unemployment

	1991	1995	2000
Denmark	8.4	7.2	4.7
France	9.5	11.7	9.5
Germany	n.d.	8.2	7.9
Great Britain	8.8	8.7	5.5
Spain	16.4	22.9	14.1
Sweden	3.1	8.8	5.9

Note: Data for unified Germany were not available for 1991.

Source: European Commission (2001).

short-term contracts would provide a distorted picture of the extent of job insecurity in some countries, undermining the comparability of the data.

A third indicator of insecurity could be levels of unemployment. It seems very plausible that the level of unemployment in the labour market will affect people's perceptions of the security of their job, even if they are not directly affected by job loss. Arguably, it is above all the change in unemployment rates across time that will affect people's sense of insecurity. As can be seen in Table 6.1, there were marked differences between our core countries both in overall levels at particular time points and in the trends in the 1990s. Spain experienced a much higher level of unemployment at each time period than the other countries. On the other hand, as with Denmark, Sweden, and Great Britain, it saw a marked decline in unemployment levels in the second half of the 1990s, whereas this was much less evident in France and Germany.

Nonetheless, the assumption that unemployment levels will directly affect perceived insecurity needs to be treated with caution. It assumes a relatively homogeneous labour market, where different categories of employee are equally at risk in times of economic downturn. Clearly, if the labour market has a strong insider–outsider structure, this may not prove to be the case. Insiders will benefit from strong employment protection regulation, while the burden of unemployment may be focused heavily on particular categories of the workforce. Unemployment data is also difficult to relate to detailed information about job tasks, making it difficult to carry out the analysis of cumulative disadvantage which is crucial for the risk of social marginalization.

Given the problems with the measures considered above, we base the analyses in this chapter on a self-report measure of job insecurity. This is available in two EU-15 wide surveys undertaken for the European Commission by DG Employment in 1996 and 2001 respectively. The surveys

Table 6.2. Country difference in job security

	1996	2001	1996/2001 combined
Great Britain	1.90	1.80	1.85
France	1.57	1.62	1.59
Germany	1.71	1.77	1.74
Sweden	1.77	1.83	1.80
Denmark	2.35	2.30	2.32
Spain	1.56	1.63	1.59

included common variables in all of the countries, and a significant proportion were included at both points in time, facilitating the analysis of the job characteristics of the insecure.

In each country, representative national surveys were carried out in which households were selected through a random walk method and face-to-face interviews were conducted in people's homes. Identical questionnaires were used in each country, with translations checked through back-translation. The chapter is based primarily on the samples of employees in Denmark, France, Germany, Great Britain, and Sweden—taken as 'critical cases' of the key institutional differences that we are examining. However, some of the arguments are further tested by grouping a wider range of countries into different types of regime. The analysis uses the pooled sample for the two years, giving unweighted sample numbers of 1,025 for Denmark, 996 for France, 1,734 for Germany, 883 for Great Britain, 668 for Spain, and 1,005 for Sweden.[1]

Country Differences and Trends in Job Security

We start by examining the basic trends in job security and the differences between countries. The measure of job security is a question that asks individuals how strongly they agree with the statement that 'My job is secure'. Answers were made against a four-point scale that runs from 0 (not at all true) to 3 (very true), with higher values indicating higher levels of job security. It can be seen in Table 6.2 that the average level of job security was very different across countries. In both 1996 and 2001 Danish employees reported the highest level of job security among all workers in the six countries. This is consistent with other data (Auer and

[1] The weights are a version provided by the survey agency INRA, with an adjustment for ISCO occupational class distribution.

Cazes 2003; Madsen 2003) for a wider set of OECD countries. Taking the data of both years combined, the average score of job security is 2.32 in Denmark. It is followed at some distance by Britain (1.85) and Sweden (1.80). By contrast, Spain and France reported the lowest levels of job security (1.59). Examining the trends over time, there appears to be no uniform direction of change: employees' perception of job insecurity declined in Britain and Denmark whilst it increased in France, Germany, Sweden, and Spain from 1996 to 2001. However, a *t*-test showed that none of these changes reached statistical significance.

Is there any evidence that different categories of employees experience different levels of job insecurity on the basis of their labour market positions? If so, how does the extent of stratification differ across countries?

Table 6.3 draws on the pooled data for 1996 and 2001 to compare the means of job security for the categories of employees for which there has been the strongest theoretical expectation of divergence. In particular, the analysis is focused on four potential lines of polarization: sex, skill (higher level managerial and professional employees vs. semi and unskilled elementary workers), industry sector (traditional transformative

Table 6.3. Means of job security by types of employee, 1996 and 2001 combined

	Great Britain	France	Germany	Sweden	Denmark	Spain
All	1.85	1.59	1.74	1.80	2.32	1.59
Occupational class						
Managers and professionals	1.92	1.80	2.17	1.93	2.41	2.09
Elementary	1.53	1.53	1.35	1.82	2.24	1.29
Ratio	1.25	1.18	1.61	1.06	1.08	1.62
Sex						
Male	1.80	1.65	1.78	1.87	2.32	1.65
Female	1.91	1.52	1.70	1.73	2.33	1.48
Ratio	0.94	1.09	1.05	1.08	1.00	1.11
Industry						
Industry	1.88	1.49	1.73	1.91	2.27	1.68
Retail and hotels	1.89	1.29	1.53	1.87	2.32	1.47
Ratio	0.99	1.16	1.13	1.02	0.98	1.14
Contract status 1						
Permanent work	1.92	1.72	1.79	1.87	2.38	1.76
Temporary work	1.15	0.83	1.02	1.02	1.81	1.05
Ratio	1.67	2.07	1.75	1.83	1.31	1.68
Contract status 2						
Full-time work	1.91	1.64	1.75	1.84	2.33	1.61
Part-time work	1.77	1.41	1.75	1.66	2.27	1.55
Ratio	1.08	1.16	1.00	1.11	1.03	1.04

industries vs. routine services), and type of employment contract (regular contracts vs. 'non-standard' contracts).

It can be seen in Table 6.3 that the most salient line of divergence in all six countries is between employees who hold temporary work contracts and those who hold permanent contracts. The situation is particularly striking in France, where the mean score of job security for permanent workers is more than twice that of temporary workers (1.72 for the former and 0.83 for the latter). By contrast, the most egalitarian scenario is found in Denmark, where the mean scores of job security for permanent and temporary workers are 2.38 and 1.81 respectively. Tendencies to polarization can also be seen through ratios of the job security scores between different groups of employees. The third row under 'contract status1' shows that the degree of polarization in job security is the least severe in Denmark while most severe in France. Britain, Spain, Germany, and Sweden emerged in the intermediate position.

Examining the degree of the polarization along the line of skill, Denmark and Sweden emerge as the most egalitarian societies where the ratios of job security score between managerial/professional employees and elementary workers are 1.08 and 1.06. By contrast, low-skilled employees fare much worse in Germany and Spain (with the ratios being 1.61 and 1.62).

Turning to sex and industry sector, Britain and Denmark showed the highest degree of sex and sectoral equality among the six countries. In both countries, there is no evidence that women perceive their jobs as more insecure than men, and the mean scores of job security are very close for employees in routine services and those in the traditional transformative industries (manufacturing, mining, energy, and construction). By contrast, France and Spain emerged as the most unequal societies both in terms of sex and of sectoral differences. Finally, with respect to segmentation by working time, Table 6.3 shows that the relative position of part-time workers is worse than full-time workers in all countries except Germany. The extent of part-time penalty is also relatively small in Denmark and Spain. By contrast, France stood out as the most polarized society as the average level of job security perceived by full-time employees is 1.16 times that of part-time employees.

The general picture revealed by Table 6.3 suggests that there are no systematic regime differences across the overall set of potentially vulnerable employees. In terms of class differences, the most egalitarian scenario is found in Denmark and Sweden, suggesting that inclusive regimes are effective in reducing differences in the security of workers with different levels of skill. But in other respects, there are no clear cut regime differences, and, indeed, Sweden and Denmark would appear to be different in their patterns.

We also examined whether the differences between categories of employee had become sharper or had attenuated over time.[2] While there were differences between countries, these again appeared to have little to do with regime differences. The differential between managers and professionals on the one hand and low-skilled workers on the other grew between 1996 and 2001 in Denmark and France, while differences between workers in manufacturing and services became stronger in Sweden. The relative position of temporary workers had improved over the period in two countries, in Britain on the one hand and in Denmark on the other, and there were no countries in which it had deteriorated. There were two interesting points of commonality between countries: in no case was there evidence of increased polarization over time either between men and women or between full-timers and part-timers.

Job Insecurity and the Quality of Job Tasks

So far our analysis has been focused on the distribution of job insecurity across different categories of employees in different countries. However, as we argued earlier, insecurity is likely to have very different implications for marginalization risks depending on the other characteristics of the employees' job. Those who experience job loss are likely to find it much more difficult to find work again if they have been in jobs that made little demands on their skills and initiative and provided few opportunities for updating their knowledge. How is job insecurity, as a distinct dimension of job quality, related to other job features? Is the general pattern one of a cumulative disadvantage in the sense that insecure jobs are also 'low-quality' jobs as measured against other job quality criteria, or are there distinct dimensions of job quality which are not necessarily correlated with job insecurity?

To answer this question, we take job security as the dependent variable and regress against it a wide range of dimensions of job quality for each of the six countries. In particular, we are concerned to take account of the core dimensions of job quality discussed in other chapters: the

---

[2] The analysis involved OLS regressions, using the pooled data for each country for the two years. The regressions included a year dummy for 2001 and year interaction terms for each of the 'vulnerable employee' categories.

opportunities for skill use and skill development, the degree of initiative the employee can take in decisions about the way the work is done, and the extent of work–family balance. The majority of the independent variables are measured against continuous numerical scales while some are dichotomized into dummy variables (e.g. opportunity to use abilities).

Table 6.4 shows that for most countries, there is indeed a strongly significant association between job security and other dimensions of job quality. Taking the first column for example, in all six countries employees' perception of job security is strongly related to whether the job provides them with opportunities to use their abilities. The association is particularly strong in Germany, whereas in Sweden and Denmark it appears to be the weakest. The only dimension of job quality which did not appear to have a strong association with job security is the level of work pressure, as the coefficient was only statistically significant for Germany. In other countries, there is no evidence that higher work pressure is linked to lower levels of job security as perceived by the employees.

To provide an overall picture that can take into account the full range of job quality measures, a scale was created by giving a score ranging from 1 to 4 to each of the items and then taking the average of the summed scores. Higher values on the summary index indicate higher levels of job quality. It can be seen in the last column of Table 6.4 that the summary index of job quality is significantly and positively associated with employees' perception of job security in all countries. It confirms the hypothesis that job security is an integral element of the overall quality of work life. However, the strength of the link varies widely across countries. The correlation between job quality and job security is the weakest in Denmark and Sweden while strongest in Germany. France, Britain, and Spain came in an intermediate position. It might be argued that the pattern reflects different compositions of the workforce across countries, for instance, with respect to the relative size of different age groups or the balance of men and women in the labour force. However, even after employees' age and sex have been taken into account, the general pattern of country divergence remains broadly similar (Table 6.5). It is notable that, although grouped by the production regime literature as part of a common category (the coordinated production regimes), the patterns for the Nordic countries and Germany are quite distinct; indeed, they are at opposite points of the spectrum.

A second way of examining the degree of divergence between different types of societies is to group the individual countries into different employment-welfare regimes. We assume that integration is partly

Table 6.4. Effects of job quality on job security by country (without controls)

	Use of abilities	Discretion	Pay satisfaction	Learn	Interesting	Skill development	Respondent development	Work pressure	Participation	WFC	Summary index
Great Britain	0.66***	0.67***	0.20***	0.44***	0.60***	0.53***	0.36***	−0.07	0.49***	0.23***	1.72***
France	0.75***	0.43***	0.34***	0.52***	0.69***	0.50***	0.34***	0.03	0.45***	0.11*	1.38***
Germany	1.01***	0.86***	0.39***	0.56***	0.94***	0.47***	0.34***	−0.18**	0.92***	0.36**	2.14***
Sweden	0.32*	0.57***	0.23***	0.25***	0.54***	0.29**	0.18	0.01	0.23***	0.09	1.16***
Spain	0.61***	0.49***	0.39***	0.50***	0.70***	0.35**	0.29*	−0.16	0.32***	0.28***	1.40***
Denmark	0.44**	0.64***	0.11**	0.20**	0.29***	0.25*	0.12	−0.05	0.33***	0.04	0.69***

Notes: *** $p < 0.001$; ** $p < 0.01$; * $p < 0.05$.

Table 6.5. Effects of job quality on job security by country (with controls of sex and age)

	Use of abilities	Discretion	Pay satisfaction	Learn	Interesting	Skill development	Respondent development	Work pressure	Participation	WFC	Summary index
Great Britain	0.71***	0.71***	0.20***	0.43***	0.60***	0.53***	0.35***	-0.06	0.52***	0.23***	1.74***
France	0.71***	0.41***	0.33***	0.52***	0.68***	0.50***	0.32***	-0.01	0.44***	0.15**	1.37***
Germany	0.98***	0.88***	0.39***	0.57***	0.95***	0.47***	0.35***	-0.19***	0.92***	0.36***	2.13***
Sweden	0.20	0.56***	0.21***	0.25***	0.53***	0.29**	0.20*	-0.01	0.22***	-0.14	1.11***
Spain	0.56**	0.46***	0.40***	0.51***	0.70***	0.40**	0.38***	-0.27***	0.29***	0.34***	1.44***
Denmark	0.40**	0.66***	0.10**	0.20**	0.30***	0.30**	0.16	-0.07	0.33***	0.03	0.69***

Notes: *** p < 0.001; ** p < 0.01; * p < 0.05.

affected by forms of employment regulation and partly by the level and form of social protection for the unemployed. Based on the theoretical argument outlined in the introduction, we distinguish between the Nordic 'inclusive' regimes and the liberal 'market' employment regimes. Denmark, Finland, and Sweden are taken as examples of inclusive regimes and the UK and Ireland of 'liberal regimes'. The countries within these groupings also share a broad similarity in their welfare arrangements for the unemployed. However, the third category of 'dualist employment regimes' include countries with rather diverse systems of social protection for the unemployed: some of an employment-centred type and others of a sub-protective type (Gallie and Paugam (eds.) 2000). In the former case unemployment benefit tends to be insurance-based, whereas in the latter protection for the unemployed is primarily left to the family. Hence we distinguish on the one hand a 'Continental' group of dualist countries, with employment-centred welfare systems—the Netherlands, Germany, France, and Belgium—and, on the other hand, a Southern group—Italy, Spain, Greece, and Portugal—which are characterized by sub-protective welfare systems for the unemployed.

Table 6.6 shows that the most egalitarian scenario is found in inclusive regimes. Although in all types of employment regimes job security is significantly linked to other dimensions of job quality, the magnitude of the correlation is the smallest for Nordic countries. This is reflected by both the coefficients of the particular aspects of job quality and that of the summary index. Also consistent with anticipation, liberal economies emerged as the most polarized societies in terms of the cumulative disadvantage resulting from low job security and poor job quality along other dimensions. In other words, employees in liberal regimes who hold insecure jobs are substantially more likely than those in Scandinavian countries to find their jobs unrewarding in other senses as well. Again, the degree of country divergence cannot be accounted for in terms of compositional effects, as the pattern remains unchanged even after controlling for employees' age and sex (Table 6.7).

Patterns of Employment Integration

Having confirmed that job security is associated with many dimensions of job quality, we turn now to consider types of employment integration defined both by employment security and by the quality of job tasks. These 'employment integration types' distinguish between high quality

Table 6.6. Effects of job quality on job security by regime type (without controls)

	Use of abilities	Discretion	Pay satisfaction	Learn	Interesting	Skill development	Respondent development	Work pressure	Participation	WFC	Summary index
Nordic	0.40***	0.63***	0.21***	0.38***	0.52***	0.29***	0.13*	−0.11*	0.31***	−0.17***	1.19***
Continental	0.77***	0.55***	0.36***	0.43***	0.74***	0.40***	0.28***	−0.06	0.55***	−0.40***	1.63***
Liberal	0.79***	0.67***	0.22***	0.58***	0.87***	0.60***	0.43***	0.09	0.44***	−0.07	1.88***
Southern	0.38***	0.55***	0.31***	0.48***	0.66***	0.21***	0.19***	−0.21***	0.29***	−0.46***	1.46***

Notes: ***p < 0.001; **p < 0.01; *p < 0.05.

Table 6.7. Effects of job quality on job security by regime type (with controls of sex and age)

	Use of abilities	Discretion	Pay satisfaction	Learn	Interesting	Skill development	Respondent development	Work pressure	Participation	WFC	Summary index
Nordic	0.32***	0.62***	0.20***	0.37***	0.51***	0.31***	0.15**	−0.12**	0.30***	−0.16**	1.17***
Continental	0.75***	0.55***	0.36***	0.44***	0.74***	0.40***	0.28***	−0.07*	0.55***	−0.41***	1.63***
Liberal	0.81***	0.69***	0.22***	0.58***	0.87***	0.59***	0.43***	0.09	0.46***	−0.07	1.89***
Southern	0.39***	0.53***	0.31***	0.50***	0.67***	0.27***	0.23***	−0.24***	0.28***	−0.47***	1.49***

Notes: *** $p < 0.001$; ** $p < 0.01$; * $p < 0.05$.

Table 6.8. Percentage of employees in job quality/job security categories by country, *1996 and 2001 combined

	HS	HI	LS	LI	Total	N
Denmark	59.4	9.4	25.3	5.9	100	1,005
Sweden	37.1	16.2	25.7	21.0	100	918
Britain	33.6	8.5	34.2	23.7	100	962
France	33.4	12.7	23.1	30.9	100	828
Germany	36.5	7.6	23.5	32.3	100	1,528
Spain	28.4	14.4	24.2	33.0	100	645
EU-15 countries	38.4	10.0	28.2	23.4	100	11,914

Notes: HS— high quality secure; HI—high quality insecure; LS—low quality secure; and LI—low quality insecure.

secure (HS) integration, high quality insecure (HI), low quality secure (LS), and low quality insecure (LI) forms of integration.[3]

Among the four types, HS integration represents the most favourable condition for employees. It both provides individuals with opportunities for self-development and offers sufficient stability to protect them from sudden life disruptions. At the opposite end of the spectrum lies LI integration, which is assumed to be the least desirable type of employment, with a high risk of cumulative disadvantage and labour market marginalization. In between the 'high quality secure' and 'low quality insecure' categories are work situations characterized either by high job task quality and low security or by poor job task quality and high security.

To construct the different types, we divided the summary index of job quality into two categories according to respondents' scores on the index. The 50 per cent of individuals (for all EU-15 countries combined) with higher scores on the index are defined as workers who hold high quality jobs, and the 50 per cent with lower scores are defined as holders of low quality jobs. Similarly, the job security variable was divided into two categories with about the same number of people in each group (defined as workers who feel secure and those who feel insecure). The four categories were then derived by cross-classifying the two variables.

Table 6.8 shows the distribution of the four types of integration in Britain, France, Germany, Sweden, Denmark, and Spain. The data for 1996 and 2001 are combined to increase the robustness of estimates. It can be seen that there are marked variations between countries. The country in which employment integration is strongest is without question Denmark:

---

[3] This typology is similar to one developed by Serge Paugam for different types of occupational integration in France (see Paugam 2000).

nearly 60 per cent are in the 'high quality secure' type, while less than 6 per cent are in the category of 'low quality insecure'. In comparison, the distribution for Spain reveals a much more disturbing situation since only 28 per cent of workers are in the 'high quality secure' type, while 33 per cent are in the 'low quality insecure' category.

Note too that the gap between Denmark and Sweden is substantial. In Sweden, 37 per cent are in the 'high quality secure' category, a difference of twenty-two percentage points compared to Denmark. In recent years, Sweden has experienced major industrial restructuring and a change of its social security system that have contributed to feelings of job insecurity. Such differences show that it is important to bear in mind the contrasts that exist within the countries that are close to the 'Nordic' model.

It should also be pointed out that the differences between Great Britain, France, and Germany are fairly small at least if one takes the percentage of the workforce in the HS category: 33.6 per cent in Great Britain, 33.4 per cent in France and 36.5 per cent in Germany. Employment in 'low quality-secure' (LS) work is more prevalent in Britain (34%) than in France or Germany (23%), but in the latter two cases more people are in the 'low quality insecure' integration category (32% in Germany, 31% in France compared to 24% in Britain). Overall, the differences between, on the one hand, Britain—close to the liberal model and, on the other hand, France and Germany (which are usually seen as belonging to quite different types of production and employment regime) do not seem very strong.

If a wider group of EU countries are classified according to an employment-welfare regime classification, the variations are again very significant (Table 6.9). The countries close to the Nordic model stand out very clearly from other groups. Working in a situation in which there are both high quality jobs and employment security is clearly much more prevalent: 48 per cent are in such a position in contrast to 34 per cent

Table 6.9. Percentage of employees in job quality/job security categories by employment regime, 1996 and 2001 combined

	HS	HI	LS	LI	Total	N
Nordic	48.3	11.9	25.9	13.9	100	2,615
Liberal	34.4	7.6	32.2	25.8	100	1,787
Continental	38.9	10.2	24.6	26.2	100	3,772
Southern	30.3	9.9	32.5	27.3	100	2,435

Notes: HS—high quality secure; HI—high quality insecure; LS—low quality secure; and LI—low quality insecure.

Table 6.10. Mean levels of job satisfaction across countries

	HS	HI	LS	LI
Great Britain	5.69	4.87	4.95	4.23
France	5.55	5.00	4.51	4.14
Germany	5.89	5.53	4.95	4.44
Sweden	5.87	5.61	4.87	4.54
Denmark	5.96	5.60	4.89	4.20
Spain	5.84	5.41	4.73	4.04
EU-15 countries	5.81	5.41	4.85	4.30

Notes: HS—high quality secure; HI—high quality insecure; LS—low quality secure; and LI—low quality insecure.

for the 'liberal' countries, 39 per cent for the 'Continental' dualist and 30 per cent for the 'southern' dualist countries. At the other extreme, only 14 per cent of those in the Nordic countries are in the 'low quality insecure' category, while this is the case for just over a quarter of those in the other regime types. These results confirm then that the degree of integration differs strongly between employment systems. In the Nordic countries, the probability of a worker being in the worst type of category ('low quality insecure') is very much lower.

Table 6.10 shows the mean levels of job satisfaction for employees in each category for the six countries. Consistent with anticipation, employees in HS work in all countries reported the highest levels of job satisfaction. They are followed by those in HI work and then by those in LS work (with the exception of Britain). The lowest level of job satisfaction is found among those in LI work. A one-way ANOVA analysis showed that differences between employees in the four categories are statistically significant for all countries, except that in Britain there is no significant difference in terms of job satisfaction between those in HI work and those in LS work. The fact that, despite the wide country variations in the prevalence of the different categories, there is such similarity between countries in the implications of each 'employment integration' type for job satisfaction reinforces the view that the categories are capturing important differences of work experience.

How are the four types of employment integration distributed across particular categories of employee in different countries? Are certain countries subject to greater risks of polarization—with the more vulnerable categories of workers (low-skilled, female, those in routine services, and those with 'non-standard' work contracts) more heavily concentrated in LI work than their counterparts in other countries?

Taking first the absolute risks of being in the worst category of work, Table 6.11 presents the percentage distributions of the four types across different categories of employees. The data again points to wide country divergence. Taking skill polarization for example, 56 per cent of German elementary workers were employed in LI work, whereas the comparable figure was 11 per cent for Denmark, 22 per cent in Sweden, 41 per cent in Britain, 43 per cent in France, and 52 per cent in Spain. The Nordic countries clearly stand out as having a particularly low proportion of the low-skilled in very poor quality work. Another salient division which emerged strongly in our earlier analysis is the divide between temporary and permanent workers. The results presented in Table 6.11 show that Denmark had the smallest proportion of temporary workers in 'low quality insecure' work (17%). But while temporary workers in Sweden were the next best placed (51%), they were not very different from those in Britain (53%), France (59%), and Spain (54%). It is Germany that stands out at the other extreme as having a particularly high proportion in low quality insecure jobs (68%).

With respect to industry sector, the theoretical expectation is that employees in the low-level services (e.g. retail and hotels), where employers are more concerned with cost minimization and numerical flexibility, should have a high risk of being in LI work. However, this hypothesis does not appear to receive strong empirical support. In most countries the percentages of workers in LI work are rather close for those in routine services and those in the traditional sector of the economy. But the proportions in the worst types of jobs were particularly low in Denmark and Sweden (3% and 14% respectively), followed by Britain (24%). In contrast, in France, Germany, and Spain close to 40 per cent of retail and hotel workers were in very poor quality work. There was even less evidence of a regime difference with respect to part-time work. Denmark again stood out as having a particularly low proportion in the poorest work category, but part-time workers in Sweden were in a very similar situation to those in other countries.

Finally, women were least likely to be in the LI jobs in Denmark and Britain, followed by Sweden. Whereas in Denmark this reflected the fact that a high proportion of women were in high quality secure work, in Britain it resulted from the fact that they were more likely to be in low quality secure jobs than women in France, Germany, and Spain.

To obtain a broader picture of the degree of divergence between societies with different types of institutional systems, the EU-15 countries are grouped into four types of employment regimes. Examining the

Table 6.11. Percentage in job security/quality categories by types of employee 1996 and 2001 combined

	Great Britain (N = 962)				France (N = 828)				Germany (N = 1528)				Sweden (N = 918)				Denmark (N = 1005)				Spain (N = 645)			
	HS	HI	LS	LI	HS	HI	LS	LI	HS	HI	LS	LI	HS	HI	LS	LI	HS	HI	LS	LI	HS	HI	LS	LI
Occupational class																								
Elementary	14.3	1.1	44.0	40.7	28.6	5.7	22.9	42.9	13.5	5.4	25.0	56.1	21.5	9.2	47.7	21.5	35.7	8.5	45.0	10.9	10.7	1.9	35.0	52.4
Managers/professionals	49.2	14.3	22.5	14.0	41.2	20.2	24.6	14.0	59.3	8.4	19.2	13.1	54.3	16.7	15.1	14.0	71.6	6.8	18.4	3.2	54.5	11.9	19.8	13.9
Sex																								
Female	32.4	10.0	36.2	21.4	27.9	11.5	27.1	33.5	30.1	8.3	26.3	35.3	32.1	15.4	27.2	25.3	58.1	10.1	26.6	5.2	24.3	17.0	23.9	34.9
Male	34.8	7.2	32.3	25.7	37.4	13.6	20.2	28.9	41.4	7.0	21.5	30.1	42.4	17.2	23.9	16.5	60.7	8.7	24.1	6.5	30.7	13.1	24.4	31.9
Industry																								
Retail and hotels	29.4	5.1	41.6	23.9	21.7	11.7	24.2	42.5	26.5	7.7	24.6	41.2	39.6	22.8	23.8	13.9	44.3	13.1	39.3	3.3	20.4	15.7	25.0	38.9
Industry	35.9	6.3	32.0	25.7	34.9	14.2	15.9	34.9	34.8	6.1	22.1	37.0	38.6	10.2	34.0	17.2	57.1	6.2	27.9	8.8	25.6	9.8	30.8	33.8
Contract status 1																								
Temporary work	9.6	7.2	30.1	53.0	11.9	13.8	15.6	58.7	9.2	4.6	18.4	67.8	12.7	19.0	17.7	50.6	48.9	18.5	15.2	17.4	11.3	16.6	17.9	54.3
Permanent work	35.9	8.6	34.5	20.9	36.7	12.5	24.2	26.7	38.2	7.8	23.9	30.2	39.4	16.0	26.4	18.2	60.4	8.4	26.4	4.8	33.6	13.8	26.1	26.5
Contract status 2																								
Part-time work	26.0	6.8	38.9	28.3	30.8	11.5	23.8	33.8	39.3	5.2	19.1	36.3	27.3	12.0	30.6	30.1	50.0	14.1	31.4	4.5	38.3	16.5	12.2	33.0
Full-time work	37.0	9.6	33.1	20.3	34.0	13.1	23.0	29.9	36.9	8.6	24.2	30.3	39.7	17.2	24.5	18.6	60.7	8.5	24.4	6.3	26.8	13.1	27.0	33.2

Notes: HS—high quality secure; HI—high quality insecure; LS—low quality secure; and LI—low quality insecure.

experience of specific categories of workers by employment regime
(Table 6.12), it can be seen that the least desirable type of employment—
LI work—is less common among all categories of those in relatively disadvantaged labour market positions in the Nordic countries than in other
employment regimes.

In absolute terms then Denmark and the broader group of Nordic
countries do particularly well in ensuring that potentially more vulnerable
categories of employee are protected from LI work, although the lower
distinctiveness of Sweden shows that there is considerable heterogeneity
within these countries. But does this reflect the fact that work quality
is generally better in these societies, benefiting in a broadly similar way
all categories of employee, or does it also lead to a reduction of the
differentials between categories? To examine this, we have calculated odds
ratios which show the relative probabilities of being in the best rather
than the worst work categories.

As can be seen in Tables 6.13 and 6.14, the differentials between managers and professionals on the one hand and elementary workers on the
other are low in Sweden and in the Nordic countries more generally
(although France also had low class differentials in this respect). A statistical test showed that, although the individual country differences were
not significant, the Nordic countries as a whole were quite clearly more
egalitarian in this respect than the other regime groupings.[4] But there is
no evidence that the Nordic countries are more egalitarian with respect
to the other potential sources of employee disadvantage. In terms of sex
differentials Denmark is similarly low to Britain, while Sweden has one
of the highest differentials. Overall, the Nordic countries come out with
the strongest relative disadvantage for women. A statistical test showed,
that relative to Britain, women in both the Nordic and the Continental
dualist countries did significantly worse. Denmark, Sweden, and the overall group of the Nordic countries showed lower disadvantage among retail
and hotels workers, but these differences were not statistically significant.
Taking workers on non-standard contracts, part-time status made least
difference in Spain and the Southern dualist societies, and although there
were no significant differences at country level, temporary workers also
appeared to be relatively least disadvantaged in the Southern countries
taken as a whole.

---

[4] A multinomial regression analysis was carried out for this (as for the other employee category divisions) in which an interaction effect for elementary workers and each country was
introduced while controlling for the broader country effects. Britain or the liberal countries
were taken as the reference group.

Table 6.12. Percentage in job security/quality categories by type of employee, 1996 and 2001 combined

	Nordic (N = 2,615)				Continental (N = 3,772)				Liberal (N = 1,787)				Southern (N = 2,435)			
	HS	HI	LS	LI	HS	HI	LS	LI	HS	HI	LS	LI	HS	HI	LS	LI
Occupational class																
Elementary	30.0	7.9	43.9	18.2	21.8	6.5	28.9	42.8	13.5	1.8	36.8	48.0	14.7	2.5	43.9	38.9
Managers/professionals	60.7	11.5	20.3	7.5	57.3	13.9	18.2	10.6	54.1	11.9	21.9	12.1	52.2	11.5	22.4	13.9
Sex																
Female	44.2	12.7	26.9	16.3	34.4	9.9	27.5	28.3	33.0	8.1	34.6	24.3	30.4	9.5	32.7	27.3
Male	52.3	11.1	24.9	11.6	42.5	10.5	22.4	24.6	35.6	7.1	30.2	27.1	30.2	10.1	32.4	27.3
Industry																
Retail and hotels	43.5	14.7	32.4	9.4	32.0	9.0	24.8	34.2	29.0	4.3	38.6	28.1	26.9	11.2	26.9	35.0
Industry	48.2	7.7	30.3	13.8	36.5	9.6	23.0	30.9	35.1	6.1	33.2	25.5	21.9	7.7	43.1	27.3
Contract status 1																
Temporary work	24.9	21.4	14.6	39.1	16.9	13.0	18.7	51.5	9.0	10.1	27.7	53.2	15.3	15.9	22.3	46.5
Permanent work	51.1	10.7	27.3	10.9	41.0	10.0	25.2	23.8	37.4	7.3	32.8	22.6	32.9	8.9	34.2	24.0
Contract status 2																
Part-time work	37.5	16.2	28.3	18.1	39.9	10.1	22.7	27.3	29.6	6.1	35.0	29.3	41.5	11.7	16.8	30.1
Full-time work	50.5	11.0	25.4	13.1	39.2	10.6	25.1	25.1	35.9	8.3	32.2	23.6	28.6	9.4	35.2	26.7

Notes: HS—high quality secure; HI—high quality insecure; LS—low quality secure; and LI—low quality insecure.

In the light of this evidence, the Nordic countries appear to be distinctive in terms of integrating the more vulnerable categories of employees (female, low-skilled, those in routine services and those in 'non-standard' work contracts) into relatively stable employment. These results are broadly consistent with the view that inclusive employment regimes, with their high degree of centralization of collective bargaining and strong welfare and quality of work policies, tend to create an environment that is most conducive to the integration of employees into the labour market. But it should be noted that there were substantial differences within the Nordic grouping, with Sweden coming out much less favourably than Denmark on most sources of disadvantage other than class. Moreover, the protection of potentially vulnerable groups did not imply that relative differences were lower in the Nordic countries except in the case of class differences. The policies that led to improved conditions for the disadvantaged also benefited other categories, with the result that differentials with respect to sex and contract status remained high.

Finally, in its dynamic sense, the concept of polarization implies that the differential between advantaged and disadvantaged grows over time. To examine this, we carried out a series of regression analyses (not shown), in which year-interaction terms were introduced to examine change over

Table 6.13. Odds of being in HS jobs against being in LI jobs by country, 1996 and 2001 combined

	Great Britain	France	Germany	Sweden	Denmark	Spain
Managers and professionals/elementary	10.03	4.39	18.88	3.88	6.83	19.60
Male/female	0.89	1.55	1.62	2.02	0.83	1.37
Industry/retail and hotels	1.14	1.96	1.47	0.79	0.48	1.46
Permanent/temporary	9.56	6.85	9.00	8.64	4.48	6.05
Full-time/part-time	1.98	1.25	1.13	2.34	0.87	0.70

Table 6.14. Odds of being in HS jobs against being in LI jobs by employment regime, 1996 and 2001 combined

	Nordic	Continental	Liberal	Southern
Managers and professionals/elementary	4.90	10.60	16.00	9.89
Male/female	1.66	1.42	0.96	1.00
Industry/retail and hotels	0.75	1.26	1.34	1.04
Permanent/temporary	7.33	5.21	9.71	4.15
Full-time/part-time	1.86	1.07	1.50	0.78

time. This indicated that the pattern remained very stable over the second half of the 1990s. There was no significant change from 1996 to 2001 in any country other than France (where polarization did increase for females, retail workers, and part-timers) in the relative risk of the disadvantaged groups of employees being in LI work.

Conclusion

Job insecurity is high in most European countries, primarily due to the high level of unemployment compared to the immediate post-war decades. Bankruptcies and the restructuring of firms resulting from international competition and the growing interdependence of markets have become so common that they are necessarily increasingly viewed as inevitable, even if they are still the source of considerable social conflict. The threat of dismissal destabilizes an important periphery of the workforce creating collective anxiety about the future. In addition to mass unemployment, there has been strong growth in some countries of jobs with short-term contracts and of underemployment. To explore this in greater depth, we have sought in this chapter to examine the hypothesis that there has been a polarization between a protected core of workers and a periphery particularly sharply exposed to insecurity.

The results show that the countries where job security is strongest are also those that where class differentials are lowest. This supports the view that an 'inclusive' employment regime allows a higher level of integration in the labour market than either a 'dualist' or 'market' regime with respect to this particular type of employee division. But there was no systematic pattern across the other types of difference between employees.

We have also shown that, although there is a correlation in every country between job insecurity and poor quality of work, the statistical relationship between these two dimensions of employment—which need to be kept analytically distinct—is notably less strong in Denmark and in Sweden than in the other countries. We were able to confirm this pattern with an analysis of a wider set of countries grouped by broad regime type. The association between the two types of disadvantage was clearly weaker in the Nordic countries, that is to say the inclusive employment regimes, than in the others.

Finally, the typology of forms of employment integration that we constructed confirmed the existence of major differences between countries. The results showed that the countries in which employment integration

tion was the most favourable for employees were quite clearly Denmark, followed by Sweden. The overall proportion of low quality insecure jobs was lower and the prevalence of such worker was less for all of the vulnerable employee categories. These differences have important implications. First, if there is a general underlying tendency for work intensity to increase alongside growing job insecurity, the country differences show that it is possible to limit the negative consequences for workers. Second, the 'success' of Denmark, and more generally of the Nordic countries, shows that it is possible to reconcile an open economy with a high level of social protection, economic efficacy with a satisfactory level of employment integration for the great majority of workers. These differences with respect to the prevalence of poor work conditions among the potentially vulnerable categories of the workforce did not, however, necessarily imply that differentials were lower in these countries. Inclusive employment policies appear to have benefited most categories of employee. It is only with respect to class differentials that the Nordic countries emerged as significantly more egalitarian.

A number of observers have noted the distinctiveness of the Danish experience. If most countries have sought to introduce targeted programmes to encourage integration in and through work, while lowering the level of social protection, the difference in the Danish case has been the attempt to develop effective employment policies without accompanying them with a reduction in social expenditure. This compromise has been defined by the now widely used expression 'flexicurity'. Denmark is characterized both by a reduction of constraints on hiring and firing in the interests of the flexibility expected by firms and by a system of unemployment benefit that protects the unemployed from poverty (Gallie and Paugam 2000).

The Danish experience fascinates policymakers as well as researchers. The idea that the Danish model can be transferred in some simple and pure form to other countries is utopian. The institutional context that led to the emergence of the Danish model is very different from that in other countries. The level of union density has reached 70 per cent. The social history of Denmark has been marked by a continuing search for compromise between divergent interests, by a culture of collective negotiation aimed at bringing about an improvement in social well-being. In comparison, French social history has consisted of conflicts, sudden social eruptions, and power struggles expressing above all the failure of dialogue between the social partners. Moreover, the Danes adhere with confidence to the institutions of a socially orientated 'State' and approve the high levels of tax necessary to fund it. Finally, the quality of public and social services assures the legitimacy of the model. Whether it is with respect to initial education or continuing training, the preferred policy is to invest collectively to support both economic effectiveness and a high quality labour market. It is clear that an attempt to imitate this model would be an impossible challenge given the specificity of the institutions that underlie it.

Nonetheless, it is possible to imagine some possibility of cross-fertilization of ideas. It is possible to look for functional equivalents of what has made a success of the Danish model and to try to reform institutions in the light of them. It is not necessarily a futile enterprise to seek to adapt the Danish experience to the specificity of other countries, notably in the spheres of training, collective bargaining and the fight against poor quality work. Recognition of a weakening of the strength of personal ties between individuals within the workplace does not necessarily mean that there is no possibility of improvement. Even in the context of an increasingly flexible and global economy, there remain margins of autonomy by which social reform may lead to greater solidarity in forms of employment integration.

7

The Quality of Work Life in Comparative Perspective

Duncan Gallie

Our objective has been to compare the quality of work life in a range of European countries with respect to five key dimensions—skill levels, training opportunities, task discretion, work–family balance, and job security. Each of the chapters has also been concerned with the differences between categories of employee within countries and the pattern of change over time. The countries upon which the chapters focused were selected to provide key contrasts with respect to two major views about the institutional mediation of economic change—namely the production and employment regime perspectives. They have examined how far changes have been common in pattern across these diverse social structural settings or have varied between countries. In this final chapter, we describe first the major findings with respect to each of the dimensions of work quality and then turn to consider their implications for the contrasting arguments about the determinants of work quality discussed in Chapter 1.

Skill Levels and Skill Trends

Most theories of the quality of work take as their starting point trends in skills. This is not just because the level of skill exercised by employees is itself a major determinant of their experience of, and capacity for self-realization through, work but because it is thought to affect most other aspects of work that define good job quality. Michael Tåhlin's chapter seeks to compare the skill profile of the different countries, to assess the pattern of change over time (in particular whether there is evidence of polarization) and to consider the implications of skill for patterns of wage inequality.

He begins by addressing the issue of how skill is best to be measured. Much of the literature (especially by economists) takes a person's own educational level as a measure of skill level. But this ignores a crucial distinction between the skill requirements of the job itself and the skill capacities of the individual. These may not be the same and indeed there has been considerable speculation about the possible growth of a mismatch between them. He opts then for measures that more directly focus on the skills required by jobs. The core components of any such measure should capture the 'learning time' needed in order to perform the work, on the assumption that this is likely to be the surest guide to the substantive complexity of the work. The most reliable estimate, he suggests, can be drawn from measures that tap three time phases of learning: pre-entry, immediate post-entry and continuing. These have recently become available for most European countries in a cross-sectional data-set, but only a couple of countries have data that allow an analysis across time.

In the absence of detailed direct measures of skill over time, it is necessary to look for a good proxy of job skill for which data is available over a longer period. Tåhlin argues that this can be found in class classifications, in particular the EGP class schema. At first sight, this might seem a controversial claim, because Goldthorpe has formally presented the schema as founded upon differences in the employment relations of different categories of the workforce rather than as based on distinctions of skill. But Tåhlin suggests that skill provides a more convincing account of the mechanisms by which class has the wide array of outcomes for people's lives that have been amply documented in the literature. Further, while there are grounds for doubts about how well class captures employment relations, the empirical relationship between class and direct measures of skill is very high indeed and there is a notable similarity in their predictive power for wages. Given this, he bases his analyses of trends in skill across time on changes in the occupational class structure.

A central issue of the book is whether trends in skill patterns have been broadly similar across countries or have differed between countries as a result of different institutional configurations. Expectations of country differences need to draw upon the growing literature on national patterns of education and initial training. As seen earlier, the production regime literature draws a contrast between the general systems of the liberal market economies (LMEs) and the specific skill formation systems of the coordinated market economies (CMEs). But there is also a substantial empirical literature that has emerged from researchers into the youth labour market that points to the importance of the degree of standardization and stratification of educational systems, and that shows that these can account for significant differences between countries in the nature of the transition from school to work. To some degree these distinctions correspond to those of production regime theory in that systems that are both highly standardized and stratified (such as the German) also tend to place a strong focus on vocational (specific skill) training, while those low on both dimensions (such as the British) do not. But at the same time, this literature cautions against overemphasizing the homogeneity of the national education systems grouped together by production regime theory. For instance, the Swedish has markedly lower levels of standardization, stratification and occupational specificity than the German.

The empirical analysis first compares the skill profiles of the different countries, using the European Social Survey (ESS) of 2004—which contains the key direct skill indicators in fully comparable form for each of the countries. This shows the importance of taking into account the full time line of skills learning in assessing the differences between countries. The conclusions differ significantly from the expectations of production regime theory. A key indicator of the specificity of skills is the extent to which the firm is involved in the process of skill formation. While Germany may have a stronger pre-entry training system, the evidence would suggest that post-entry learning is more frequent in Britain. The importance of this is not only confirmed by employees' reports of the time spent in post-entry learning in jobs, but also by the wage markup received for post-entry learning. In short, the apparently stark differences between the systems appear considerably less striking when different phases of the skill formation cycle are taken into account.

Production regime theory would predict that, in countries where specific skills are more important, women would be more disadvantaged because of the reluctance of employers to invest in what they see as 'shorter-term' employees. In general the gender effect for pre-entry learning requirements is relatively small, and only significant in Germany and Spain. Further the assumption that women should be particularly disadvantaged in higher level occupations (where the requirements for specific skills are likely to be greater) is not borne out. Where gender does make a major difference, however, is with respect to post-job-entry learning. Women are in jobs that involve much shorter learning periods.

But this appears to be common across all the countries, rather than linked to any specific national institutional configuration.

The other potential lines of division that are a focus of the book are those of industrial sector and contract status. Tåhlin's data confirm that employees in the consumer services (for instance retail and hotels) have lower job entry requirements than those in manufacturing jobs, although there is little difference in post-entry learning requirements. But the view that employees on non-standard contracts form a particularly low-skilled periphery gets less support. Once other characteristics are controlled for, temporary and part-time workers are no less skilled in terms of pre-entry learning requirements than other employees—with the exception of part-time workers in Sweden who have relatively low-skilled jobs. But temporary workers were in jobs requiring less post-entry learning in Germany, Spain, and Sweden, while this was also the case for part-time workers in Germany and Britain. Overall, it is clear that it is difficult to generalize about the relative skill position of non-standard employees; rather their labour market position varies significantly between countries.

Turning to the longer-term pattern of change, Tåhlin's findings broadly confirm the more optimistic scenarios of skill change. Taking the pattern from the 1970s, overall skill requirements increased in all countries, and in all countries, but Britain, this was true across both the manufacturing and service sectors. In Britain it was particularly marked in the service sector and there was a small decline in skill level among production occupations. Partly as a result of this, Britain was distinctive in being the only country in which there was evidence of a marked polarization of the skills structure. The general rise in skill levels was particularly beneficial for women, whose skills rose more rapidly than men's in all countries other than France. Again Britain was distinctive in that there was a tendency to a polarization of women's skills, a pattern that contrasted particularly with Sweden where there was some narrowing of the distribution. But there was no evidence that skill change had a major impact in reducing sex differences in types of skills as reflected in gender segregation. There was some evidence of an increase in horizontal segregation in Germany and France and of a decline of vertical segregation in Britain and Sweden, but the overall pattern suggests remarkable stability across time.

Finally, Tåhlin assesses the implications of skill differences for pay inequalities between different categories of employee. Class pay inequalities were notably higher in Britain than in other countries, while, in contrast, in Sweden they were exceptionally low. He finds that most of class wage gap can be accounted for by differences in skill and this is the case for all countries. This is just what would be expected given his view that class is effectively a broad proxy for skill. In sharp contrast, only a minor part of the gender wage gap is skill-related and this is largely due to differences in post-entry learning rather than pre-entry. The relatively minor role of skill in accounting for pay disadvantage is also evident in the case of the difference between manufacturing and consumer services and between regular employees and those on non-standard contracts.

Overall, the analysis of skills confirms arguments that emphasize the general tendency to upskilling in advanced societies. The major point on which it supports the predictions of theories of country difference is in the distinctive character of the trends in Britain which alone experienced a degree of polarization of the skills structure. This is an expectation that can be derived from both production regime theory (with its emphasis on skills formation systems) and employment regime theory (with its emphasis on the principles of employment regulation). But the analysis has called into question the characterization of countries in terms of the emphasis on skill specificity, thereby casting doubt on the explanatory account offered by production regime theory.

Employer Training

Given the importance of skills for employees' life chances, the availability of employer training is necessarily a fundamental aspect of the quality of a job. Changes in employment and the labour market since the early 1980s have accentuated this. Rapid technological change, and its concomitant of frequent organizational change, requires continuous adaptation of employee skills. At the same time, a more fragile labour market has highlighted the importance of updating skills and maintaining employees' learning capacity if they are to avoid job loss and subsequent labour market marginalization. There has been substantial research at national level on the determinants of training participation and its implications for careers (at least in the sense of pay progression), but relatively little is known about the extent to which processes are similar or vary between countries.

In Chapter 3, Dieckhoff, Jungblut, and O'Connell are concerned with whether institutional differences between countries in skill formation systems affect the overall incidence of training, the extent and type of inequalities in access to training and finally the financial returns to training. Their point of departure is production regime theory. Although this gave a central explanatory place to skills formation systems, the principal focus was on initial training and its proponents have given very little consideration to continuing training. But Dieckhoff, Jungblut, and O'Connell suggest that the arguments can be readily extended. Given the emphasis on diversified quality production and on the importance of specific skills in CMEs, one could expect the countries in this category to be distinctive both in the volume of training provided and in the opportunities provided for those lower in the skill ladder. They argue, however, that these differences should be even more accentuated in the Nordic countries, as a result of greater union strength and a more compressed wage structure. Liberal market economies, in contrast, are thought to be based on a polarized skill structure, combining a highly trained elite with extensive use of low-skilled labour. This should result in relatively restricted training provision, focused on the highly skilled, and leading to exceptionally high levels of inequality in training opportunities.

The empirical analysis makes use of the first EU longitudinal study—the ECHP—that provides detailed information on training histories. Great Britain and Ireland are taken as examples of liberal regimes, and Denmark, Finland (given the absence of Sweden from the ECHP data-set) and Germany as examples of coordinated regimes. Although France and Spain are difficult to classify in terms of the production regime typology, they are also included for comparison as 'dualist employment systems', where the incidence of training could again be expected to be relatively low and its distribution highly polarized as a result of their strong insider–outsider structures.

Taking first the incidence of training, the authors show that it is only the Nordic countries that stand out as having exceptionally high rates of training. This was the case both in the mid- and in the late 1990s. Whereas close to half of Danish and Finnish employees had received some vocational training, this was the case for less than a quarter of employees in other countries in the mid-1990s and less than a third in 2000. The other country usually classified as a CME, Germany, was much closer to the pattern to be found in Great Britain than it was to that of the Nordic countries. The LMEs—Great Britain and Ireland—also showed a sharp divergence in training levels, and it was only in Ireland that the expectation of a very low volume of training was confirmed. The evidence, however, did support the view that France and Spain, with their 'dualist employment systems', would both have low levels of training. Overall, the pattern suggests that it is the employment regime rather than the production regime that best accounts for the extent of training in a country.

Indeed, although the Nordic countries are an extreme case, the institutional factors that have been argued to account for their distinctiveness—in particular, the strength of unions and the extent of wage compression—would appear to have a wider efficacy. The authors explore their effect through a multilevel analysis that takes account of variations in these factors across different economic sectors within countries. Even when the data for the different countries are pooled, and controls are introduced for the major individual predictors of training involvement, it is clear that higher union density and greater wage compression significantly raise the chances of receiving training. The union effect is plausibly due to the implications of stronger membership for the capacity of unions to bargain for better employment conditions for their members, while a more compressed wage structure may increase the incentives for employers to provide training since it reduces the amount they have to reward trained employees.

However, if institutional factors are related to the overall incidence of training, they would appear to make little difference to its distribution. Previous research on training has pointed to the importance of taking account of processes of selection into training, including the potential role of unobserved factors such as ability and motivation. While there was some evidence, at least for the mid-1990s, that the Nordic countries had more equal opportunities for employees of different skill levels, the analysis that takes account of selection effects finds no systematic difference between countries in different production or employment regime categories. Class inequalities in access to training would appear to be pervasive and broadly similar across capitalist societies with very different institutional structures. Although there were country differences, there were also no evident regime variations with respect either to contract status or employment in the public or private sector.

Finally, the authors turn to the issue of the financial rewards for training in different countries. They point out that employment regime theories could lead to two radically different expectations. The first is that in employment regimes where collective bargaining is strong the quality of training would be higher and as a result pay rewards to training would be greater. The second is that, because wage compression would tend to be greater in these same countries, they would be characterized by lower returns to training. (As seen earlier, it was precisely because of this that employers were thought to have a greater incentive to provide training in these countries). The issue of possible bias due to processes of selection into training is also relevant here. Trained employees may come to receive higher pay, not because of the value of the training per se, but because of other characteristics that they have as employees that are also responsible for the fact that they received training. The authors' initial analyses, which did not take account of possible selection effects, supported the wage compression argument. Of the seven countries, Denmark and Finland were the only cases where receiving training (including employer-provided training) was not associated with increased pay. However, the distinctiveness of these countries was reduced once selection factors were taken into account. These analyses suggested that even in those countries where training did appear to have a pay effect, this was due more to the personal characteristics of trained employees than to the training itself. Even longer periods of training appeared to have an effect only in the case of France.

Overall, the clearest evidence of an institutional effect lay in the volume of continuing training, with countries with more inclusive employment systems providing higher overall levels of training. In contrast, class inequalities in access to training appeared to be similarly high across very diverse institutional systems and there was no systematic pattern with respect to the disadvantage of those on non-standard contracts. The countries also showed a remarkable similarity in terms of the financial rewards of training—there was no pay advantage, whatever the production or employment regime.

Task Discretion

Task discretion, or job autonomy, has had a central place in discussions of job quality among writers with very different visions of the developing pattern of work. Its importance derives from the fact that it provides employees with a means both to make use of their individual creativity in work and to develop their abilities over time. It has also been shown to be a strong predictor of job satisfaction and, more recently, of psychological health in work. It is usually seen as integrally linked to changes in skill levels. The more skilled the work, it is suggested, the greater the knowledge of the work process held by the employee rather than by management. The employer has a strong interest in giving more decision-making scope to higher skilled employees to ensure that work is carried out as effectively as possible. Theorists with different views about the evolution of skills in capitalist societies have tended then to give very different predictions about likely future trends in task discretion. But the assumption they have in common is that such trends will be broadly similar across advanced capitalist societies.

Chapter 4 examines both the level and trends in task discretion, focusing primarily on France, Germany, Great Britain, Spain, and Sweden. The initial comparison of different countries makes use of a survey of work conditions in EU countries that provides identical indicators for the different countries, but (with the exception of Spain) the analysis of trends and in particular their differences between specific categories of employee is based upon larger national surveys that both allow a longer-time perspective and provide much more robust sample sizes for subcategories of the workforce. In the case of Germany, such longer-term evidence was only available for the former West Germany.

The evidence suggests that there are very wide variations between European countries in the discretion that employees are allowed to exercise at work. The comparative surveys measure task discretion through questions on the ability of employees to choose or change the order of their work tasks, their methods of work and their speed or rate of work. Viewed in the context of all EU-15 countries, Sweden, together with the other Nordic countries, has one of the highest levels of task discretion, while Spain has a particularly low level. Great Britain, France, and Germany come in an intermediate position. The pattern of country differences in the EU-15 does not appear to be a result of differences in economic development, reflected in the size of different occupational classes or of different industrial sectors, but it does relate significantly to the strength of trade unions and to the salience of national policies of work life reform.

Turning to the trends over time, the notable point is that there was no common pattern across the countries but marked differences in trends. In both Britain and Spain there was an overall decline in task discretion in the 1990s, in France there was no significant change, in Germany it rose (after a period of decline in the 1980s), while in Sweden there was a continuing increase in task discretion for the whole period between the 1970s and 1990s. Given Tåhlin's finding in Chapter 2 that overall skill requirements increased in all countries over this period, it is clear that any straightforward assumption that task discretion will increase in line with trends in skills is incorrect. The only consistent evidence of increase is in the country with the most strongly institutionalized labour movement and strong quality of working life policies. The two countries where there was an overall decline had low or very rapidly falling union density, together with the absence of national quality of work life programmes. France also had low union density but it witnessed very substantial state intervention in the industrial relations scene with the introduction of the Lois Auroux.

Overall trends can conceal important differences in the experiences of different categories of the workforce and it is this that is the central concern of the remainder of the chapter. It examines in particular whether there is evidence of polarization between relatively privileged and relatively vulnerable sectors of the workforce. It considers in turn the differences by occupational class between the relatively highly skilled categories of professionals and managers on the one hand and semi- and unskilled employees on the other; between workers in manufacturing and those in the consumer services (retail and hotels); between employees on 'standard' contracts (full-time and permanent employees) and those on 'non-standard' contracts (part-timers and temporary employees) and finally between men and women.

Taking first the differences by occupational class, it is notable that the two countries that had seen an overall decline in task discretion— Britain and Spain—were also the only countries to experience a significant polarization in the experiences of different classes, with an increasing gap between the discretion allowed to the low skilled compared with professionals and managers. In contrast, France, Germany, and Sweden saw a measure of convergence between classes (though in Sweden the evidence suggests that this primarily occurred in the early 1990s and then levelled off).

In contrast to the case for occupational class, there was little evidence of either polarization or convergence with respect to industry or sex. Employees in hotels and retail had more not less discretion in the way they carried out their work than workers in manufacturing. In Germany, Sweden, and Spain their relative advantage actually increased in the 1990s. Even in France, where their position deteriorated, they were still notably better placed than their manufacturing colleagues. There was also no evidence of polarization by sex. The only country in which women appeared to be at a relative disadvantage to men with respect to task discretion was Sweden, but there was no accentuation of (or improvement in) these differences in the 1990s.

Some of the more influential arguments about polarization in work and employment conditions have focused on the difference between employees on 'standard' and 'atypical' contracts. The latter are often depicted as a flexible workforce that is unlikely to receive either the rewards or level of trust of 'core' employees. The pattern with respect to the differences between part-time and full-time employees in practice varies considerably between countries. Part-timers were certainly disadvantaged in Britain and Sweden, but they had similar levels of task discretion to full-timers in France and even higher levels of task discretion in Germany and Spain. The only country where there was a change in the relative position of part-timers and full-timers was Britain, where the position of part-timers deteriorated, but this could be accounted for by compositional changes in part-time work rather than by the nature of the contractual position itself.

The other, and most frequently highlighted, source of contractual vulnerability is short-term contract status. The high turnover and dispensability of such employees could be expected to lead to severe disadvantage in terms of responsibilities with respect to work. In all countries temporary workers did indeed have lower task discretion than permanent employees. But it was only in Britain and Germany that the evidence suggested that their position grew worse in the course of the 1990s. In Britain this appeared to be due to changes in other characteristics of temporary workers, but in Germany it would appear to have been more tightly linked to their status as temporary workers.

Overall, the only clear cases of polarization were with respect to class in Britain and Spain and to contract status in Germany. In other countries, any polarization tendencies were effectively contained. Indeed in France, Germany, and Sweden, there was some sign of class convergence. Any institutional interpretation of these differences in country pattern can only be tentative. The focus must be on potential safety nets that could protect the relatively vulnerable from deterioration in their position. There is no obvious explanation in terms of our initial theoretical expectations of the relative decline of the position of temporary workers in Germany. But with respect to country divergences in class patterns, it is arguments based on the importance of the skills formation system that would seem to provide the most satisfactory account of the empirical pattern. Both Britain and Spain, which experienced class polarization, were distinctive in having general initial skills formation systems, which provided lower-level employees with little specialized vocational expertise before taking their job. In contrast, the countries where there was evidence of class convergence had 'specific skill' systems where employees entered their jobs already equipped with considerable technical knowledge (and arguably with strong occupational identities). As has been suggested in the literature, where the vocational training system gives employees greater expertise and stronger occupational identity, employers are likely to find greater resistance to modifications of work organization that threaten to undermine the control they can exercise over their jobs.

Work–Family Balance

The growth of women's employment placed the issue of work–family balance firmly on the agenda of the quality of work. How far are current patterns of working life compatible with people's commitments to their partners and their caring responsibilities for family members? What are the main features of the work situation that place pressure on family life? And how far can they be offset by institutional arrangements that facilitate flexibility over working hours or give greater caring support for parents? European societies differ very substantially both in employment rights with respect to control of working time and leave provision and in the level of support for childcare provided by the welfare state. They provide then a good setting for investigating the causes and sources of mediation of work–family conflict.

Scherer and Steiber address these issues by focusing on six countries. In addition to our 'core' countries of France, Germany, Great Britain, Spain, and Sweden, they include the Netherlands as the country that has gone furthest in developing opportunities for part-time work for employees. Their principal data source is the 2002 International Social Survey (ISSP), but for the analysis over time they also bring into play data from two Eurobarometer studies conducted by DG Employment to assess changes in the quality of work. Their study reveals well the technical complexity of this type of analysis, and in particular the need to pay due attention to selection effects that may mean that the composition of the female workforce differs between countries, with important implications for the risk of work–family conflict.

The country differences in the experience of work–family conflict were far from what might be expected on the assumption that high welfare provision would be reflected in reduced difficulty in reconciling work and family life. In terms of welfare support for employment, Sweden usually emerges as an exemplar country. But the level of work–family conflict among Swedish women was second only to that of Spanish women and notably higher than that for women in Britain where welfare support was relatively rudimentary. The country that stood out as most successfully balancing work and family life was the Netherlands.

The authors argue that the explanation for the apparent paradox of high welfare associated with high work–family stress lies precisely in the efficacy of the welfare system in making it possible for women in general, and mothers in particular, to enter and remain in the labour market. Whereas in the Netherlands the participation rate of mothers is as low as 37 per cent, it reaches 85 per cent in Sweden. As a result, the employment system in Sweden incorporates a much higher proportion of women who are likely to find it particularly difficult to combine work and family life. The authors formally test this using a selection model that takes account of the differing characteristics of employed women in the various countries. When this is done, Swedish women are no longer distinctive, while women in Spain still remain more severely affected than those in other countries.

Turning to the factors about the work situation that give rise to problems of work–family balance, the most powerful determinants proved to be quite simply the length of working hours and the pressure under which people carried out their jobs. For men it was particularly those working very long hours (45 hours or more) who experienced severe difficulty, whereas for women the length of working hours had a more progressive effect. The time pressures of work underlay many other apparent sources of work–family tension. Once these were taken into account, there was no evidence that people in more highly skilled jobs, or with greater supervisory responsibility, found it more difficult to combine work and home than others. Similarly, these factors accounted for the lower levels of work–family conflict among men in the public sector. It was the fact that they tended to work shorter hours that explained why, contrary to the authors' initial expectation, women did not appear to suffer more severely than men. Indeed, it was the relatively low working hours associated with the prevalence of part-time work that explained the fact that women in the Netherlands experienced exceptionally low levels of conflict compared to those in other countries.

The authors also examine whether problems are more severe as a result of the form of household in which people live. Focusing on coupled workers, they construct a detailed classification of household types in terms of the combinations of working hours of partners. The effects are particularly striking for women. The highest level of work–family pressure is felt by women who either are 'female breadwinners', with main responsibility for the household income, or are members of 'dual high commitment households' where both partners work more than 40 hours a week. For women the type of household remains important even when account has been taken of their personal work demands. For men, however, apparent household effects could be explained by their own work schedules. Rather surprisingly the presence of children was not related in a direct way to the severity of work–family conflict. This again was largely due to the fact that the mothers of small children tended to work fewer hours. Controlling for hours worked, mothers (but not fathers) were clearly under greater pressure. A more equal sharing of domestic labour did not reduce significantly the difficulties women faced, although a higher household income (which presumably provided the opportunity for 'outsourcing' housework) did make a difference. It is clear then that the nature of the household has to be taken into account in any overall understanding of work–family conflict, but it remains the case that, even when household characteristics are controlled for, work-related factors still have a very strong determining effect.

The relatively high levels of work–family conflict in Sweden showed that strong welfare provision is not necessarily associated with lower levels of conflict, if only because of its success in drawing into the labour market those who are likely to find it particularly difficult to resolve conflicting demands. But the authors do nonetheless find support for the view that institutional factors can make a difference. The degree of influence that employees have over the timing of their work hours has a significant effect: greater control makes it easier to cope with family demands. In particular, a high level of discretion over work time reduces the negative effects of long work hours on women's work–life balance. Similarly, more extensive state policies to support women's employment are beneficial for women working particularly long hours. The authors suggest that the low level of employee discretion over work time may help to account for the particularly severe problems of work–family conflict experienced by Spanish women.

Finally, Scherer and Steiber turn to the issue of whether the difficulty of reconciling work and family life has been growing greater over time as a result of an intensification of work. In practice, they find that in most countries there was very little change over the second half of the 1990s and indeed that among French and British men and Spanish women, the level of work–family conflict declined. The general pattern is consistent with evidence that shows that there was no increase in work pressure in the later 1990s (in contrast to the early 1990s), while in most countries there was a small decrease in the length of average working hours. For

French men a particularly sharp reduction in working hours was probably attributable to the reduction of work hours, following the progressive introduction of the 35-hour week.

Looking at specific categories of employee, across a somewhat wider range of countries clustered by broad welfare regime type, the notable point is that employees normally classified as 'peripheral' did not experience disadvantage in this particular aspect of their working lives. In particular, female part-time workers tended to report significantly lower levels of work–family conflict. The pattern of change over time was diverse. For instance, comparing employees of different skill levels, there was a tendency for work–family conflict to diminish most among those in low-skilled occupations in the 'Southern' countries, whereas, in the 'liberal' countries, it was those in professional and managerial occupations who benefited from an improvement in work–life balance. Temporary workers experienced some erosion of their more favourable position in the mid-1990s, and, similarly, the advantage of female part-timers relative to full-timers diminished over the second half of the 1990s. But overall it is clear that there can be no strong argument for polarization with respect to work–family conflict.

Job Insecurity

The final empirical chapter takes up the issue of job insecurity. Job insecurity has been shown to be highly detrimental for employees' psychological well-being. It has also been seen as a particularly important aspect of the quality of work given its wider implications for the risk of social marginalization. Insecure jobs tend to be associated with a higher likelihood of experiencing unemployment and this in turn triggers a greater risk of poverty and, on some accounts of, social isolation. A vicious circle of social exclusion may set in, which makes re-entry to the labour market increasingly difficult.

Paugam and Zhou, however, argue that job insecurity alone is unlikely to be the critical factor that precipitates marginalization. If employees are in relatively high quality jobs, where they have opportunities to renew their skills and use their initiative, the fact that they are in an insecure job may have less severe psychological consequences. It is also likely to pose less risk of social marginalization since they have the competencies required to get back into employment within a reasonable period. Rather it is where job insecurity is combined with work tasks that are of low quality that risks of marginalization are substantial since those affected will have to confront loss of work with skills of low market value and often without the learning skills to adapt to new job tasks. The authors' underlying concern then is with the extent of, and trends in, job insecurity in the context of poor quality work tasks. Their approach directly links the analysis of job insecurity with the other dimensions of work quality that have featured in the book and leads them into a broader discussion of the prevalence of low quality employment.

An initial issue is the choice of indicator of insecurity. They reject job tenure on the basis that it fails to distinguish voluntary and coerced job quits. But they are also sceptical of the current preoccupation with temporary work on the grounds that it can take very different forms (with different implications for long-term insecurity), while at the same time neglecting the possibility of widespread insecurity in so-called 'permanent' jobs. Similarly, unemployment experience may underestimate the prevalence of insecurity among those in work. They opt then for a self-report measure of insecurity, as providing the most comprehensive picture and one that is directly comparable across countries. Their analysis draws on data from two EU-wide surveys carried out in 1996 and 2001 respectively that provide a wide range of indicators of job task quality. In addition to the countries that have featured in most other chapters, they include the case of Denmark. Denmark and Sweden represent interesting variants of an 'inclusive' employment regime with respect to labour market regulation. In contrast to the relatively high level of job protection provided to existing employees in Sweden, Denmark has a more flexible labour market in which employers have powers of hiring and firing that are not dissimilar to those in the liberal market regime of Great Britain. The key difference is that this is accompanied by an exceptionally generous welfare system in the event of unemployment and by strong activation policies that facilitate re-entry to work and protect against longer-term marginalization. It is the exemplar case of what has come to be termed 'flexicurity'.

Taking first the overall country differences in job insecurity, there is some evidence of a broad link with the level of unemployment. For instance, Spain and France had the highest levels of unemployment both in the mid-1990s and at the end of the decade and also the highest level of job insecurity. Denmark had the lowest unemployment in both periods and the lowest insecurity. But the relationship is far from perfect. Britain, Germany, and Sweden had broadly similar unemployment rates in the mid-1990s, but rather different levels of job insecurity. A notable point is how employees in Denmark, despite the formally weak protection of their jobs, have by far the highest level of security of the countries considered in both periods, a difference far greater than might be anticipated simply on the basis of the unemployment rates. A comparison of the two points in time showed no clear general trends in insecurity: it rose in some countries and declined in others.

To what extent did job insecurity vary between different categories of employee? In general the theoretical expectations about sources of labour market disadvantage were confirmed: those in jobs with lower-skill, women, workers in the consumer service sector, part-time workers and above all those on short-term contracts had lower levels of security in most countries. But there were marked country variations in the sharpness of these differences. Denmark and Sweden were particularly successful in limiting differences in job security between occupational classes, but Britain had relatively low differentials in terms of sex and industry sector. Indeed, confirming evidence from unemployment studies, Britain was the only country where women had somewhat higher job security than men. The dualist regimes of France, Germany, and Spain had particularly sharp differentials with respect to industry sector, although they were not particularly distinctive in the disadvantage associated with contract status.

In turning to the way job insecurity relates to other aspects of job quality, the authors reveal a strong general association between low security and poor job task quality. In all countries, those in insecure jobs also tended to be in jobs where they were less able to make use of their abilities, exercise discretion in work, develop their skills, and participate in decisions in their workplace. They also had lower satisfaction with pay and greater difficulties in balancing work and family life. The only aspect of work that was unrelated to insecurity was work pressure. These results were confirmed in an analysis of a broader range of countries grouped into 'regime' types.

There were also, however, substantial differences between countries in the extent to which the disadvantages of insecurity and low quality job tasks cumulated. The relationship was particularly weak in the Nordic countries, while it was strongest in Britain and, above all, in Germany. This led to very different distributions between countries in types of employment situation when employees were classified in terms of both dimensions. The authors distinguish four main types of employment integration: where high task quality was combined with security; where task quality was high but employment insecure; where employment was secure but the quality of tasks was poor and finally employment that suffered from the double disadvantage of both insecurity and poor task quality. It is the last of these that they regard as presenting the greatest risk to the ability to remain in stable employment. It is notable that the job satisfaction of employees differed significantly depending on the nature of the employment situation. In all countries, it was highest among those in 'high quality secure' work, followed by those in 'high quality insecure' work, and then by those in 'low quality secure' work. The lowest level of job satisfaction was among those in 'low quality insecure' work.

The worst of these work situations—'low quality insecure' work—was relatively rare in both Denmark and Sweden (6% and 21% respectively). It was most common in Spain, France, and Germany—where it constituted over 30 per cent of all jobs. Contrary to some views Britain did not stand out as having an exceptionally high level of poor jobs in these terms. Rather it is distinctive in that it has a particularly high proportion of employees in jobs that have poor job task quality, but where employment is relatively secure. The distinctiveness of the Nordic countries compared to other EU countries was confirmed by an analysis that involved a wider range of countries.

There were also notable differences between countries in the prevalence of the types of employment integration among the most vulnerable categories of employee. Taking first occupational class, only 11 per cent of Danish low-skilled workers and 22 per cent of Swedish were in 'low quality insecure' jobs, while the proportions rose to 52 per cent in Spain and 56 per cent in Germany. While women were more likely to be in the worst type of jobs in all countries other than Britain and Denmark, this affected only 5 per cent of female employees in Denmark but over a third in France, Germany, and Spain. A similar pattern emerged for consumer services and part-time employees. In all countries other than Denmark, more than half of temporary workers were in 'low quality insecure' jobs, but the proportion was particularly high in France (59%) and in Germany (68%). But despite such divergences, there was little evidence, in any of the countries other than France, that there was a process of polarization in the sense of differences between more and less advantaged categories of employee growing greater over time. Rather the notable finding was the high level of stability over time of differentials within each country.

The authors conclude that the Nordic countries stand out as quite distinctive in their high levels of employment integration. They differ markedly from Germany, and the other Continental European countries examined, in both the overall level of integration and in their effectiveness at raising the employment conditions of the most vulnerable sectors of the workforce. They conclude that the pattern is broadly consistent with the expectations that an inclusive employment regime will lead to relatively good employment conditions and a broader-based integration into work. However, it is notable that this did not imply that differentials between employee categories were necessarily less great. The Nordic countries were more egalitarian with respect to class, but not with respect to other lines of employee division.

Economic Change, Institutional Regimes, and the Quality of Work

Chapter 1 in the volume introduced three broad perspectives on the factors affecting work quality. The first were theories of a universalistic kind emphasizing the common trends in economic change either in advanced industrial societies as a whole, or at least in advanced capitalist societies. The former tended to emphasize the importance of technological developments in determining the nature of work, whereas the latter pointed to an underlying logic of the capitalist division of labour in a context of increasing economic competition. The second broad approach—the production regimes perspective—took issue with the assumption that the implications of economic processes were likely to be similar even across capitalist societies and argued instead for the mediating effect of specific institutional configurations involving different patterns of coordination of the major economic actors and differences in the core mechanisms of skill formation. Finally, a third approach—the employment regimes perspective— while also underlining the importance of institutional effects, pointed rather to the importance of the role of organized labour in a society and the prevalence of institutional mechanisms designed to enhance integration both in the workplace and in stable employment.

With evidence from a relatively limited number of countries, and given the ideal-typical nature of the different regime constructs, the chapters have not sought to test these theories in any strict sense. Rather they have posed the issue of how far the different perspectives are consistent with, and can illuminate, the empirical patterns that have been uncovered. While it may be the case that key arguments would display their explanatory power more effectively with a different choice of countries, those that have been the focus of the book—France, Germany, Great Britain, Spain, and Sweden—have been taken because they have been regarded in the literature as exemplars of different institutional arrangements. If the arguments are uninformative about the critical cases selected, then there must be some doubt about their more general plausibility. Further, some chapters have brought to bear a wider range of examples to check the robustness of particular conclusions.

Common Patterns

The scenarios presented by the universalistic theories, while sharing the assumption that economic and social processes will be broadly similar across societies, differ fundamentally in their specific predictions. Theories of advanced industrial societies, in their successive forms (most recently theories of knowledge-based and informational societies), have tended to present an optimistic vision of the long-term trends of change, whereas theories of capitalist society have typically presented a darker image of the evolution of work. In both cases, however, the major proximate driver of change is the trend in the development of skills. While, in the former case, the prediction was of a general process of upskilling of the workforce, in the latter, the emphasis has been on long-term deskilling of intermediate and lower-level employees and growing polarization in the skills structure. For both versions of the thesis, however, skill has been seen as a key determinant of other features of work quality, most notably task discretion, access to further training opportunities and job security.

The evidence presented on trends in skill in Chapter 2 strongly confirms the more optimistic scenario of skill change. Across all of the countries examined there has been a substantial increase in skill demand and this has been the case both for men and for women. Indeed, the skill requirements in women's jobs have tended to rise more rapidly than those of men and there has been a significant convergence in skill requirements for men and women across countries as diverse as Germany, Great Britain, and Sweden.

But while the industrialism/knowledge society arguments fit well with aggregate skills trends, it provides a much less satisfactory account of other aspects of work experience. It cannot account for the diverse patterns of polarization with respect to class or for the different experiences between countries of employees with different contract statuses. Moreover, the assumption that skill trends would largely condition other aspects of work quality was clearly incorrect. Writers from this perspective have tended to assume that rising skills would lead to greater control by employees over the way they carried out their jobs. But, in practice, a general process of rising skills was accompanied by very varied trends in task discretion. There was also no evidence that the upskilling of the workforce was accompanied by greater employment security. Rather this varied considerably between countries and these differences remained stable across time.

There is, moreover, one common feature that is more in line with a scenario premised on a 'capitalist' logic of the employment relationship. It is notable that most of the chapters found major class inequalities in the quality of work. Those in higher class positions had greater opportunities to acquire new skills, they had considerably more control over their work tasks, and they had greater job security. It was only with respect to work–family balance that there was no evidence of class advantage—there were no class differences for men, while women in higher positions were under particularly severe pressure in reconciling the demands of work and family.

However, the key polarization arguments associated with the pessimistic scenario received little support. It was only in Britain that there was evidence of class polarization with respect to skill, and there was no general pattern of growing class divergence with respect to employer training, task discretion or job security. Arguments that emphasized new lines of workforce division in terms of industry sector fared little better. Workers in the consumer services were indeed lower skilled in terms of pre-entry job requirements, but they had similar levels of task discretion to workers in manufacturing and there was no consistent pattern of disadvantage (or trend in differentials) with respect to job insecurity.

Those on non-standard contracts were also not systematically disadvantaged across different aspects of work quality and there was no evidence that their position grew worse over time. Once compositional differences had been taken into account, part-time workers were not significantly less skilled in terms of pre-entry skill requirements than those with standard jobs and they were only more likely to be in jobs offering less task discretion in Britain and Sweden. In most of the countries examined, they were less likely to receive employer training and more likely to be in insecure jobs, but there was no general evidence that their position grew worse across time. Temporary workers were not disadvantaged in terms of pre-entry skill requirements, and it was only in some countries that they were less likely to receive training. Certainly, in all countries they were in jobs with less task discretion and greater job insecurity, but it was only in Germany that their relative position grew worse (and only with respect to task discretion). In sum, there is no general evidence of polarization along any of the key dimensions proposed, whether they be class, industry sector, or contractual status.

Production Regimes

In contrast to such universalistic theories, production regime theory emphasized the existence of 'varieties of capitalism' and the stability of distinct institutional syndromes, each offering specific types of competitive economic advantage. However, of the two main types of regime presented—LMEs, on the one hand, and CMEs on the other—it was the CMEs that were held to offer the major benefits to the wider workforce in terms of the quality of job and employment conditions. In contrast to the LMEs, they were thought to encourage a less polarized skill structure with higher levels of skill specialization among those in intermediate and lower class positions, which in turn led to greater devolution of responsibility to employees and higher levels of job security. The proximate determinant of these differences was the nature of the skills formation systems, which emphasized the development of specific skills (rather than the general skill formation systems prevalent in the LMEs).

An initial issue with respect to production regime theory is whether the classification scheme captures the empirical differences between countries with respect to its major explanatory factor—the skills formation regime. The production regimes literature took as its point of departure differences in initial skills formation, that is to say prior to full entry in employment. In those terms its categorization of the coordinated countries as grouping the Scandinavian countries and Germany seems empirically well founded in that they share relatively developed systems of initial vocational training—albeit with important differences in the role attributed to the workplace in the learning process and to the degree of specialization of courses. Similarly, the main European example of a liberal market regime—Britain—indeed has a system of pre-entry education that is predominantly 'general' in type.

But the picture gets more complicated when one takes account of the fact that skills formation may be a continuing process in people's work careers rather than being uniquely determined before entering the labour market. Taking this broader view of skills formation, the Scandinavian societies and Germany are less similar because the former has considerably more extensive continuing learning provision (whether one takes measures of post-entry learning time or of employer training). This may help account for the fact that skill demand in Sweden increased more rapidly than in Germany. Further, the characterization of Britain as a general skills regime becomes problematic, given that it has more extensive workplace learning than Germany (presumably in part to compensate for the lack of vocationally orientated specialization during the period of formal education). There may be issues about the precise character of the skills acquired through workplace learning, but, as Tåhlin shows, they are sufficiently valuable for employers to pay for them. The importance of firm-based learning (the formal training element of which appears to have increased over the 1990s) is doubtless related to the fact that Britain comes out from the analysis of skills trends as the country that saw the most rapid rise in job skills of the countries considered.

There are respects in which the predictions of production regime theory are consistent with the comparative evidence. As an example of a LME, it was anticipated that Britain would be characterized by a higher degree of inequality. Britain indeed stood out strongly from the pattern for Germany, France, and Sweden in being the only country where there was evidence of polarization of the skill structure over time. It was also the country with the greatest pay gap between classes. However, given the problematic nature of the assumptions about skills formation which provide the main mechanism for explaining this pattern in the production regimes perspective, this can be regarded as only weak support for the thesis. It should be noted that the same predictions are also derived from the employment regime perspective, which we turn to later.

A more convincing case for the explanatory potential of the production regimes perspective emerges from the analysis of task discretion. The view that countries with strong specific-skill pre-entry vocational training would provide conditions in which lower-level employees were less at risk of losing responsibility for making decisions about their work, was supported by the fact that France experienced no reduction and Germany and Sweden some increase in overall task discretion, while all three countries saw a measure of class convergence across the 1990s. In contrast, Britain (together with Spain) saw declining task discretion and class polarization. There are very plausible mechanisms by which the different pre-entry skill formation systems are likely to affect this. Where employees develop a relatively high level of specialized technical skill before being recruited by an employer, and can appeal to wider professional norms about how the work should be carried out, they will be in a stronger position in defining the nature and scope of job tasks than where the employer alone provides the requisite skills training. In addition, specialized vocational training systems are likely to encourage a stronger sense of occupational identity and greater sensitivity to attempts to encroach upon traditional job rights. Taken together, greater relative power and a stronger occupational identity will provide employees with greater leverage to defend the discretion they can exercise over their work.

In sharp contrast, production regime theory provides little insight into the patterns we found with respect to job security. The expectation was that, given the investment in the development of specific skills and the need to ensure that employees were highly motivated since they had a significant degree of discretion over their jobs, workers in the coordinated regimes would experience higher levels of jobs security. In contrast, employers in liberal market regimes, making extensive use of workers with low-level general skills, would be in an easier position to hire and fire, leading to relatively widespread job insecurity. In practice, the country differences in levels of job insecurity did not fit this pattern at all well. Although Denmark (a CME) did have an exceptionally high level of job security, Britain (a LME) was the next highest, while German employees had relatively low security.

Employment Regimes

The third broad approach to the determinants of work quality—the employment regimes perspective—emphasized the institutionalized role of organized labour in decision-making at both national and workplace level and the extent to which work and employment regulation facilitated the integration of potentially more vulnerable labour market groups. A distinction was drawn between inclusive regimes (such as the Scandinavian countries) where policies were designed to extend both work and employment rights as widely as possible through the population of working age, dualist regimes (such as Germany, France, and Spain) where the central concern was to guarantee strong rights to a core workforce of longer-term employees and market regimes (such as Britain) that emphasized minimal employment regulation. The assumption was that work quality would be substantially better in the inclusive employment regimes than in either the dualist or market regimes.

With respect to the conflicting claims of the production regimes and employment regimes perspectives, a critical case is Germany which is usually regarded as the paradigm example of a CME in the production regimes literature, but would be identified as a 'dualist' regime from an employment regimes perspective. Whereas in the former case, there should be broad similarity between the Scandinavian countries and Germany, in the latter they could be expected to be very different.

The principal expectation with regard to skill would be that inclusive regimes would devote more attention to continuing skills development to ensure that people could remain in stable employment despite a rapidly changing technological environment. Such measures would be particularly targeted on the lower skilled and others in potentially more vulnerable labour market positions. The evidence was certainly consistent that the Scandinavian countries had much more extensive provision for in-career learning. In Chapter 2, it was shown that Sweden was distinctive in combining a system of specialized skill formation before labour market entry, with widespread continuing learning during working life, whereas skills formation in Germany was primarily pre-entry. This was confirmed by the evidence on more formal employer training in Chapter 3, which showed that the provision of training was by far the highest in the inclusive employment regimes of Denmark and Finland, while Germany was one of the countries with the smallest proportion of employees receiving continuing training. In terms of overall provision, then, the Scandinavian countries would appear to be quite different in pattern from Germany. A major qualification to the expected pattern, however, is that class inequalities in access to training were not lower in the Scandinavian countries than in others. While the lower skilled in the Scandinavian countries certainly benefited from more extensive training provision than in other countries, so too did their colleagues in higher class positions.

There was also some support for the employment regime perspective from the pattern with respect to country differences in task discretion. Sweden and the other Scandinavian countries were exceptional in the extent to which employees were in jobs that allowed them to take initiative and exercise discretion in their work. This is likely to have reflected not only the strength of trade unionism, but also the policy importance given to programmes to improve the work environment. Germany, on the other hand, came relatively low in terms of task discretion, indeed below the EU-15 average and below Britain. Further Sweden was distinctive in combining high levels of task discretion with strong protection against polarization across the different sectors of the workforce. In Germany, in contrast, there was a marked deterioration over time in the relative position of the 'periphery' of temporary workers compared to the 'core' workforce of permanent employees.

Further, the evidence about job security and employment integration was consistent with the argument that inclusive employment regimes would have higher work quality. It was not so much that job security per se was higher (though it was high in both Denmark and Sweden, and indeed highest of all countries in Denmark), but rather that job insecurity did not go hand in hand with poor quality job tasks in the Scandinavian countries. As a result, in these countries much lower proportions not only of all employees but also of employees in potentially vulnerable labour market positions were in the type of 'low quality insecure' work that posed the greatest risks for integration into stable employment. But again the evidence was less consistent that countries approximating the inclusive regime type had reduced differentials in employment conditions between different categories of worker. They appear to have been relatively successful in reducing class differentials in job insecurity and employment integration (although there were marked differences between Nordic countries) and the differences between employees in manufacturing and in consumer services were relatively low. But (although Denmark was a special case in having generally low differentials), Sweden and the wider group of Nordic countries had relatively high differentials with respect to temporary workers, women, and part-time workers. It was through a general improvement of employment conditions, rather than through reduced differentials, that the Nordic countries improved the position of these types of employee.

One initially attractive feature of employment regime theory compared to production regime theory is that it included an expectation of differences in work–family balance. Given the greater resources devoted by countries of this type to facilitating the stable employment of women through more generous leave provisions and more accessible childcare, it might be expected that they would have considerably lower levels of work–family conflict. But our evidence suggests that this was not the case. Taking a simple comparison of reported levels of work–family conflict, Swedish women came out as having relatively high work–family stress, indeed the highest after Spanish women. Scherer and Steiber offer (and empirically defend) an intriguing explanation of this apparent paradox of high welfare accompanied by high work–family conflict. It is precisely because these societies are so successful in supporting women's entry into stable employment that work–family conflicts may be high. This is because they enable even those with very difficult domestic situations, who in other countries would leave the labour market, to remain in employment. But it should also be noted that work stress was high among Swedish women, suggesting that the programmes of work reform associated with inclusive regimes may be more effective in providing job interest and responsibility than in reducing work pressures. At all events, there are no grounds for thinking that inclusive employment regimes guarantee easier reconciliation of work and family life.

While the countries with more inclusive employment regimes were different in a number of ways, the distinction between dualist and market regimes did not correspond to any broad differences between countries with respect to work quality. The expectation was that market regimes would have particularly sharp differentials with respect to skill and dualist regimes with respect to sex and contract status. Britain, as a market regime, did stand out as the country with the highest level of class pay inequality and the only country that experienced class polarization over time. Its relatively low level of regulation, and its experience of deregulation in recent decades, provides a plausible account of why that is the case. But while there were numerous country differences in the degree of disadvantage experienced by women and employees on non-standard contracts, they related to very specific aspects of the work situation and cross-cut regime differences. Again the employment regime typology is primarily useful in relation to class differentials.

As has been seen, each of the major perspectives on the determinants of work quality can claim supportive evidence with respect to particular issues. The universalistic thesis of a very general trend to upskilling was confirmed for all countries. The emphasis on skills formation systems in the production regime perspective provided the most plausible interpretation of country differences in the extent of class polarization in task discretion. Overall, however, the employment regime perspective helped to illuminate a wider range of differences in work quality than the production regime argument and the important differences between Germany and the Scandinavian countries were also clearly in its favour. The countries closest to the inclusive regime type were distinctive in their patterns of skill formation, in their level of task discretion and in the prevalence of work conditions that were conducive to stable employment integration. They supported weaker categories of the workforce through their general improvements in work and employment conditions. But there was less consistent evidence that they were particularly successful in reducing differentials between employee categories. They were effective in some respects in reducing class differentials (namely in relation to pay, task discretion and job security), but they were not more egalitarian with respect to differences between other types of employee.

It is clear from the country comparisons that such regime categorizations are at best very broad brush. There are important variations between countries even within the inclusive regime category. An understanding of the factors that underlie such differences may be impeded by too strong an emphasis on analysis focusing on regime types. Regime analysis can complement, but not substitute for, the older tradition of 'societal' analysis which takes seriously the specificity of the historically derived institutional frameworks of particular countries.

APPENDIX: DATA SOURCES

The chapters draw on a range of surveys—some of which were designed as comparative cross-national surveys, others of which are single nation surveys. The cross-national surveys included: the European Social Survey (ESS); the European Community Household Panel (ECHP); the European Foundation for the Improvement of Living and Working Conditions' European Working Conditions (EWCS) 1995 and 2000 surveys; the Eurobarometer (EB) surveys 44.3 (1996) and 56.1 (2001); and the International Social Survey Programme (ISSP) 2002 survey. The national surveys included: the German BIBB/ IAB surveys conducted by the Federal Institute for Vocational Education and Training (BIBB) and by the Institute for Employment Research (IAB); the British Skills Survey series; the French Enquêtes Conditions de Travail; and the National Swedish Survey of Living Conditions (ULF). Some technical details of the surveys are given below.

The European Social Survey (ESS)

The European Social Survey (ESS) is an academically driven multi-country bi-annual survey, so far carried out three times (2002, 2004, 2006) with a fourth wave scheduled for 2008. In ESS-2 (2004), the most recent available data set, 26 nations were covered: Austria, Belgium, the Czech Republic, Denmark, Estonia, Finland, France, Germany, Greece, Hungary, Iceland, Ireland, Italy, Luxembourg, the Netherlands, Norway, Poland, Portugal, Slovakia, Slovenia, Spain, Sweden, Switzerland, Turkey, the United Kingdom, and Ukraine.

ESS was funded by the European Commission's 5th Framework Programme, the European Science Foundation (ESF), and national funding bodies in each country. Principal investigator is Roger Jowell at the Centre for Comparative Social Surveys, City University, London.

The purpose of the survey is to develop a series of European social indicators; in so doing, to advance and consolidate improved methods of cross-national survey measurement in Europe and beyond; and to distribute the resulting data to the general social science community. The data are freely available (in anonymous form) at the Norwegian Social Science Data Services (NSD).[1]

[1] See http://ess.nsd.uib.no

Table A.1. Sample sizes and response rates in five countries, ESS wave 2, 2004

	Germany	Spain	France	UK	Sweden
Sample size	5,456	3,033	4,145	3,746	2,962
Respondents	2,870	1,663	1,806	1,897	1,948
Response rate	0.526	0.548	0.436	0.506	0.658

Source: ESS2-2004 Documentation Report, ed. 3.1 (available at: http://ess.nsd. uib.no/index.jsp?year=2005&module=documentation&country). In general, see www.europeansocialsurvey.org

ESS is cross-sectional with random probability sampling, rigorous translation protocols, and face-to-face interviews (of about one hour's duration). The sample in each participating country is drawn from a population consisting of all persons age 15 and over (no upper age limit) resident within private households, regardless of nationality, citizenship, language, or legal status. Core modules of the questionnaire are repeated across waves, supplemented at each occasion by single-wave or rotating modules designed by external research teams selected by the ESS Scientific Advisory Board after an open call for proposals.

The total number of respondents in ESS-2 (2004) is 47,537. Data from five countries are used in Chapter 2 of the present volume: Germany, Spain, France, the United Kingdom, and Sweden. Response rates and other sample statistics for these countries are shown in Table A.1.

The European Community Household Panel (ECHP)

The European Community Household Panel (ECHP) was conducted under the responsibility of Eurostat, the Statistical Office of the European Communities. It is a large-scale comparative survey, involving interviews with the same households and individuals over eight years. It was designed to contribute to the development of comparable social statistics on income and other social indicators relating to the living conditions of both households and individuals.

ECHP data were collected by 'National Data Collection Units' (NDUs). In the first wave (1994) a sample of some 60,500 nationally representative households, approximately 130,000 adults aged 16 years and over, were interviewed in 12 member states: Germany, Denmark, the Netherlands, Belgium, Luxembourg, France, the United Kingdom, Ireland, Italy, Greece, Spain, and Portugal. Austria was added in the second wave (1995) and Finland in the third wave (1996). From 1997 onwards Sweden provided cross-sectional data derived from the Swedish Living Conditions Survey.

In the first wave of the ECHP (1994), for each country, with the exception of the Netherlands and Belgium, a new random sample was selected from the target population of private households. In most of the countries, a two-stage sampling procedure was adopted. In Germany, Luxembourg, and the UK the original ECHP surveys were stopped in 1996. In these countries the first three ECHP waves ran parallel to already existing panels with similar content. These panels were then used and harmonized ex-post. The 'cloned' data for Germany and the UK are available from 1994 onwards (and for Luxembourg from 1995 onwards). In the Netherlands and Belgium, the panel was based from the start on two modified pre-existing panels. In the Netherlands this was the Socio-Economic Panel survey (SEP) which had started in 1984. The result is considered to be a set of nationally representative random samples of private households, involving, overall, interviews with around 60,000 households and 130,000 adults in the European Union. A break down of the sample numbers by country is given in Table A.2 (Verma and Clemenceau 1996). The data files contain weights to be applied in analysis of the data. There are three types of weights: cross-sectional and longitudinal weights for each individual and a household weight for each household.

Table A.2 gives response rates for the wave 1 and wave 2 samples, distinguishing between those where the ECHP began in 1994 and those where it was integrated into existing national panels (Verma and Clemenceau 1996). The average response rates of around 70 percent are comparable to those generally found in comparable complex surveys on household budgets. The rates were much higher in the South, 90 percent in Greece and Italy, than in the North (< 50 percent in Germany and Luxembourg). In the two pre-existing panels, Belgium and the Netherlands, the original (first wave) response rate was around 50 percent. The Netherlands panel was able to interview 92 percent of the households already in the sample but only 36 percent of new entrants. In Belgium, all ECHP Wave 1 sample cases came from the pre-existing panel, of which 80 percent were interviewed.

Face-to-face personal interviews were carried out with a 'reference person' providing information on the household questionnaire and each individual in the household was asked to answer the personal questionnaire. The *Household Questionnaire* asked for information on migration status of the household, tenure of accommodation, housing amenities, possession of durable goods, major sources of income, details of the household's income, and various indicators of financial situation. The more detailed *Personal Questionnaire* was designed to include information on a number of different life domains. It covered economic activity and personal income in detail and also a range of topics including social relations, health, personal characteristics, education, and levels of satisfaction with various aspects of life and work. Economic activity was collected both for current status and retrospectively for the previous calendar year. For the previous year, people were asked to recall their main activity in each successive month, using a list of pre-coded options. Being in paid employment was defined as working 15 hours or more.

Table A.2. ECHP response rates, waves 1 and 2

	Wave 1				Wave 2				
	Households selected	Household interviews completed	Personal interviews completed	Household response rate %	Target for interview	Number interviewed	Response rate %	Interviewed in Waves 1 and 2	Attrition rate % WI to W2
New panels									
Italy	7,841	7,115	17,730	90.7	7,844	7,128	90.9	6,697	5.1
Greece	6,131	5,523	12,492	90.1	5,897	5,219	88.5	5,060	7.7
Portugal	5,492	4,881	10,054	88.9	5,436	4,916	90.4	4,654	3.6
France	9,239	7,344	14,331	79.5	7,548	6,723	89.1	6,518	10.7
UK	8,104	5,779	10,517	71.3	5,398	4,549	84.3	4,405	23.3
Spain	7,108~	7,206	17,908	87.0	7,505	6,521	86.9	6,295	12.4
Denmark	5,580	3,482	5,903	62.4	3,847	3,228	83.9	3,014	11.5
Ireland	7,252	4,048	9,915	55.8	4,369	3,587	82.1	3,433	14.4
Germany	10,604	5,054	9,887	47.7	5,177	4,755	91.8	4,657	7.7
Luxembourg	2,485	1,011	2,046	40.7	1,027	962	93.7	945	6.2
*Existing national panels**									
Netherlands	5,926	5,187	9,408	87.5		5,067			
Belgium	4,963	4,189	7,852	84.4	4,596	3,988	86.8	3,723	10.3
EU (12)	83,293	60,819	128,043	73.0					

Notes: ~ Spain, Selected households, 7108 + 4822 substitutes. * Response rates are for the national panel wave 1. Original first wave rates in both countries were around 50%.

Sources: V. Verma and A. Clemenceau (1996).

The European Surveys on Working Conditions

The European Surveys on Working Conditions are conducted by the European Foundation for the Improvement of Living and Working Conditions. An initial survey was carried out in 1990/1, followed by subsequent waves in 1995/6 and 2000. The later two surveys are used in the analyses in the book, as these provide acceptable levels of comparability.

The surveys have covered all countries that were members of the EU at the time of the survey. They consist of representative samples of the total population in employment (employees and self-employed), including those temporarily absent from their work and family workers. The sample was obtained through multi-stage random sampling, using a random walk procedure for the selection of final addresses. One eligible individual of 15+ years was interviewed at each address on a face-to-face basis. Interviews were carried out in member states of the European Union, with a target number of interviews of 1,500 per country (500 in Luxembourg).

For most countries the sample was weighted to be consistent with the Labour Force Survey on a range of variables: region, city size, gender, age, economic activity (NACE), and occupation (ISCO). However, in 1995, LFS data was not available for Austria, Finland, and Sweden and information was obtained from other data on population structure. Response rates are given in Table A.3.

The aim of the EWCS is to provide an overview of the state of working conditions in the EU, to identify major issues and changes affecting the workplace and to contribute to a better monitoring of the quality of work and employment in Europe. The number of questions and issues covered has expanded with successive surveys, but a core set of questions has remained unchanged in order to enable the study of trends in working conditions. The main focus of the survey over the years has been on physical working conditions, in particular hazardous conditions, but also included questions on autonomy in work, information, training, support from colleagues and managers, wage incentives, and hours of work.

Eurobarometer Surveys 44.3 (1996) and 56.1 (2001)

Eurobarometer surveys are the regular representative face-to-face surveys of the European Commission conducted since 1973. In spring and autumn of each year questions are asked of representative samples of the resident (non-institutional) population aged 15 years and over in each of the European Union Member States. The regular sample is 1,000 people per country except in Luxembourg (600) and in the UK (1,000 in Great Britain and 300 in Northern Ireland). Moreover, to monitor German re-unification, since 1990 1,000 persons have been sampled each in East and West Germany.

The data used in Chapters 5 and 6 are drawn from two special modules introduced into Eurobarometers 44.3 (1996) and 56.1 (2001), that were commissioned by DG Employment (formerly DGV) to investigate the extent and determinants

Table A.3. Response rates for the EWCS surveys

	1995/6	2000
Belgium	58	56
Denmark	35	42
Germany	67 (E); 70 (W)	76
Greece	47	47
France	79	74
Ireland	70	58
Italy	43	39
Luxembourg	60	68
Netherlands	37	41
Austria	81	67
Portugal	66	68
Finland	55	56
Sweden	N.A.	58
UK	58	56

Source: EWCS User Guide at: http://www.esds.ac.uk/findingData/snDescription.asp?sn=5604

of social precarity and social exclusion. The questionnaire for the module in 1996 was drawn up by Duncan Gallie and, for the 2001 module, by Duncan Gallie and Serge Paugam. In 1996, two samples were drawn for the EB 44.3—a basic sample of each member state and a booster sample of job seekers. The chapters draw on the first of these samples. The 2001 survey only included the basic sample. Following the standard fieldwork practice of Eurobarometer Surveys, a random multi-stage probability sample was drawn in each country, with an initial stratified sample of administrative regional units followed by a random route selection of addresses within sampling points. The respondents were then drawn at random within households. Eligibility is restricted to nationals of the particular member state. All interviews were conducted face-to-face in people's homes and in the national language.

The overall national sample sizes and the size of the sample in paid work are shown in Table A.4. Chapter 5 is based on the sub-sample of those in paid work, while Chapter 6 focuses on the sub-sample of employees.

Eurobarometer Surveys tend to suffer from two problems: the small size of the country samples, which makes it difficult to carry out detailed within-country analyses; and the variable nature of the response rates. Both for the EB 44.3, and the EB 56.1, there were marked variations between countries in response rates, with particularly low response rates in the Netherlands in 1996 (Gallie 1997) and Great Britain in 2001 (Gallie and Paugam 2002). For the descriptive analysis, the data have been weighted to provide a representative picture of the population for each country.

Table A.4. Eurobarometer Surveys 44.3 and 56.1, sample sizes and response rates

	Un-weighted sample sizes				Response rates (a)	
	Overall (a)		People in paid work			
	1996	2001	1996	2001	1996	2001
Denmark	1,000	1,001	565	544	40%	36%
France	1,001	1,002	609	501	80%	72%
Germany (E)	1,046	1,000	479	552	69%	75%
Germany (W)	1,028	1,009	485	471	71%	76%
Great Britain	1,051	999	551	459	53%	21%
Netherlands	1,023	1,006	489	473	24%	49%
Spain	1,000	1,000	445	430	77%	73%
Sweden	1,000	1,000	568	553	52%	50%

Sources: Gallie (1997) and Gallie and Paugam (2002).

Note: (a) in 1996 this refers to basic sample.

International Social Survey Programme (ISSP 2002)

The *International Social Survey Programme (ISSP)* is a continuing programme of cross-national collaboration that has conducted annual cross-sectional surveys since 1985. The third module on *'Family and Changing Gender Roles'* was fielded in 2002, as a partial replication of the 1998 and 1994 modules. Questions cover respondents' attitude to gender roles and the gainful employment of women, the number of hours per week the respondent and the cohabiting partner each spend on gainful work and unpaid housework, and the respondents' experience with work–family balance.

There is considerable variation across countries in the procedures used to collect data. Of the 34 countries that participated in 2002, 22 fielded this ISSP module, not as a survey of its own, but as part of a larger survey (of the countries focused on in Chapter 5, this concerns Germany, Britain, and the Netherlands). The mode of administration also differed between the countries (see Table A.5): Spain completed the survey as face-to-face interviews, whereas Britain, France, the Netherlands, and Sweden applied a self-completion format. Germany, which fielded the module together with the ALLBUS 2002, combined several modes, administering the background variables for both surveys face-to-face and the substantive questions as self-completion with interviewer involvement. Telephone interviews are not permitted in the ISSP.

Also the sampling procedure differs from country to country (Table A.5). ISSP surveys are generally probability samples of adults in each respective country, partly simple and partly multi-stage stratified random samples of respondents aged 18 or above. Of the countries under special consideration in Chapter 5, only the Netherlands used quota procedures (Klein and Harkness 2004). A lack of sufficient detail in survey documentation makes it difficult to establish detailed response rates in the ISSP and no cross-country comparative figures have been published to date. The raw figures for eligible samples and realized interviews indicate, nevertheless, that national differences are considerable (see Table A.5). Finally, some but not all countries provide weights to correct for selection or response bias (e.g. Britain and France, but not Spain, Sweden, Germany or the Netherlands).

BIBB/IAB-Surveys

The *BIBB/IAB-Surveys* are large-scale representative surveys of the German labour force conducted jointly by the Federal Institute for Vocational Education and Training (BIBB) and by the Institute for Employment Research (IAB). They started in 1979 when around 30,000 German employees were interviewed, and were repeated in 1985/96, 1991/2 (for the first time including East Germany) and 1998/9. The aim of the studies is to obtain representative information about the acquisition and use of vocational qualifications in Germany. The general focus is on the qualification profile and occupational history of individuals (cross-sectional survey design but retrospective data on education, training, and work history), but each of the individual surveys has a special focus subject, such as occupational mobility in 1979, the spread of new technologies in 1985/6, and an East–West comparison in 1990/1. In 1998/9, when also the Federal Institute for Occupational Safety and Health (BAuA) participated, the emphasis was on structural changes in the world of work and their impact on working conditions, work demands, and individual mobility behaviour.

The sample of the BIBB/IAB-Surveys generally includes people aged 15 or above, who are in gainful employment and work at least ten hours per week (including those doing internships or voluntary work), but it excludes apprentices and other trainees in the dual education system as well as those doing their military or civilian service. In each of the four waves for which data is available to date,[2] about 30,000 interviews were successfully conducted (for details on target population which differs across waves and sample sizes, see Table A.6). This amounts to a sample of about 0.1 percent of the German work force (multi-stage stratified random-route sampling on household basis, face-to-face interviews, since 1998/9 CAPI). The gross response rate for the fourth wave was 58 percent.[3] The data are weighted in a multi-stage iterative weighting scheme, taking account of the variables, 'Bundesland', size of municipality, sex, age, and occupation. The data are available form the Central Archive (ZA) at the University of Cologne.

[2] In 2005/6 a new BIBB/BAuA-Survey was conducted (20,000 employed people interviewed, CATI). These data will be available from the ZA in Cologne from early 2008.

[3] 'Abschlussbericht zum Forschungsprojekt 1.1.006. Erwerb und Verwertung beruflicher Qualifikationen—BIBB/IAB-Erhebung 1998/99', available at: http://www2.bibb.de/tools/fodb/pdf/eb_11006.pdf

Table A.5. The ISSP 'Family and Changing Gender Roles' Module, ISSP 2002

	Survey context	Sampling procedure	Data collection methods	Sample size	Response rate
DE	Part of larger survey	Two-stage random sample	Face-to-face and self-completion with interviewer involvement *	DE-W: 936 DE-E: 431	DE-W 46% DE-E 46%
GB	Part of larger survey	Stratified clustered random sample	Self-completion with interviewer involvement	1,960	52%
ES	Individual survey	Three-stage stratified random sample	Face-to-face	2,471	—
FR	Individual survey	Two-stage random sample	Self-completion by mail	1,951	ca. 20%
NL	Part of larger survey	Two-stage with quota procedures	Self-completion with interviewer involvement	1,249	25%
SE	Individual survey	Random sample	Self-completion by mail	1,080	men 53%, women 61%

Notes: The response rates were calculated as the eligible sample divided by the effective sample size, as reported in the survey documentation. * Face-to-face for background variables and self-completion with interviewer involvement for substantive variables.

Sources: Klein and Harkness (2004) for France and the Netherlands; Scholz, Harkness and Klein (2003) for Germany; Edlund and Svallfors (2002) for Sweden; and individual study description for Britain and Spain (available at: www.za.uni-koeln.de/data/en/issp/nspub/ZA3880_StudyDescriptions.pdf).

Table A.6. The BIBB/IAB-Surveys, sample composition and size

Year	Sample	Available for analysis
1979	Employed, unemployed, no foreigners or apprentices/trainees	28,828
1985/6	Employed, excluding the unemployed, foreigners or apprentices/trainees—two separate surveys by the BIBB and the IAB with, in part, different questionnaires	26,515 IAB: 15,000 BIBB: 11,515
1991/2	Old Länder: employed (including foreigners with knowledge of German language, excluding the unemployed, apprentices/trainees) New Länder: employed and unemployed (excluding foreigners, apprentices/trainees)	34,277 Old Länder: 24,090 employed New Länder: 7,851 employed, 1,880 unemployed and 456 in re-education
1998/9	Employed plus foreigners with sufficient knowledge of German language, excluding apprentices/trainees	34,343 (of which 32,896 with German citizenship)

Source: http://www.bibb.de/dokumente/pdf/a22_bibb-iab-1998-1999_ueberblick.pdf see also Dostal, W. and Jansen, R. (2002); Parmentier K. and Dostal, W. (2002).

The British Skills Surveys

The British Skills Surveys series consists of a number of cross-sectional surveys that have measured skills trends and their implications for work experience during the 1990s. The surveys were separately funded and differed in the scope of their concerns, but they included a common core of questions on a wide range of key issues. The surveys used in the book were carried out in 1992, 1997, and 2001 respectively (a new survey will later become available for 2006).

The 1992 Employment in Britain (EIB) survey was co-sponsored by an Industrial Consortium, the Employment Department, the Employment Service, and the Leverhulme Trust. The principal investigators were Duncan Gallie, Nuffield College, Oxford, and Michael White, Policy Studies Institute, London. The aim of the survey was to provide a representative picture of the nature of work and the employment relationship in Britain in the early 1990s. The overall programme consisted of three large-scale national surveys of people in the labour market aged 20 to 60 (employees, self-employed, and unemployed). Its focus was on the skills required of employees in their jobs, together with extensive information about job quality. The interview for employed people was divided into three parts: a questionnaire on individuals' work histories, which traced their labour market experiences from the time that they first left full-time education; a main questionnaire covering employees' current and recent experience of work; and a self-completion questionnaire which contained items of a relatively sensitive or personal nature. The survey achieved a response rate of 72 percent in the case of the employed sample, resulting in a sub-sample of 3,869 individuals (Table A.7).

Table A.7. The EIB, 1997 and 2001 Skills surveys: sample composition, size, and response rate

Survey	Sample	Gross response rate (%)	Available for analysis
1992 Employment in Britain Survey	Employed, self-employed and unemployed, aged 20–60	72	3,869
1997 Skills Survey	Employed, aged 20–60	67	2,467
2001 Skills Survey	Employed, aged 20–60	72	4,470

Sources: Felstead, A., Gallie, D., and Green, F. (2002); Gallie, D., White, M., Cheng, Y., and Tomlinson, M. (1998).

The sample results were weighted according to two factors: the primary weighting factor was the number of eligible individuals at each pre-selected address, given the fact that only one person was interviewed at each address regardless of the number of eligible people at that dwelling unit; gender was introduced as the second weighting factor to correct for a slight over-representation of women in the sample.

The 1997 Skills Survey, funded by ESRC as part of its 'Learning Society' research programme, was designed to extend the evidence about trends across time in broad skills while providing more detailed knowledge about particular skills. The principal investigators were Alan Felstead (then of the University of Leicester) and Francis Green, University of Kent. It was a nationally representative survey of 2,467 individuals who were aged 20 to 60 and classified as in paid work at the time of the interview, with a response rate of 67 percent (Table A.7). The designers of the questionnaires built into the survey a wide range of questions that were directly comparable to the 1992 EIB survey. The primary innovation of the survey was that it enabled the measurement of ten generic skills and in addition computing skills.

The 2001 Skills Survey was a partial repeat survey, funded by the UK Government's Department for Education and Skills and the Centre for Skills Knowledge and Organizational Performance (SKOPE) at the Universities of Oxford and Warwick. The principal investigators were Alan Felstead, University of Leicester, Duncan Gallie, Nuffield College, Oxford; and Francis Green, University of Kent. All the key questions on job analyses and skill requirements were repeated identically. The survey thereby enabled an updating of the picture of the distribution of and trends in broad skill requirements, and for the first time gave measures of the trends in utilization of generic skills. The survey extended the work of the 1997 survey by including a richer set of measures of other aspects of job quality that allowed comparisons with the 1992 EIB survey. It achieved a gross response rate of 72 percent and the resulting sub-sample was 4,470 employed individuals (Table A.7). Like the EIB survey, the sample was weighted to take into account the differential probabilities of sample selection according to the number of eligible interview respondents at each address.

Overall the series constructed to date provides us with broad measures of job skill in terms of the qualifications required for recruitment to jobs, the accumulated required training time, and the required learning time. It has also provided evidence for change in generic skills for the period 1997 to 2001. Finally, it offers a wide range of measures over time of the quality of the work task and of the work context. All the three datasets and further information are available at the UK Data Archive (http://www.data-archive.ac.uk/).

Enquêtes complémentaires à l'enquête emploi: Conditions of Work, France

The French work conditions surveys are carried out under the responsibility of the Ministry of Employment, Dares, and INSEE (the National Institute of Statistics). They are periodic modules based on sub-samples drawn from the main annual labour force surveys, namely from the third leaving the sample in that year. The surveys used in Chapter 4 were carried out in 1984, 1991, and 1998. They focus broadly on working conditions—in particular, the hours of work, the nature of the work task, and physical hazards in working conditions. Background data on individuals is drawn from the original Labour Force Surveys.

While the objective is to observe work conditions as perceived by those in work, the questions are designed to tap factual issues rather than opinions. The main focus is on the prevalence of constraints in the work situation. The surveys seek to maintain reasonable continuity between years in the contents of the questionnaires, but vary to some degree between surveys to address new issues or to increase the depth of information on particular topics. The 1984 survey focused on three broad themes: working hours and the organization of work time; work organization; and physically hazardous work conditions. The 1991 survey centred on four broad themes—in addition to those above, it included a larger question set on the contents of work. It also extended the question coverage on the use of machines and new technologies. The 1998 questionnaire maintained the same basic structure, but again included additional question on the mental demands of work, new technologies, and work accidents.

The sample in 1984 was drawn to be representative of employees, while those of 1991 and 1998 were drawn to be representative of people in work (whether or not employees). All active people in the selected households were interviewed in face-to-face interviews at home. Proxy interviews were not allowed. Sample sizes were: 17,602 in 1984; 19,220 in 1991 and 20,067 in 1998. Chapter 4 uses the sub-samples of employees for each survey.

Further information is available from LASMAS (http://www.iresco.fr).

The National Swedish Survey of Living Conditions (ULF)

The ULF is a broad social survey covering areas such as work environment, housing conditions, economic conditions, health, leisure activities, social relations, employment conditions, transport and communications patterns, sense of safety and security, and education. The survey has been conducted annually by Statistics Sweden since 1975. The questionnaire consists of rotating themes that appear for at least two consecutive waves.

For each wave, an eight year rotating panel component and a cross-sectional component of equal shares is pooled. Each component is formed of a national representative systematic sample stratified by age of all 16–84-year-olds domiciled in Sweden. The sampling procedure closely resembles a stratified random sample.

Effective sample sizes were initially around 11,500, but were adjusted to 6–7,000 from 1980 onwards. The response rates declined from 87 to 75 percent during the period 1980 through 2005. Precision is improved by post-stratification weights based on approximately 82 strata defined by sex, age intervals, place of living, and marital status.

The analyses in Chapter 4 are based upon the sub-sample of employees. Further information can be sourced from Statistics Sweden (2006).

References

Acemoglu, D. (2002). 'Technical Change, Inequality, and the Labor Market', *Journal of Economic Literature*, 40(1): 7–72.

—— and Pischke, J. S. (1998). 'Why Do Firms Train? Theory and Evidence', *Quarterly Journal of Economics*, 113(1): 79–119.

—— —— (1999a). 'Beyond Becker: Training in Imperfect Labour markets', *Economic Journal*, 109(453): F112–F42.

—— —— (1999b). 'The Structure of Wages and Investment in General Training', *Journal of Political Economy*, 107(3): 539–72.

Addison, J. T., Bellmann, L., Schnabel, C., and Wagner, J. (2002). 'German Works Councils Old and New: Incidence, Coverage and Determinants', *IZA Discussion Paper*, No.495, Bonn Germany: Institute for the Study of Labor.

—— Schnabel, C., and Wagner, J. (2006). 'The (Parlous) State of German Unions', *IZA Discussion Paper:* No. 2000, Bonn Germany: Institute for the Study of Labour.

Allmendinger, J. (1989). 'Educational Systems and Labor Market Outcomes', *European Sociological Review*, 5(3): 231–50.

Almeida-Santos, F. and Mumford, K. (2005). 'Employee Training and Wage Compression in Britain', *Manchester School*, 73(3): 321–42.

Aoyama, Y. and Castells, M. (2002). 'An Empirical Assessment of the Informational Society: Employment and Occupational Structures of G7 Countries, 1920–2000', *International Labour Review*, 141(1–2): 123–59.

Argyris, C. (1964). *Integrating the Individual and the Organisation*. New York: Wiley.

Arrowsmith, J. (2006). *Temporary Agency Work in an Enlarged European Union*. Dublin, Ireland: European Foundation for the Improvement of Living and Working Conditions.

Artiles, A. M. (2005). *Reconciliation of Work, and Family Life for Women in Spain*. European Industrial Relations Observatory On-line. Dublin: European Foundation for the Improvement of Living and Working Conditions (available at: http://eurofund.europa.eu/eiro/2005/04/feature/cs0504205f.html).

Arulampalam, W. and Booth, A. L. (1998). 'Training and Labour Market Flexibility: Is There a Trade-Off?', *British Journal of Industrial Relations*, 36(4): 521–36.

Aryee, S., Field, D., and Luk, V. (1999). 'A Cross-Cultural Test of a Model of the Work–Family Interface', *Journal of Management*, 25: 491–511.

Ashford, S. J., Lee, C., and Bobko, P. (1989). 'Content, Causes, and Consequences of Job Insecurity: A Theory-Based Measure and Substantive Test', *Academy of Management Journal*, 32(4): 803–29.

Ashton, D., Davies, B., Felstead, A., and Green, F. (1999). *Work Skills in Britain*. Oxford: Centre for Skills, Knowledge and Organisational Performance.

Atkinson, J. (1984). 'Manpower Strategies for Flexible Organisations', *Personnel Management*, 15(8): 28–31.

Auer, P. and Cazes, S. (2003). 'Introduction', in P. Auer and S. Cazes, (eds), *Employment Stability in an Age of Flexibility*. Geneva, Switzerland: International Labour Office.

Autor, D. H., Levy, F., and Murnane, R. J. (2003). 'The Skill Content of Recent Technological Change: An Empirical Exploration', *The Quaterly Journal of Economics*, 118: 1279–333.

Åberg, R. (2004). 'Vilka jobb har skapats på den svenska arbetsmarknaden de senaste decennierna?', *Ekonomisk Debatt*, 34: 37–46.

Bainbridge, S., Murray, J., Harrison, T., and Ward, T. (2004). *Learning for Employment. Second Report on Vocational Education and Training Policy in Europe*. Luxembourg: Office for Official Publications of the European Communities.

Barker, K. and Christensen, K. (ed.) (1998). *Contingent Work: American Employment Relations in Transition*. Ithaca, NY: Cornell University Press.

Barling, J. and Kelloway, E. K. (1996). 'Job Insecurity and Health: The Moderating Role of Workplace Control', *Stress Medicine*, 12(4): 253–59.

Barrett, A. and O'Connell, P. (2001). 'Does Training Generally Work? The Returns to In-Company Training', *Industrial and Labor Relations Review*, 54: 647–62.

Bassanini, A. (2006). 'Training, Wages and Employment Security: An Empirical Analysis on European Data', *Applied Economics Letters*, 13(8): 523–27.

—— and Brunello, G. (2003). 'Is Training More Frequent When Wage Compression is Higher?' IZA Discussion Paper Series No.839. Bonn, Germany: Institute for the Study of Labour.

—— Booth, A. L., Brunello, G., De Paola, M., and Leuven, E. (2005). 'Workplace Training in Europe', IZA Discussion Paper Series, No.1640. Bonn, Germany: Institute for the Study of Labour.

Batt, R. and Valcour, P. M. (2003). 'Human Resource Practices as Predictors of Work–Family Outcomes and Employee Turnover', *Industrial Relations*, 42(2): 189–20.

Becker, G. S. (1964). *Human Capital: A Theoretical and Empirical Analysis with Special Reference to Education*. New York: Columbia University Press.

Begg, I. (2004). 'Policy Responses to Marginalization: The Changing Role of the EU', in D. Gallie (ed.), *Resisting Marginalization*. Oxford: Oxford University Press.

Bell, D. (1974). *The Coming of Post-Industrial Society*. London: Heinemann.

Bellmann, L. and Düll, H. (1999). 'Die Bedeutung des beruflichen Bildungsabschlusses in der betrieblichen Weiterbildung. Eine Analyses auf der Basis des IAB Betriebspanels 1997 fuer West- und Ostdeutschland', in L. Bellmann and V. Steiner (eds), *Panelanalysen zur Lohnstruktur, Qualifikation und*

Beschaeftigungsdynamik. Nuernberg, Germany: IAB, Beitraege zur Arbeitsmarkt- und Berufsforschung.

Berg, P., Appelbaum, E., Bailey, T., and Kalleberg, A. L. (2004). 'Contesting Time: International Comparisons of Employee Control of Working Time', *Industrial & Labor Relations Review*, 57(3): 331–49.

Berger, S. and Piore, M. (1980). *Dualism and Discontinuity in Industrialised Societies*. Cambridge: Cambridge University Press.

Bishop, J. (1997). 'Expertise and Excellence: Skill Development in the United States', in B. W. M. Hövels, W. J. Nijhof, A. M. L. van Wieringen, and M. van Dyck (eds), *Beroepsonderwijs en Volwasseneneducatie Nader Bekeken*. Den Haag, the Netherlands: VUGA Uitgeverij.

Black, S. and Lynch, L. (1997). 'How to Compete: The Impact of Workplace Practices and Information Technology on Productivity', NBERWorking Paper No. 6120. Cambridge, MA: National Bureau of Economic Research.

Blanchflower, D. and Freeman, R. B. (ed.) (2000). *Youth Unemployment and Joblessness in Advanced Countries*. Chicago, IL: University of Chicago Press/NBER.

Blau, F. D. and Kahn, L. M. (1996). 'Wage Structure and Gender Earnings Differentials: An International Comparison', *Economica*, 63(250): S29–S62.

Blauner, R. (1964). *Alienation and Freedom: The Factory Worker and his Industry*. Chicago, IL: University of Chicago Press.

—— (1967). 'Work Satisfaction and Industrial Trends in Modern Society', in R. Bendix and S. M. Lipset (eds), *Class, Status and Power: Social Stratification in Comparative Perspective*. London: Routledge and Kegan Paul.

Blossfeld, H.-P., Klijzing, E., Mills, M., and Kurz, K. (eds) (2005). *Globalization, Uncertainty and Youth in Society*. London: Routledge.

Blundell, R., Dearden, L., and Meghir, C. (1996). *The Determinants and Effects of Work-related Training in Britain*. London: Institute For Fiscal Studies.

Booth, A. (1993). 'Private Sector Training and Graduate Earnings', *Review of Economics and Statistics*, 76: 164–70.

—— and Bryan, M. L. (2005). 'Testing Some Predictions of Human Capital Theory: New Training Evidence from Britain', *Review of Economics and Statistics*, 87(2): 391–4.

—— Francesconi, M., and Zoega, G. (2003). 'Unions, Work-related Training and Wages: Evidence for British Men', *Industrial and Labour Relations Review*, 57: 68–91.

—— —— and Frank, J. (2003). 'A Sticky Floors Model of Promotion, Pay and Gender', *European Economic Review*, 47: 295–322.

Bosch, G. (1999). 'Working Time: Tendencies and Emerging Issues', *International Labour Review*, 138(2): 131–49.

Bratberg, E., Dahl, S.-A., and Risa, A. E. (2002). 'The Double Burden: Do Combinations of Career and Family Obligations Increase Sickness Absence among Women?' *European Sociological Review*, 18(2): 233–49.

References

Braverman, H. (1974). *Labor and Monopoly Capital. The Degradation of Work in the Twentieth Century*. New York: Monthly Review Press.

Breen, R. and Luijkx, R. (2004). 'Social Mobility in Europe between 1970 and 2000', in R. Breen (ed.), *Social Mobility in Europe*. Oxford: Oxford University Press.

Brinton, M. C. (2005). 'Education and the Economy', in N. J. Smelser and R. Swedberg (eds), *Handbook of Economic Sociology*, 2nd edn. Princeton, NJ: Princeton University Press and Russell Sage Foundation.

Brunello, G. (2001). 'On the Complementarity between Education and Training in Europe', in D. Checchi and C. Lucifora (eds), *Education, Training and Labour Market Outcomes in Europe*. New York: Macmillan.

Bullock, L. (1977). *Report of the Committee of Inquiry on Industrial Democracy. Cmnd 6706*. London: HMSO.

Burchell, B., Lapido, D., and Wilkinson, F. (2002). *Job Insecurity and Work Intensification*. London: Routledge.

Burri, S., Opitz, H. C., and Veldman, A. G. (2003). 'Work–Family Policies on Working Time Put into Practice: A Comparison of Dutch and German Case Law on Working Time Adjustment', *International Journal of Comparative Labour Law and Industrial Relations*, 19: 321–46.

Byron, K. (2005). 'A Meta-Analytic Review of Work–Family Conflict and Its Antecedents', *Journal of Vocational Behavior*, 67(2): 169–98.

Caplan, R. D., Cobb, S., French, J. R. P. J., Harrison, R. V., and Pinneau, S. R. (1980). *Job Demands and Worker Health: Main Effects and Occupational Differences*. Ann Arbor, MI: Institute for Social Research.

Cappelli, P., Bassi, L., Katz, H., Knoke, D., Osterman, P., and Useem, M. (1997). *Change at Work*. Oxford: Oxford University Press.

Castells, M. and Aoyama, Y. (1994). 'Paths towards the Informational Society: Employment Structure in G-7 Countries, 1920–90', *International Labour Review*, 133(1): 5–33.

Charles, M. and Grusky, D. B. (2004). *Occupational Ghettos: The Worldwide Segregation of Women and Men*. Stanford, CA: Stanford University Press.

Christensen, K. E. and Staines, G. L. (1990). 'Flextime: A Viable Solution to Work/Family Conflict?' *Journal of Family Issues*, 11: 455–76.

Clark, A. (2005). 'Your Money or Your Life: Changing Job Quality in the OECD Countries', IZA Discussion Paper No. 1610.

Clark, S. C. (2001). 'Work Cultures and Work/Family Balance', *Journal of Vocational Behavior*, 58: 348–65.

Clarkberg, M. and Merola, S. (2003). 'Competing Clocks: Work and Leisure in Dual-Earner Couples', in P. Moen (ed.), *It's about Time: Couples and Careers*. Ithaca, NY: Cornell University Press.

Cousins, C. R. and Tang, N. (2004). 'Working Time and Work and Family Conflict in the Netherlands, Sweden and the UK', *Work, Employment and Society* 18(3): 531–49.

Crompton, R. (2002). 'Employment, Flexible Working and the Family', *British Journal of Sociology*, 53 (4): 537–58.

—— and Jones, G. (1984). *White-Collar Proletariat*. London: Macmillan.

—— and Lyonette, C. (2005). 'Work–Life "Balance" in Europe', GeNet Working Paper No. 10, October.

Cruz-Castro, L. and Conlon, G. P. P. (2001). 'Initial Training Policies and Transferability of Skills in Britain and Spain', Instituto Juan March de Estudios e Investigaciones Working Paper No.2001/162.

Davis, K. and Moore, W. E. (1945). 'Some Principles of Stratification', *American Sociological Review*, 10: 242–49.

Dekker, S. W. A. and Schaufeli, W. B. (1995). 'The Effects of Job Insecurity on Psychological Health and Withdrawal: A Longitudinal-Study', *Australian Psychologist*, 30(1): 57–63.

Dex, S. and Smith, C. (2002). *The Nature and Pattern of Family-friendly Employment Policies in Britain*. Bristol, UK: Policy Press.

—— and Bond, S. (2005). 'Measuring Work–Life Balance and Its Covariates', *Work, Employment & Society*, 19(3): 627–37.

DiPrete, T. A., de Graaf, P. M., Luijkx, R., Thalin, M., and Blossfeld, H.-P. (1997). 'Collectivist versus Individualist Mobility Regimes? Structural Change and Job Mobility in Four Countries', *American Journal of Sociology*, 103: 318–58.

—— Goux, D., Maurin, E., and Tablin, M. (2001). 'Institutional Determinants of Employment Chances: The Structure of Unemployment in France and Sweden', *European Sociological Review*, 17(3): 233–54.

Doeringer, P. and Piore, M. (1971). *Internal Labor Markets and Manpower Analysis*. Lexington, MA: D. C. Heath.

Dostal, W. and Jansen, R. (2002). 'Qualifikation und Erwerbssituation in Deutschland—20 Jahre BIBB/IAB-Erhebungen', *Mitteilungen aus der Arbeitsmarkt- und Berufsforchung*, 35(2): 232–53 (available at: http://doku.iab.de).

Durkheim, E. (1930). *De la division du travail soci*. Paris: PUF/Quadrige.

Dustmann, C. and Pereira, S. (2005). 'Wage Growth and Job Mobility in the UK and Germany', IZA Discussion Paper No.1586.

Duxbury, L., Higgins, C., and Lee, C. (1994). 'Work–Family Conflict: A Comparison by Gender, Family Type, and Perceived Control', *Journal of Family Issues*, 15(3): 449–66.

Edlund, J. and Svallfors, S. (2002). 'ISSP 2002: Family and Gender III'. Codebook for machine-readable datafile, umeå University (available at: www.umu.se).

Edwards, R. C. (1979). *Contested Terrain: The Transformation of the Workforce in the Twentieth Century*. New York: Basic Books.

Engelbrech, G. and Jungkunst, M. (2001). 'Erwerbsbeteiligung von Frauen: Wie bringt man Beruf und Kinder unter einen Hut?', 1st edn. AB Kurzbericht 7/200, Nürnberg, Germany: IAB.

References

Ericson, T. (2004). 'The Effects of Wage Compression on Training: Swedish Empirical Evidence', Working Paper Series 2004: 15. IFAU: Institute for Labour Market Policy Evaluation.

Erikson, R. and Goldthorpe, J. H. (1992). *The Constant Flux: A Study of Class Mobility in Industrial Societies*. Oxford: Oxford University Press.

—— and Jonsson, J. O. (1998). 'Qualifications and the Allocation Process of Young Men and Women in the Swedish Labour Market', in Y. Shavit and W. Müller (eds), *From School to Work: A Comparative Study of Educational Qualifications and Occupational Destinations*. Oxford: Clarendon Press.

—— Goldthorpe, J. and Portocarero, L. (1979). 'Intergenerational Class Mobility in Three Western European Societies: England, France and Sweden', *British Journal of Sociology*, 30: 415–41.

Esping-Andersen, G. (1990). *The Three Worlds of Welfare Capitalism*. Cambridge: Polity Press.

Estevez-Abe, M. (2005). 'Gender Bias in Skills and Social Policies: The Varieties of Capitalism Perspective on Sex Segregation', *Social Politics*, 12(2): 180–215.

—— Iversen, T., and Soskice, D. (2001). 'Social Protection and the Formation of Skills: A Reinterpretation of the Welfare State', in P. A. Hall and D. Soskice (eds), *Varieties of Capitalism: The Institutional Foundations of Comparative Advantage*. Oxford: Oxford University Press.

European Commission (2000). *Communication from the Commission to the Council, the European Parliament, the Economic and Social Committee and the Committee of Regions*. Social Policy Agenda, Brussels: Commission of the European Communities.

—— (2001a) 'Employment and Social Policies: A Framework for Investing in Quality'. Communication from the Commission to the Council, the European Parliament, the Economic and Social Committee, and the Committee of the Regions. COM (2001) 313 final.

—— (2001b). *Employment in Europe 2001 Recent Trends and Prospects*. Luxembourg: Office for Official Publications of the European Communities.

—— (2002). *Joint Report on Social Inclusion*. Luxembourg: Office for Official Publications of the European Union.

—— (2003). 'Improving Quality in Work: A Review of Recent Progress', Communication from the Commission to the Council, the European Parliament, the Economic and Social Committee and the Committee of the Regions, COM(2003) 728.

—— (2004). *Industrial Relations in Europe 2004*. Luxembourg: Office for Official Publications of the European Communities.

—— (2006). *Joint Report on Social Protection and Social Inclusion*. Luxembourg: Office for Official Publications of the European Communities.

Eurostat (2006). 'Expenditure on Labour Market Policies in 2004', *Statistics in Focus: Population and Social Conditions*, 12: 1–7.

Evans, J. M., Lippoldt, D. C., and Marianna, P. (2001). 'Trends in Working Hours in OECD Countries', No.45 edn. OECD Labour Market and Social Policy Occasional Papers. Paris: OECD.

Evertsson, M. (2004). 'Formal On-the-job Training: A Gender-typed Experience and Wage-related Advantage?', *European Sociological Review*, 20(1): 79–94.

Eyraud, F. and Tchobanian, R. (1985). 'The Auroux Reforms and Company Level Industrial Relations in France', *British Journal of Industrial Relations*, 23(2): 241–58.

Fagan, C. (2004). 'Gender and Working Time in Industrialised Countries', in J. Messenger (ed.), *Working Time and Workers' Preferences in Industrialized Countries: Finding the Balance*. London: Routledge.

—— and Hebson, G. (2004). 'Making Work Pay: Debates From a Gender Perspective: A Comparative Review of Some Recent Policy Reforms in Thirty European Countries', Employment Directorate (DGV), European Commission, Brussels, Co-ordinators' report for the EU Expert Group on Gender, Social Inclusion and Employment Expert Group (EGGSIE) to the Equal Opportunities Unit.

—— Hegewisch, A., and Pilinger, J. (2006). 'Out of Time: Why Britain Needs a New Approach to Working-time Flexibility', Research paper for the TUC.

Farkas, G., England, P., Vicknair, K., and Kilbourne, B. S. (1997). 'Cognitive Skill, Skill Demands of Jobs, and Earnings among Young European American, African American, and Mexican American Workers', *Social Forces*, 75(3): 913–38.

Felstead, A. and Jewson, N. (1999). *Global Trends in Flexible Labour*. Basingstoke, UK: Macmillan.

—— Gallie, D., and Green, F. (2002). *Work Skills in Britain 1986–2001*. Nottingham, UK: DfES Publications.

Finegold, D. and Wagner, K. (1999). 'The German Skill Creation System and Team Based Production: Competitive Asset or Liability?', in P. D. Culpepper and D. Finegold (eds), *The German Skills Machine: Sustaining Comparative Advantage in a Global Economy*. New York: Berghahn Books.

—— and Soskice, D. (1998). 'The Failure of Training in Britain: Analysis and Prescription', *Oxford Review of Economic Policy*, 4(3): 21–53.

Fligstein, N. and Byrkjeflot, H. (1996). 'The Logic of Employment Systems', in J. Baron, D. Grusky, and D. Treiman (eds), *Social Differentiation and Stratification*. Boulder, CO: Westview Press.

French, J. R. P. J., Caplan, R. D., and Harrison, R. V. (1982). *The Mechanisms of Job Stress and Strain*. Chichester, UK: John Wiley & Sons.

Fricke, W. (2003). 'Thirty Years of Work Life Programmes in Germany', *Concepts and Transformation*, 8(1): 43–68.

Frick, K. and Wren, J. (2000). 'Reviewing Occupational Health and Safety Managment: Multiple Roots, Diverse Perspectives and Ambiguous Outcomes', in

K. Frick, P. L. Jensen, M. Quinlan, and T. Wilthagen (eds), *Systematic Occupational Health and Safety Management Systems*. Oxford: Elsevier Science.

—— Jensen, P. L., Quinlan, M., and Wilthagen, T. (2000). *Systematic Occupational Health and Safety Management Systems*. Oxford: Elsevier Science.

Friedmann, G. (1946). *Problemes humains du machinisme industriel*. Paris: Gallimard.

Frohlich, D. and Pekruhl, U. (1996). *Direct Participation and Organisational Change. Fashionable but Misunderstood: An Analysis of Recent Research in Europe, Japan and the USA*. Luxembourg: Office for Official Publications of the European Communities.

Frone, M. R., Russel, M., and Cooper, M. L. (1992*a*). 'Antecedents and Outcomes of Work–Family Conflict: Testing a Model of the Work-Family Interface', *Journal of Applied Psychology*, 77(1): 65–78.

—— —— —— (1992*b*). 'Prevalence of Work–Family Conflict: Are Work and Family Boundaries Asymmetrically Permeable?' *Journal of Organizational Behavior*, 13(7): 723–9.

—— Yardley, J. K., and Markel, K. S. (1997). 'Developing and Testing an Integrative Model of the Work–Family Interface', *Journal of Vocational Behavior*, 50(2): 145–67.

Gallie, D. (on behalf of the European Commission) (1997). 'Employment, Unemployment and the Quality of Life: The Employment in Europe Survey 1996'. Paper given at the University of Oxford, Oxford, June (available at: http://ec.europa.eu/public_opinion/archives/eb/ebs_098_en.pdf).

—— (2003). 'The Quality of Working Life: Is Scandinavia Different?' *European Sociological Review*, 19(1): 61–79.

—— (2005). 'Work Pressure in Europe 1996–2001: Trends and Determinants', *British Journal of Industrial Relations*, 43: 351–75.

Gallie, D. and Paugam, S. (eds) (2000). *Welfare Regimes and the Experience of Unemployment in Europe*. Oxford: Oxford University Press.

—— —— (2002). 'Social Precarity and Social Integration', Report for the European Commission based on Eurobarometer 56. 1, October (available at: http://ec.europa.eu/public_opinion/archives/eb/ebs_098_en.pdf).

—— White, M., Cheng, Y., and Tomlinson, M. (1998). *Restructuring the Employment Relationship*. Oxford: Clarendon Press.

Gangl, M. (2001). 'European Patterns of Labour Market Entry: A Dichotomy of Occupationalized versus Non-Occupationalized Systems?', *European Societies*, 3: 471–94.

Gatter, J. (1999). 'Continuing Occupational Training in an Ageing German Economy', in P. D. Culpepper and D. Finegold (eds), *The German Skills Machine: Sustaining Comparative Advantage in a Global Economy*. New York/Oxford: Berghahn Books.

Gauthier, A. H. and Bortnik, A. (2001). Comparative Maternity, Parental and Childcare Database, Version 2 (University of Calgary). Online available at http://www.soci.ucalgary.ca/FYPP/images/DOCUMENTS/Maternity-database-v2.xls

Gelderblom, A. and de Koning, J. (2002). 'Exclusion of Older Workers, Productivity and Training', in K. Schömann and P. J. O'Connell (eds), *Education, Training and Employment Dynamics*. Cheltenham, UK: Edward Elgar.

Gerfin, M. (2004). 'Work-related Training and Wages: An Empirical Analysis of Male Workers in Switzerland', IZA Discussion Paper Series No.1078. Bonn, Germany: Institute for the Study of Labour.

Gershuny, J. and Sullivan, O. (2003). 'Time Use, Gender, and Public Policy Regimes', *Social Politics*, 10(2): 205–28.

Goetschy, J. (1998). 'France: The Limits of Reform', in A. Ferner and R. Hyman, (eds), *Changing Industrial Relations in Europe*. Oxford: Blackwell.

Goldthorpe, J. (2000). 'Social Class and the Differentiation of Employment Contracts', in J. Goldthorpe, (ed.), *On Sociology: Numbers, Narratives, and the Integration of Research and Theory*. Oxford: Oxford University Press.

Goos, M. and Manning, A. (2007). 'Lousy and Lovely Jobs: The Rising Polarization of Work in Britain', *Review of Economic and Statistics*, 89: 118–33.

Gornick, J. C. (1999). 'Gender Equality in the Labour Market: Women's Employment and earnings', in D. Sainsbury (ed.), *Gender and Welfare State Regimes*. Oxford: Oxford University Press.

—— and Meyers, M. K. (2003). *Families that Work: Policies for Reconciling Parenthood and Employment*. New York: Russell Sage Foundation.

—— —— and Ross, K. E. (1997). 'Supporting the Employment of Mothers: Policy Variation across Fourteen Welfare States', *Journal of European Social Policy*, 7: 45–70.

—— —— —— (1998). 'Public Policies and the Employment of Mothers: A Cross-National Study', *Social Science Quarterly*, 79: 35–54.

Gottfredson, L. S. (1985). 'Education as a Valid but Fallible Signal of Worker Quality: Reorienting an Old Debate about the Functional Basis of the Occupational hierarchy', in A. C. Kerckhoff (ed.), *Research in the Sociology of Education and Socialization*, vol. 5.

Gourevitch, P., Martin. A., Ross, G., Bornstein, S., Markovits, A., and Allen, C. (1984). *Unions and Economic Crisis: Britain, West Germany and Sweden*. London: George Allen & Unwin.

Goux, D. and Maurin, E. (2000). 'Returns to Firm-provided Training: Evidence from French Worker–Firm Matched Data', *Labour Economics*, 7(1): 1–19.

Granquist, L. and Persson, H. (1999). 'Career Mobility and Gender', in H. Persson (ed.), *Essays on Labour Demand and Career Mobility*. Stockholm: Swedish Institute for Social Research.

Green, F. (2001). 'It's Been a Hard Day's Night: The Concentration and Intensification of Work in late 20th Century Britain', *British Journal of Industrial Relations*, 39(1): 53–80.

—— (2002). 'Why has Work Effort Become More Intense?', *Studies in Economics* 0207, Department of Economics, University of Kent.

Green, F. (2006). *Demanding Work: The Paradox of Job Quality in the Affluent Economy.* Princeton, NJ: Princeton University Press.

—— and McIntosh, S. (2001). 'The Intensification of Work in Europe', *Labour Economics*, 8: 291–308.

Greenhaus, J. H. and Beutell, N. J. (1985). 'Sources of Conflict between Work and Family Roles', *Academy of Management Review*, 10(1): 76–88.

Gregg, P. and Wadsworth, J. (1996). 'It Takes Two: Employment Polarisation in the OECD', CEP Discussion Paper No. 304. London: Centre for Economic Performance, LSE.

—— Hansen, K., and Wadsworth, J. (2000). 'Measuring the Polarisation of Work Across Households', Working paper, CEP. London: LSE.

Gremion, P. and Piotet, F. (2004). *Georges Friedmann: un sociologue dans le siecle 1902–1977.* Paris: CNRS Editions.

Grönlund, A. (2004). 'Flexibilitet eller friktion? Om inflytande över arbetstiden och konflikten mellan arbete och familj', *Sociologisk Forskning*, 1(1): 35–54.

Grubb, D. and Wells, W. (1993). 'Employment Regulation and Patterns of Work in EC Countries', *OECD Economic Studies*, 21(Winter): 7–56.

Grusky, D. B. (ed.) (2001). *Social Stratification: Class, Race, and Gender in Sociological Perspective.* Boulder, CO: Westview Press.

Gunningham, N. and Johnstone, R. (2000). 'The Legal Construction of OHS Management Systems', in K. Frick, P. L. Jensen, M. Quinlan, and T. Wilthagen (eds), *Systematic Occupational Health and Safety Management Systems.* Oxford: Elsevier Science.

Gustavsen, B. (1983). 'The Norwegian Work Environment Reform: The Transition from General Principles to Workplace Action', in C. Crouch and F. A. Heller (eds), *International Yearbook of Organisational Democracy, i. Organisational Democracy and Political Processes.* Chichester, UK: John Wiley & Sons.

—— Hofmaier, B., Philips, M. K., and Wikman, A. (1996). *A Concept-driven Development and the Organisation of the Process of Change: An Evaluation of the Swedish Working Life Fund.* Amsterdam, the Netherlands/Philadelphia, PA: John Benjamins Publishing Company.

Gutek, B. A., Searle, S., and Klepa, L. (1991). 'Rational versus Ggender Role Explanations for Work–Family Conflict', *Journal of Applied Psychology*, 76(4): 560–568.

Haas, B. and Wallace, C. (2004). 'Comparing the Relationship between Flexibility and Control of Work in Eight European Countries', Cross-National Research Papers, Seventh Series (3): Learning from Employment and Welfare Policies in Europe.

Hall, P. A. and Soskice, D. (ed.) (2001a). *Varieties of Capitalism: The Institutional Foundations of Comparative Advantage.* Oxford: Oxford University Press.

—— —— (2001b). 'An Introduction to Varieties of Capitalism', in P. A. Hall and D. Soskice (eds), *Varieties of Capitalism: The Institutional Foundation of Comparative Advantage.* Oxford: Oxford University Press.

Hartley, J., Jacobson, D., Klandermans, B., and van Vuuren, T. (1991). *Job Insecurity: Coping with Jobs at risk*. London: Sage.

Heckman, J. J. (1979). 'Sample Selection as a Specification Error', *Econometrica*, 47(1): 153–161.

Herrigel, G. and Sabel, C. F. (1999). 'Craft Production in Crisis: Industrial Restructuring in Germany during the 1990s', in P. D. Culpepper and D. Finegold (eds), *The German Skills Machine: Sustaining Comparative Advantage in a Global Economy*. Oxford/New York: Berghahn Books.

Hill, E. J., Yang, C., Hawkins, A. J., and Ferris, M. (2004). 'A Cross-Cultural Test of the Work–Family Interface in 48 countries', *Journal of Marriage and Family*, 66(5): 1300–16.

Hochschild, A. R. (1989). *The Second Shift*. New York: Avon.

Hunter, J. E. (1986). 'Cognitive-ability, Cognitive Aptitudes, Job Knowledge, and Job-performance', *Journal of Vocational Behavior*, 29(3): 340–62.

Huzzard, T. (2003). *The Convergence of the Quality of Working Life and Competitiveness*. Stockholm: National Institute for Working Life.

Hvid, H. (1999). 'Development of Work and Social (ex)inclusion', in J. Lind and I. H. Moller (eds), *Inclusion and Exclusion: Unemployment and Non-Standard Employment in Europe*. Aldershot, UK: Ashgate Publishing.

Iversen, T. and Soskice, D. (2001). 'An Asset Theory of Social Policy Preferences', *American Political Science Review*, 95(4): 875–93.

Jacobs, J. A. (2003). 'Changing Hours of Employment in American Families', Paper presented at the 'Workforce/Workplace Mismatch? Work, Family, Health, and Well-Being' Conference in Washington, DC, 16–18 June (Maryland Population Research Center).

—— and Gerson, K. (2001). 'Overworked Individuals or Overworked Families? Explaining Trends in Work, Leisure and Family Time', *Work and Occupations*, 28(1): 41–63.

Jefferys, S. (2003). *Liberte, Egalite and Fraternite at Work: Changing French Employment Relations and Management*. Basingstoke, UK: Macmillan.

Jick, T. D. (1985). 'As the Axe Fails: Budget Cuts and the Experience of Stress in Organizations', in T. A. Beehr and R. S. Bhagat (eds), *Human Stress and Cognition in Organizations: An Integrated Perspective*. New York: John Wiley & sons.

Johnson, J. V. and Johansson, G. (ed.) (1991). *The Psychosocial Work Environment: Work Organization, Democratization and Health: Essays in Memory of Bertil Gardell*. Amityville, NY: Baywood Publishing Company.

Joshi, H. and Paci, P. (1998). *Unequal Pay for Men and Women: Evidence from the British Birth Cohort Studies*. Cambridge, MA: The MIT Press.

Juhn, C., Murphy, K. M., and Pierce, B. (1991). 'Accounting for the Slowdown in Black–White Wage Convergence', in M. H. Kosters (ed.), *Workers and Their Wages*. Washington, DC: AEI Press.

Kamerman, S. B. (2000). 'International Journal of Educational Research Early Childhood Education and Care (ECEC): An Overview of Developments in the OECD Countries', *International Journal of Educational Research*, 33: 7–29.

Kangas, O. (1991). *The Politics of Social Rights: Studies on the Dimensions of Sickness Insurance in OECD Countries*. Stockholm: Stockholm University Press.

Karageorgiou, A., Jensen, P. L., Walters, D., and Wilthagen, T. (2000). 'Risk Assessment in Four Member States of the European Union', in K. Frick, P. L. Jensen, M. Quinlan, and T. Wilthagen (eds), *Systematic Occupational Health and Safety Management Systems*. Oxford: Elsevier Science.

Karesek, R. and Theorell, T. (1990). *Healthy Work: Stress, Productivity and the Reconstruction of Work Life*. New York: Basic Books.

Kelloway, E. K., Gottlieb, B. H., and Barham, L. (1999). 'The Source, Nature, and Direction of Work and Family Conflict: A Longitudinal Investigation', *Journal of Occupational Health Psychology*, 4(4): 337–46.

Kerckhoff, A. C., Raudenbush, S. W., and Glennie, E. (2001). 'Education, Cognitive Skill, and Labor Force Outcomes', *Sociology of Education*, 74(1): 1–24.

Kerr, C., Dunlop, J. T., Harbison, F., and Myers, C. A. (1960). *Industrialism and Industrial Man*. Cambridge, MA: Harvard University Press.

Kinnunen, U. and Mauno, S. (1998). 'Antecedents and Outcomes of Work–Family Conflict Among Employed Women and Men in Finland', *Human Relations*, 51(2): 157–77.

Kjellberg, A. (1998). 'Sweden: Restoring the Model?', in A. Ferner and R. Hyman (eds), *Changing Industrial Relations in Europe*. Oxford: Blackwell.

Klein, S. and Harkness, J. (2004). 'The International Social Survey Programme', Study Monitoring 2002, ZUMA (available at: www.za.uni-koeln.de).

Kodz, J., Davis, S., Lain, D., Strebler, M., Rick, J., Bates, P., Cummings, J., Meager, N., Anxo, D., Gineste, S., Trinczek, R., and Pamer, S. (2003). 'Working Long Hours: A Review of the Evidence', The Institute for Employment Studies, Volume 1—Main report, Department of Trade and Industry.

Kohn, M. and Schooler, C. (1983). *Work and Personality: An Inquiry into the Impact of Social Stratification*. Norwood, NJ: Ablex Publishing Corporation.

Korpi, W. (1978). *The Working Class in Welfare Capitalism: Work, Unions and Politics in Sweden*. London: Routledge and Kegan Paul.

—— (1983). *The Democratic Class Struggle*. London: Routledge and Kegan Paul.

Kossek, E. and Ozeki, C. (1998). 'Work–Family Conflict, Policies, and the Job-Life Satisfaction Relationship: A Review and Directions for Organizational Behavior-Human Resources Research', *Journal of Applied Psychology*, 83: 139–49.

Ladipo, D. and Wilkinson, F. (2002). 'More Pressure, Less Protection', in B. Burchell, D. Ladipo, and F. Wilkinson (eds), *Job Insecurity and Work Intensification*. London: Routledge.

Lane, C. (1987). 'Capitalism or Culture? A Comparative Analysis of the Position in the Labour Process and Labour Market of Lower White-collar Workers in the Financial Services Sector of Britain and the Federal Republic of Germany', *Work, Employment & Society*, 1(1): 57–83.

Latack, J. C. and Dozier, J. B. (1986). 'After the Axe Falls: Job Loss on a Career Transition', *Academy of Management Review* , 11: 375–92.

Lazarus, R. S. and Folkman, S. (1984). *Stress Appraisal and Coping*. New York: Springer.

Lehto, A.-M. and Sutela, H. (1999). *Efficient, More Efficient, Exhausted: Findings of Finnish Quality of Work Life Surveys 1977–1997*. Helsinki: Statistics Finland.

Leuven, E. (2005). 'The Economics of Private Sector Training: A Survey of the Literature', *Journal of Economic Surveys*, 19(1): 91–111.

Leuven, E. and Osterbeek, H. (2002). 'A New Approach to Estimate the Returns to Work-Related Training'. Unpublished working paper, IZA Discussion Paper Series No. 1122, Institute for Study of Labour, Bonn.

Lewis, J. (1992). 'Gender and the Development of Welfare Regimes', *Journal of European Social Policy*, 2(3): 159–73.

Lilja, K. (1998). 'Continuity and Modest Moves towards Company-level Corporatism', in A. Ferner and R. Hyman (eds),*Changing Industrial Relations in Europe*. Oxford: Blackwell.

Lynch, L. (1994). *Training and the Private Sector: International Comparisons*. Chicago, IL: University of Chicago Press.

Madsen, P. K. (2003). ' "Flexicurity" through Labour Market Policies and Institutions in Denmark', in P. Auer and S. Cazes (eds), *Employment Stability in an Age of Flexibility*. Geneva, Switzerland: International Labour Office.

Mandel, H. and Semyonov, M. (2005). 'Family Policies, Wage Structures, and Gender Gaps: Sources of Earnings Inequality in 20 Countries', *American Sociological Review*, 70(6): 949–67.

—— —— (2006). 'A Welfare State Paradox: State Intervention and Women's Employment Opportunities in 22 Countries', *American Journal of Sociology*, 111 (6): 1910–49.

Mangan, J. (2000). *Workers Without Traditional Employment: An International Study of Non-Standard Work*. Cheltenham, UK: Edward Elgar.

Manning, A. (2004). 'We Can Work it Out: The Impact of Technological Change on the Demand for Low-skill Workers', Centre for Economic Performance Discussion Paper No.640.

Mares, I. (2003). *The Politics of Social Risk: Business and Welfare State Development*. New York: Cambridge University Press.

Marsden, D. (1986). *The End of Economic Man? Custom and Competition in Labour Markets*. Brighton, UK: Wheatsheaf.

—— (1990). 'Institutions and Labour Mobility: Occupational and Internal Labour Markets in Britain, France, Italy and West Germany', in R. Brunetta and C. Dell'Aringa (eds), *Labour Relations and Economic Performance*. Houndmills, Basingstoke, UK: Macmillan.

—— (1999). *A Theory of Employment Systems: Micro-Foundations of Societal Diversity*. Oxford: Oxford University Press.

Marshall, T. H. (1964). 'Citizenship and Social Class', *Class, Citizenship and Social Development*. Chicago, IL: University of Chicago Press.

Martin, D. (1994). *Democratie industrielle: la participation directe dans les entreprises*. Paris: Presses Universitaires de France.

Matysiak, A. and Steinmetz, S. (2006). 'Who Follows Whom? Female Employment Patterns in West Germany, East Germany and Poland', Mannheimer Zentrum für Europäische Sozialforschung, Mannheim, Working Paper No.94.

Maurice, M., Sellier, F., and Silvestre, J. J. (1986). *The Social Foundations of Industrial Power: A Comparison of France and Germany*. Cambridge, MA: The MIT Press.

Maurin, E. and Thesmar, D. (2003). 'Changes in the Functional Structure of Firms and the Demand for Skill', CEPR Discussion Paper No. 3831.

McCall, L. and Orloff, A. (2005). 'Introduction to Special Issue of Social Politics: Gender, Class, and Capitalism', *Social Politics*, 12(2): 159–69.

Murray, G., Belanger, J., Giles, A., and Lapointe, P.-A. (ed.) (2002). *Work and Employment Relations in the High–performance Economy*. London: Continuum.

Müller, W. and Gangl, M. (2003). 'The Transition from School to Work: A European Perspective', in W. Müller and M. Gangl (eds), *Transitions from Education to Work in Europe: The Integration of Youth into EU Labour Markets*. Oxford: Oxford University Press.

—— and Shavit, Y. (1998). 'The Institutional Embeddedness of the Stratification Process: A Comparative Study of Qualifications and Occupations in Thirteen Countries', in Y. Shavit, and W. Müller (eds), *From School to Work: A Comparative Study of Educational Qualifications and Occupational Destinations*. Oxford: Clarendon Press.

Netemeyer, R. G., McMurrian, R., and Boles, J. S. (1996). 'Development and Validation of Work–Family Conflict and Family–Work Conflict Scales', *Journal of Applied Psychology*, 81(4): 400–10.

Nichols, T. and Beynon, H. (1977). *Living with Capitalism*. London: Routledge and Kegan Paul.

Nielson, K. T. (2000). 'Organizational Theories Implicit in Various Approaches to OHS Management', in K. Frick, P. L. Jensen, M. Quinlan, and T. Wilthagen (eds), *Systematic Occupational Health and Safety Management Systems*. Oxford: Elsevier Science.

Nilsson, A. and Svärd, B. (1991). 'The Quantitative Development of Vocational Education in Sweden 1950–1990', Lund Papers in Economic History No.12/1991, Dept. of Economic History, Lund University.

Nolan, B., Hauser, R., and Zoyem, J. P. (2000). 'The Changing Effects of Social Protection on Poverty', in D. Gallie and S. Paugam (eds), *Welfare Regimes and the Experience of Unemployment in Europe*. Oxford: Oxford University Press.

O'Connell, P. (1999). *Adults in Training: An International Comparison of Continuing Education and Training*. Paris: OECD Centre for Educational Research and Innovation.

—— (2002). 'Does Enterprise-Sponsored Training Aggravate or Alleviate Existing Inequalities? Evidence from Ireland', in K. Schömann and P. J. O'Connell (eds), *Education, Training and Employment Dynamics*. Cheltenham, UK: Edward Elgar.

OECD (1997a). *Employment Outlook July 1997*. Paris: OECD.

—— (1997b). 'Is Job Insecurity on the Increase in OECD Countries?', in OECD (ed.), *OECD Employment Outlook July*. Paris: Office for Economic Cooperation and Development.

—— (1998). *Employment Outlook 1998—Working Hours: Latest Trends and Policy Initiatives*, Chapter 5 edn. Paris: Organization for Economic Cooperation and Development.

—— (1999a). *Preparing Youth for the 21st Century: The Transition from Education to the Labour Market*. Paris: OECD.

—— (1999b). *Employment Outlook*. Paris: OECD.

—— (2002). *Employment Outlook 2002*. Paris: Organisation for Economic Co-operation and Development.

—— (2004). *Employment Outlook*. Paris: OECD.

—— (2005). *Society at a Glance: OECD Social Indicators 2005*. Paris: Organisation for Economic Co-operation and Development.

Ok, W. and Tergeist, P. (2003). 'Improving Workers' Skills: Analytical Evidence and the Role of the Social Partners', OECD Social, Employment and Migration Working Papers No. 10.

Palme, J. (1990). *Pension Rights in Welfare Capitalism: The Development of Old-Age Pensions in 18 OECD Countries 1930–1985*. Stockholm: Swedish Institute for Social Research.

Paoli, P. and Merlli, D. (2001). 'Third European Survey on Working Conditions', European Foundation for the Improvement of Living and Working Conditions. Luxembourg: Office for Official Publications of the European Communities.

Parasuraman, S. and Simmers, C. A. (2001). 'Type of Employment, Work–Family Conflict and Well-being: A Comparative Study', *Journal of Organizational Behavior*, 22(5): 551–68.

Parmentier, K. and Dostal, W. (2002). 'Qualifikation und Erwerbssituation in Deutschland: Konzeption und Inhaltliche Schwerpunkte der BIBB/IAB-Erhebungen', in G. Kleinhenz (ed.) *IAB-Kompenclium Arbeitsmarkt- und Berufsforschung*, Nürnberg, p. 31–44. Beiträge cur Arbeitsmarkt- und Berufsforschung No.250 (available at: http://doku.iab.de).

Paugam, S. (2000). *Salarié de la précarité: les nouvelles formes d'intégration professionnelle*. Paris: Presses Universitaires de France.

—— and Russell, H. (2000). 'The Effects of Employment Precarity and Unemployment on Social Isolation', in D. Gallie, and S. Paugam (eds), *Welfare Regimes and the Experience of Unemployment in Europe*. Oxford: Oxford University Press.

Piore, M. J. and Sabel, C. F. (1984). *The Second Industrial Divide: Possibilities for Prosperity*. New York: Basic Books.

References

Piotet, F. (1988). 'L'amélioration des conditions de travail entre échec et institutionnalisation', *Revue Francaise de Sociologie*, 29(1): 19–33.

Pischke, J. S. (2001). 'Continuous Training in Germany', *Journal of Population Economics*, 14(3): 523–48.

Platenga, J. (2002). 'Combining Work and Care in the Polder Model: An Assessment of the Dutch Part-time Strategy', *Critical Social Policy*, 22(1): 53–71.

Pleck, J. H., Staines, G. L., and Lang, L. (1980). 'Conflicts between Work and Family Life', *Monthly Labor Review*, 103: 29–32.

Polavieja, J. G. (2001). 'Insiders and Outsiders: Structure and Consciousness Effects of Labour Market Deregulation in Spain (1987–1997)', D.Phil. thesis, Nuffield College, University of Oxford.

Procter, S. J., Rowlinson, M., McArdle, L., Hassard, J., and Forrester, P. (1994). 'Flexibility, Politics and Strategy: In Defence of the Model of the Flexible Firm', *Work, Employment and Society*, 8(2): 221–42.

Promberger, M. (2001). 'Industriebeschäftigte in hochflexiblen Arbeitszeitarrangements [English Title: Flexible Working Hours for Blue-Collar Workers]', WSI-Mitteilungen 10/2001.

Quinn, R. P. and Staines, G. L. (1979). *The 1977 Quality of Employment Survey*. Ann Arbor, MI: Institute of Social Research.

Quintin, O. and Faverel-Dapas, B. (1999). *L'Europe sociale: enjeux et réalités*. Paris: La Documentation Francaise.

Raffe, D. and Müller, W. (2002). 'An Overview of the Catewe Project: Comparative Analysis of Transitions from Education to Work in Europe', paper to the European Research Network on Transitions in Youth, Florence.

Riedmann, A. (2006). *Working Time and Work Life Balance in European Companies: Establishment Survey on Working Time 2004–2005*. Dublin, Ireland: European Foundation for the Improvement of Living and Working Conditions.

Rodrigues, M. J. (ed.) (2002). *The New Knowledge Economy in Europe: A Strategy for International Competitiveness and Social Cohesion*. Cheltenham, UK: Edward Elgar.

—— (2003). *European Policies for a Knowledge Economy*. Cheltenham, UK: Edward Elgar.

Roehling, P. V., Moen, P., and Batt, R. (2003). 'Spillover', in P. Moen (ed.), *It's about Time: Couples and Careers*. New York: Cornell University Press.

Rose, M. (ed.) (1987). *Industrial Sociology: Work in the French Tradition*. London: Sage.

Rosenbaum, P. R. and Rubin, D. B. (1983). 'The Central Role of the Propensity Score in Observational Studies for Causal Effects', *Biometrica*, 70: 41–55.

Rosenberg, S. (1989). 'From Segmentation to Flexibility', *Labour and Society*, 14(4): 363–407.

Rubery, J. (1988). 'Employers and the Labour Market', *Employment in Britain*. Oxford: Blackwell.

Ryan, P. (2001). 'The School-to-work Transition: A Cross-National Perspective', *Journal of Economic Literature*, 39(1): 34–92.

Sandberg, A., Broms, G., Grip, A. et al. (1992). *Technological Change and Co-Determination in Sweden*. Philadelphia: Temple University Press.

Scheuer, S. (1998). 'Denmark: A Less Regulated Model', in A. Ferner and R. Hyman (eds), *Changing Industrial Relations in Europe*. Oxford: Blackwell.

Scholz, E., Harkness, J., and Klein, S. (2003). 'ISSP 2002 Germany: Family and Changing Gender Roles III', ZUMA Report on the Germany Study, ZUMA Methodenbericht 15/2003, December (available at: www.gesis.org).

Schooler, C., Mulatu, M. S., and Oates, G. (2004). 'Occupational Self-direction, Intellectual Functioning, and Self-directed Orientation in Older Workers: Findings and Implications for Individuals and Societies', *American Journal of Sociology*, 110(1): 161–97.

Schröder, L. (2000). 'Ungdomsarbetslösheten i ett internationellt perspektiv. [Youth Unemployment in International Perspective.]', *Research Report* 2000: 4, Institute for Labour Market Policy Evaluation (IFAU), Uppsala.

Shavit, Y. and Müller, W. (ed.) (1998). *From School to Work: A Comparative Study of Educational Qualifications and Occupational Destinations*. Oxford: Clarendon Press.

Sorensen, A. (2001). 'Gender Equality in Earnings at Work and at Home', Income Study Working Paper No.251, Luxemburg.

Soskice, D. (1994). 'Reconciling Markets and Institutions: The German Apprenticeship System', in L. Lynch (ed.), *Training and the Private Sector: International Comparisons*. Chicago, IL: University of Chicago Press and NBER.

—— (1999). 'Divergent Production Regimes: Coordinated and Uncoordinated Market Economies in the 1980s and 1990s', in H. Kitschelt (ed.), *Continuity and Changes in Contemporary Capitalism*. Cambridge: Cambridge University Press.

—— (2005). 'Varieties of Capitalism and Cross-national Gender Differences', *Social Politics*, 12(2): 170–79.

Sørensen, A. B. (1991). 'On the Usefulness of Class Analysis in Research on Social Mobility and Socioeconomic Inequality', *Acta Sociologica*, 34: 71–87.

—— (2000). 'Toward a Sounder Basis for Class Analysis', *American Journal of Sociology*, 105(6): 1523–58.

Spitz-Oener, A. (2006). 'Technical Change, Job Tasks, and Rising Educational Demands: Looking Outside the Wage Structure', *Journal of Labor Economics*, 24(2): 235–70.

Staines, G. L. and Pleck, J. H. (1986). 'Work Schedule Flexibility and Family-life', *Journal of Occupational Behaviour*, 7(2): 147–53.

Statistics Sweden (1998). *Sysselsattning, arbetstider och arbetsmiljo 1994–5* [Employment, Working Hours and Work Environment 1994–5] Report No.92. Stockholm: Statistics Sweden.

—— (2006). *Living Conditions: Appendix 16 The Swedish Survey of Living Conditions— Design and Methods*. Stockholm: Statistics Sweden.

Steiber, N. (2005). 'Work Humanisation Programmes in Germany in the 1990s', Changequal Working Paper, Nuffield College, University of Oxford.

References

Stephens, J. D. (1979). *The Transition from Capitalism to Socialism*. London: Macmillan.

Stern, D. and Wagner, D. (eds) (1999). *International Perspectives on the School-to-work Transition*. Creskill, NJ: Hampton Press.

Stier, H. and Lewin-Epstein, N. (2001). 'Welfare Regimes, Family-supportive Policies, and Women's Employment along the Life-course', *American Journal of Sociology*, 106: 1731–60.

Streeck, W. (1992). *Social Institutions and Economic Performance: Studies of Industrial Relations in Advanced Capitalist Economies*. London: Sage.

Sverke, M., Hellgren, J., and Naswall, K. (2006). *Job Insecurity: A Literature Review*. Stockholm: National Institute for Working Life.

Tausig, M. and Fenwick, R. (2001). 'Unbinding Time: Alternate Work Schedules and Work–Life balance', *Journal of Family and Economic Issues*, 22(2): 101–19.

Taylor, P. and Urwin, P. (2001). 'Age and Participation in Vocational Education and Training', *Work, Employment and Society*, 15(4): 763–79.

Taylor, R. (2002). 'Britain's World of Work: Myths and Realities', ESRC Future of Work Programme Seminar Series.

Tåhlin, M. (2006). 'Class Clues', Manuscript, Swedish Institute for Social Research (SOFI), Stockholm University.

Theorell, T. and Karesek, R. (1996). 'Current Issues Relating to Psychosocial Job Strain and Cardiovascular Disease Research', *Journal of Occupational Health and Psychology*, 1: 9–26.

Theorell, T. (1998). 'Job Characteristics in a Theoretical and Practical Health Context', in C. L. Cooper (ed.), *Theories of Organizational Stress*. Oxford: Oxford University Press.

Thorsrud, E. (1984). 'The Scandinavian Model: Strategies of Organizational Democracy in Norway', in B. Wilpert and A. Sorge (eds), *International Yearbook of Organizational Democracy, ii : International Perspectives on Organizational Democracy*. Chichester, UK: John Wiley & Sons.

Thurow, L. (1975). *Generating Inequality*. New York: Basic Books.

Uunk, W., Kalmijn, M., and Muffels, R. (2005). 'The Impact of Young Children on Women's Labour Supply: A Reassessment of Institutional Effects in Europe', *Acta Sociologica*, 48(1): 41–62.

Van Bastelaer, A., Lemaître, G., and Marianna, P. (1997) *The Definition of Part-Time Work for the Purpose of International Comparisons*. Labour Market and Social Policy Occasional Papers No.22. Paris: OECD.

Van de Velde, C. (2005). 'Public Action and Working Conditions in France: The ANACT in the Last Three Decades', Changequal Working Paper, Nuffield College, University of Oxford.

Van der Doef, M. and Maes, S. (1999). 'The Job Demand–Control (–Support) Model and Psychological Well-being: A Review of 20 Years of Empirical Research', *Work and Stress*, 13(2): 87–114.

Van der Lippe, T., Jager, A., and Kops, Y. (2006). 'Combination Pressure: The Paid Work–Family Balance of Men and Women in European Countries', *Acta Sociologica*, 49: 303–19.

Verma, V. and Clemenceanu, A. (1996). 'Methodology of the European Community Household Panel', *Statistics in Transition*, 2(7): 1023–62.

Visser, J. (2002). 'The First Part-time Economy in the World: A Model to be Followed?' *Journal of European Social Policy*, 12(1): 23–42.

—— (2003). 'Unions and Unionism Around the World', in J. T. Addison and C. Schnabel (eds), *The International Handbook of Trade Unions*. Cheltenham, UK: Edward Elgar.

—— (2006). 'Union Membership Statistics in 24 Countries', *Monthly Labor Review*, 129(1): 38–49.

Voydanoff, P. (1988). 'Work Role Characteristics, Family Structure Demands, and Work/Family Conflict', *Journal of Marriage and the Family*, 50: 749–61.

Walton, R. E. (1985*a*). 'From Control to Commitment in the Workplace', *Harvard Business Review*, 85(2): 77–84.

—— (1985*b*). 'Towards a Strategy of Eliciting Employee Commitment Based on Policies of Mutuality', in R. E. Walton and J. R. Lawrence (eds), *HRM: Trends and Challenges*. Boston, MA: Harvard Business School.

Warr, P. (1987). *Work, Unemployment and Mental Health*. Oxford: Clarendon Press.

—— (1991). 'Mental Health, Well-being and Job Satisfaction', in B. Hesketh and A. Adams (eds), *Psychological Perspectives on Occupational Health and Rehabilitation*. Australia: Harcourt Brace Jovanovich Ltd.

White, M., Hill, S., McGovern, P., Mills, C., and Smeaton, D. (2003). ' "High-performance" Management Practices, Working Hours and Work—Life Balance', *British Journal of Industrial Relations*, 41(2): 175–95.

Wilthagen, T., Tros, F., and van Lieshout, H. (2003). 'Towards "Flexicurity"? Balancing Flexibility and Security in EU Member States', Invited paper prepared for the 13th World Congress of the International Industrial Relations Association (IIRA), Berlin, September.

Winter-Ebmer, R. and Zweimüller, J. (1997). 'Unequal Assignment and Unequal Promotion in Job Ladders', *Journal of Labour Economics*, 15: 43–71.

Wright, E. O. (ed.) (2005). *Approaches to Class Analysis*. Cambridge: Cambridge University Press.

—— and Dwyer, R. (2002). 'The Patterns of Job Expansions in the USA: A Comparison of the 1960s and the 1990s', *Socio-Economic Review*, 1: 289–325.

—— and Singelmann, J. (1982). 'Proletarianization in the Changing American Class Structure', in M. Burawoy and T. Skocpol (eds), *Marxist Enquiries*. Chicago, IL: University of Chicago Press.

Zuboff, S. (1988). *In the Age of the Smart Machine: The Future of Work and Power*. New York: Basic Books.

Author Index

Subject Index